As a pastor who has witne____
shifts in America, I find ____
for our times. Troy Anders____ ....ully articulated a narrative
that intertwines prophecy, historical events, and the miraculous survival of President Donald Trump following an assassination attempt.
This book is not merely a recounting of events but a profound call
to spiritual awakening. Anderson's insights into America's Nineveh
moment, inspired by the prophetic words of world-renowned evangelist Billy Graham, resonate deeply with the urgency of our national
repentance and prayer. *The Trump Code* is a timely reminder of
God's hand in our nation's history and a compelling guide for those
seeking to understand the spiritual dimensions of our current era.

—DR. ROBERT JEFFRESS
SENIOR PASTOR, FIRST BAPTIST CHURCH, DALLAS

Troy Anderson's ability to navigate through the annals of time in
The Trump Code reveals hidden prophetic secrets. The comparisons
between the Baron Trump novels of the 1800s and today's President
Donald Trump era will cause you to consider Nikola Tesla's time
travel theories. A tantalizing must-read.

—PASTOR PAUL BEGLEY
HOST, *THE COMING APOCALYPSE*

Troy Anderson has done it again with *The Trump Code*. This fascinating read uses Anderson's top-notch skills as an investigative
journalist to sort through an enduring mystery that has major implications for the world. It should be considered essential reading.

—ALEX NEWMAN
SENIOR EDITOR, *THE NEW AMERICAN*

The Trump Code is a unique book that intertwines biblical prophecy,
politics, and divine intervention. Troy Anderson has woven a narrative that is both insightful and inspiring, connecting end-times
events and offering a picture of what the future may hold for Israel
and America. As a rabbi, I am particularly moved by *The Trump
Code's* exploration of America's "Nineveh moment" and the call for
national repentance. This book is a powerful testament to the belief

that God's providence is guiding our nation. *The Trump Code* is a must-read for anyone seeking to grasp the spiritual underpinnings of our contemporary political landscape.

—RABBI JONATHAN BERNIS
PRESIDENT AND CEO, JEWISH VOICE MINISTRIES INTERNATIONAL

What an interesting book. I know it will give you a hope and a future. We all stand in agreement on the bottom line that Jesus Christ is Lord of lords and King of kings and He will make a way when there seems to be no way. He is our rock, our firm foundation. We put our trust in Him. Our personal prayers on all the concerns in our lives will move the hand of God. He has no favorites. He loves the same all who have faith in Him. Troy Anderson has been a joy in my life as we pray at 8 a.m. most every morning and ask the Holy Spirit to lead and guide our lives and make us a blessing to all we connect with, because He is the answer to every question, and we trust Him now and forever. Join us in our faith in Him.

—REV. JERRY MOSES
FORMER MEGACHURCH PASTOR
FORMER ASSISTANT TO THE PRESIDENT AT MOVIEGUIDE, CBN,
AND BENNY HINN MINISTRIES

THE TRUMP CODE

TROY ANDERSON

FRONT LINE

THE TRUMP CODE by Troy Anderson
Published by FrontLine, an imprint of Charisma Media
1150 Greenwood Blvd., Lake Mary, Florida 32746

While the author has made every effort to provide accurate, up-to-date source information at the time of publication, statistics and other data are constantly

For more resources like this, visit MyCharismaShop.com and the author's website at www.troyanderson.us.

Cataloging-in-Publication Data is on file with the Library of Congress.
International Standard Book Number: 978-1-63641-439-3
E-book ISBN: 978-1-63641-440-9

1 2024
Printed in the United States of America

Most Charisma Media products are available at special quantity discounts for bulk purchase for sales promotions, premiums, fund-raising, and educational needs. For details, call us at (407) 333-0600 or visit our website at www. charismamedia.com.

DEDICATION

This book is dedicated to the courageous and indomitable spirit of America, a nation God has used to spread the good news of Jesus Christ throughout the world for over four centuries. From the Pilgrims who sought religious freedom in 1620, to the Founding Fathers and patriots who risked their lives and fortunes in the Revolutionary War, to the brave heroes who halted the demonic Nazi onslaught in World War II, God has continually demonstrated His prophetic destiny for America on the world stage.

As the Bible declares, He is the God of the impossible. If we rise to the occasion with humble repentance before our Creator at this critical hour, we will witness not only a miraculous turnaround in America and the world but also the great end-times revival and awakening that millions are praying for. This is God's heart for humanity. He loves us so much that "He gave His one and only Son, that whoever believes in Him shall not perish but have eternal life" (John 3:16, NIV). It is a choice all of us must make—judgment or revival, heaven or hell.

CONTENTS

FOREWORD

I N AMERICAN HISTORY, some moments compel us to look beyond the surface for deeper, prophetic meanings. One such moment was the near-assassination of President Donald Trump. As my esteemed colleague and long-time coauthor, Troy Anderson, explores in *The Trump Code*, this incident transcends politics.

On July 13, 2024, Trump faced an event that could have altered history—a bullet narrowly missed his head, grazing his ear and leaving him stained with blood. This incident invites us to explore its deeper significance, especially through the lens of ancient biblical practices and prophecies.

The parallels between Trump's experience and the ancient consecration rites of priests described in Leviticus 8 are compelling, as *New York Times* bestselling author Rabbi Jonathan Cahn pointed out in his YouTube video "The Mystery Behind the Trump Assassination Attempt."[1]

Just as the blood of a sacrifice was placed on the right ear, thumb, and big toe of a priest, Trump's actions during the incident—raising his right hand to his bloodied ear—mirror this biblical ritual. The removal of his shoes during the event echoes the biblical practice of priests ministering shoeless, highlighting that they were on holy ground.

The location of the incident, Butler, Pennsylvania, is also significant. The word *butler* derives from the word *cupbearer*, a role historically associated with protecting a king from assassination.[2] This adds another layer of meaning to the event.

These spiritual insights urge us to look beyond the immediate and the political, considering the possibility of a higher purpose at work. Could this incident be a form of divine consecration for Trump, calling him to hear God's voice, perform His work, and walk in His ways? As believers we are reminded of our own call to consecration, to seek God's guidance and to fulfill His purposes in our lives.

In *The Trump Code*, Troy Anderson delves into these themes, offering readers an exploration of the spiritual dimensions of current events. This book is not just a political analysis; it is an exploration of biblical prophecies, of prophecies regarding Trump and America's future, of the curious Baron Trump novels by nineteenth-century lawyer and author Ingersoll Lockwood, and of Trump's enigmatic connection to famed inventor Nikola Tesla and the fascinating topic of time travel. It is a call to prayer and a reminder that God is sovereign over human affairs.

AMERICA AND THE INTERDIMENSIONAL WAR

America and the world are currently engulfed in the greatest interdimensional war in history. Unlike traditional conflicts, this war transcends the dimensions of our physical senses. Quantum physics, discovered by pioneers like Max Planck, Niels Bohr, and Albert Einstein, revealed that our reality consists of dimensions beyond our perception. String theorists propose that our universe contains at least ten dimensions, most of which we cannot perceive.

From both a biblical and a quantum physics perspective, God exists beyond time and space. The Bible teaches about the spiritual realm, where angels and demons are engaged in a monumental battle for the souls of humanity.

America and the American dream originate in consciousness—in an idea, dream, or vision—which, according to quantum physics, is an electromagnetic frequency projected into our reality from another dimension. These divine streams of consciousness, thoughts, ideas, visions, and dreams are sacred because, as the Bible says, "Where there is no vision, the people perish" (Prov. 29:18, KJV).

The energy that flows from unseen dimensions, creating a thought, idea, vision, or dream, can contain a divine spark. This spark can be perceived as coming from our imagination, energized by God, His Word, His love, or the forces of darkness.

A free America, blessed with freedom of religion, speech, and the press, stems from these divine ideas, inspired by our Creator and reflected in the Declaration of Independence, the US Constitution, and the Bill of Rights.

The promise of America—freedom, liberty, justice, and prosperity—has allowed us to spread the good news of Jesus Christ worldwide for over two centuries and to support Israel since its birth in 1948. This promise was birthed in the spiritual realm and projected into our geopolitical reality.

Acts 2:17 says: "In the last days, God says, I will pour out my Spirit on all people. Your sons and daughters will prophesy, your young men will see visions, your old men will dream dreams."

THE MYSTERY BEHIND THE TRUMP ASSASSINATION ATTEMPT

The attempted assassination of Donald Trump is a pivotal event in understanding the spiritual battle we face.

Trump spoke at the rally in Butler, Pennsylvania, on national television, during which multiple bullets were fired at him. I am convinced that this very real assassination attempt was thwarted due to the massive number of prayers for Trump going out day and night. The intent was to "blow Trump's head off, Kennedy-style, live on television," but God's people intervened through spiritual warfare and prayer.

Many mainstream television networks had stopped airing Trump rallies years ago to censor and control his message. However, for some reason many decided to broadcast this particular rally live. Could it be they broadcast this rally live because they knew an armed attempt on his life was planned and they wanted to televise it?

While some Christians and conservatives are confused, the deep state and globalist elite are not. Trump is their number one target because they see him as the primary threat to their agenda. Following the years of Trump campaigns, many powerful individuals have openly called for his death, assassination, and imprisonment. This groupthink is not only evil but pathological. These individuals seem to be able to say anything without legal accountability, as if their collective calls for his murder and death are protected by people in very high places.

THE NEXT PRESIDENT AND "MYSTERY BABYLON"

In this multidimensional war, the next president of the United States is crucial—whether it will be Donald Trump, who champions the Constitution and rational nationalism, or a globalist democrat aligned with the World Economic Forum's "Great Reset" plan. This plan envisions a Luciferian one-world government, religion, and economic system, described by the apostle John as a Mystery Babylon in Revelation 17–18. (See Revelation 17:5.)

John depicted our emerging globalist/transhumanist system as "Mystery

Babylon" due to its occult links to ancient Babylon and the Tower of Babel (Gen. 11:1–9), an interdimensional portal for fallen angels.

In the 2015 bestselling book I coauthored with Troy Anderson, *The Babylon Code: Solving the Bible's Greatest End-Times Mystery*, we explored this prophetic enigma, revealing a biblical code predicting a global government, cashless society, and universal religion in the end times. This mystery starts with the Tower of Babel in Genesis and ends with the battle of Armageddon in Revelation. We argued that an elite group of globalists is orchestrating the creation of a new world order, echoing the apostle John's "Mystery Babylon."

We presented evidence that today's global crises are harbingers of the apocalyptic events prophesied in the Bible. These signs indicate the approach of the seven-year tribulation period, marked by chaos and the rise of a global dictator—the Antichrist.

We also looked at how ancient Babylonian occult practices have influenced secret societies throughout history, fueling the push for global governance. We urged people to recognize these signs and prepare for Christ's return, when He will overthrow the false new world order and establish a divine order during His millennial reign, followed by judgment day and the creation of a new earth, new heaven, and a new Jerusalem.

MIT PROFESSOR JOHN TRUMP'S ACCESS TO NIKOLA TESLA'S SECRET FILES

Former President Trump was significantly influenced by his uncle, John Trump, a professor of engineering at the Massachusetts Institute of Technology. Following Nikola Tesla's death in 1943, John Trump was given access by the federal government to Tesla's secret technologies, including zero-point, or unlimited, energy.

Tesla invented a technology capable of extracting unlimited energy from another dimension, potentially rendering expensive energy sources like petroleum, coal, and nuclear power obsolete. These interdimensional energy sources include scalar waves, etheric field dimensions, and electromagnetic energy. However, globalist billionaires who profit from conventional energy have concealed Tesla's discoveries, seizing his blueprints and prototypes.

As a young boy, Donald Trump was exposed to his uncle's knowledge of these classified technologies. The Federal Bureau of Investigation tasked John Trump with reviewing Tesla's research and inventions, meaning Trump likely learned about them firsthand. It is highly probable that Trump has access to secret Tesla technologies, which he could potentially release to solve the global energy crisis and advance futuristic scientific innovations.

SCIENCE IN RELEASING THE THIRD GREAT AWAKENING

Accessing Tesla's technologies involves integrating biblical truth, which upholds the American dream. Amid the spiritual war for freedom, America uniquely offers individuals the possibility of realizing this dream.

While America was founded by Bible-believing pilgrims and Christians who laid the groundwork for God's end-times vision, sinister forces led by Sir Francis Bacon, an occultist and head of the Rosicrucians, sought to establish America as the head of a new world order. Despite Bacon's plans, the pilgrims and puritans followed Christ's command to "occupy the spiritual land," aiming to ultimately ignite a last-days revival and turn the tide of spiritual battle in America (Luke 19:13).

The supernatural power of Jesus Christ is released when believers obey and engage in high-level spiritual warfare. In 2013, Troy Anderson interviewed evangelist Billy Graham about the possibility of an end-times great spiritual awakening. This interview, which went viral, was featured in *The Babylon Code*, where we extensively researched globalism from Genesis to Revelation 17 and 18. A prominent pastor was so inspired that he personally delivered copies of *The Babylon Code* to Trump and his team, perhaps leading to the adoption of the phrase, "Americanism, not globalism, will be our credo," as Trump's campaign platform in 2016.

This phrase encapsulates the core conflict of our time. The Bible opposes globalism, portraying it as a Luciferian system from Genesis to Revelation. The statement "Americanism, not globalism" challenges and seeks to reverse the flawed logic promoting globalism.

The Trump Code documents how few contemporary Americans, including influential figures, understand the implications of globalism on our freedoms, except for leaders like Trump. The majority of Americans have been subjected to social engineering, brainwashing, and thought control, referred to as "sorcery" in the Book of Revelation. The globalist elite, who are Luciferians, wield occult technology and demonic power to control the world.

UNDERSTANDING THE PROPHETIC IMPLICATIONS

It is crucial for every person, secular or Christian, and every leader in politics, culture, economy, and spirituality to grasp the prophetic implications of America's direction and of its next president. Troy Anderson's intriguing book *The Trump Code* offers a prophetic analysis and documents the seismic impact of this upcoming presidential election on America and the world.

The Trump Code details the consequences if Trump wins or loses the presidency. It also addresses how enemies of America, like the deep state and globalist elite, could derail the election through crises such as national power failures, internet crashes, pandemics, natural disasters, and other catastrophic events.

America is under an all-out attack aimed at its total destruction. If conservatives, libertarians, humanists, and Christians had the proper discernment, they would see that the nation is under siege by communist, Marxist, transhumanist, totalitarian, fascist, occult, and globalist forces. These enemies aim to transform America into a dictatorship, leading to economic collapse, military rule, and mass arrests of Christians and others for reeducation in concentration camps.

This warning is not fearmongering or fatalism but a call to action. If concerned citizens, including Christians, do not become active and peacefully engage in law-abiding activities, the deep state and globalist elite will succeed in their plans. Their goal is to create a dystopian, artificial intelligence–generated communist Chinese social credit system that tracks every American.

THE SECRET SPIRITUAL WEAPON TO DEFEAT THE ADVERSARY

Scripture reveals a great end-times battle before Christ's return, described in the Book of Daniel and also in Revelation 17:5 (KJV) as "Mystery, Babylon the Great, the Mother of Harlots and Abominations of the Earth." These accounts depict fallen angels and their technology battling God and His followers. They also foresee a last-days revival, enabling God's people to participate in this spiritual awakening. The Antichrist will rise, claiming worship in Jerusalem's rebuilt temple, with the false prophet establishing a one-world religion and economy, deceiving many with signs and wonders, possibly through technological deceptions.

The term "Tower of Babel" in ancient Babylon signifies interdimensional spiritual portals. These doorways allow angels, demons, and other entities to traverse between dimensions.

In this spiritual warfare, God calls His people to engage with Holy Spirit–led accuracy, employing a non–New Age version of remote viewing to focus on divinely revealed targets. Renewing our minds, believing in God's omnipotence, and remembering, "For where two or three gather in my name, there am I with them" (Matt. 18:20, NIV), empowers us. Boldly approaching the throne of grace by faith, we trust His promise: "Greater is he that is in you, than he that is in the world" (1 John 4:4, KJV).

As Trump runs for president, expect all-out attacks from multiple directions. Victory lies in unwavering faith, in taking the land and occupying it until Christ returns. Failure is not an option.

A CALL TO CONSECRATION

As you turn the pages of *The Trump Code*, may you be inspired to look beyond the headlines and see the hand of God at work. May you be moved to pray for our leaders, for our nation, and for a revival that can only come from divine intervention. Most importantly, may you be encouraged to consecrate your own life to God's service, walking in His ways and fulfilling His purposes.

—PAUL MCGUIRE
SENIOR PASTOR, PARADISE MOUNTAIN CHURCH INTERNATIONAL
HOST, *THE PAUL MCGUIRE REPORT*
COAUTHOR, *THE BABYLON CODE* AND *TRUMPOCALYPSE*

TRUMP'S PROPHETIC ODYSSEY

I N WHAT WAS described beforehand as the "shot heard around the world" by international prophetic voice Joseph Z, President Donald J. Trump survived an assassination attempt on July 13, 2024—sending shock waves around the globe.[1] Later, he credited God for His miraculous hand of protection that saved his life.

As millions watched the campaign rally near Butler, Pennsylvania, Trump providentially turned his head at precisely the right moment, causing the bullet that likely would have killed him to miss and instead graze his right ear. Hearing the sounds of bullets whizzing by and feeling "something hit me really, really hard," Trump reached up to touch his bloodied ear and quickly took cover before the Secret Service's sniper team returned fire, killing Thomas Matthew Crooks. Tragically, Crooks killed firefighter Cory Comperatore, who used his body to protect his family, and injured two other people.[2]

"Bullets were continuing to fly as very brave Secret Service agents rushed to the stage...and pounced on top of me so that I would be protected," Trump recalled a few days afterward at the Republican National Convention. "There was blood pouring everywhere, and yet in a certain way I felt very safe because I had God on my side."[3]

After learning the failed assassin had been killed, Secret Service agents helped Trump to his feet. Upon seeing thousands of people "breathlessly waiting" to see if he had survived the fusillade of bullets, Trump shouted, "Fight, fight, fight."[4]

A journalist captured a photo of the bloodied Trump pumping his fist in the air with an American flag in the background—an iconic image that helped catapult Trump to being what famed wrestler Hulk Hogan described as a "real American hero" at the convention.[5] Hogan, during his speech, proclaimed, "I'm here tonight because I want the world to know that Donald Trump is a real American hero," after dramatically tearing off his shirt to reveal a Trump-Vance tank top, stirring the audience into thunderous applause.[6]

"You say, 'How did that happen?' But I got lucky. God was with me, I tell you," Trump said at the premiere of a film, *Trump's Rescue Mission: Saving America*, broadcast during the convention in Milwaukee, Wisconsin. "That's what they call a close call. That was an amazing, horrible thing. Amazing thing. And in many ways, it changes your attitude, your viewpoint on life. And I think, honestly, I think you appreciate God even more. I really do."[7]

This life-altering event is just one in a series of extraordinary occurrences surrounding Trump, a man who has become a focal point in modern American history—a political figure many faith leaders believe God has raised up for a divine mission at this critical point in time.

His rise to power began on June 16, 2015, when the world watched in wonder as he descended the Trump Tower escalator with his wife, Melania. The real estate titan, entertainment superstar, and American patriot was entering a new realm: the swamp of Washington, DC, politics and corruption.

What ensued over the following years, a mixture of sneers, lies, and hostility from elites, pundits, and the mainstream media, was met with cheers, excitement, and hope from everyday folks, businesspeople, and conservative and Christian media.

Not many knew that his shocking win in 2016, equally shocking loss in 2020, third run at the presidency, and now a stunning assassination attempt would signal the shift into a hyperdeceptive time of fake news, wokeness, cancel culture, artificial intelligence, soaring inflation, and looming nuclear war.

The chaos unleashed by Trump's presence in politics and media is unprecedented but not unforeseen. This book is about those who had prophetic insights into what was going to happen and what the future holds.

The Trump Code: Exploring Time Travel, Nikola Tesla, the Trump Lineage, and America's Future offers a unique perspective, delving into the connections between the obscure but eerie Baron Trump novels written by a largely unknown lawyer and author in the late 1800s, the enigmatic Trump family legacy, and Trump's curious link to Nikola Tesla, the prolific inventor whose missing research papers on time travel and other "forbidden science" have raised questions about top-secret government programs along with a myriad of modern technologies and advanced weaponry.

This book also uncovers a web of historical events and divine providence. Drawing from biblical passages about Moses, Enoch, Elijah, Ezekiel, the apostle John, and the Mount of Transfiguration, along with theories of time travel by Albert Einstein, Tesla, and others, *The Trump Code* connects the pieces of this riveting puzzle, revealing uncanny parallels between the novels, modern-day prophetic voices, and events that have unfolded and will unfold very shortly.

The Trump Code is not just a literary curiosity; it's an investigative journey into the supernatural signs and wonders unfolding all around us, and even the growing hope of an end-times awakening and turnaround in America and the world.

Through the lens of investigative journalism, *The Trump Code*—featuring interviews with high-profile political and faith leaders, as well as highly respected experts in various fields—invites you to discern the deeper truths hidden within the pages of Scripture, history, and world events.

INTRODUCTION
STRANGER THAN FICTION

*Truth is stranger than fiction, but it is because Fiction
is obliged to stick to possibilities; Truth isn't.*
—MARK TWAIN, *FOLLOWING THE EQUATOR: A JOURNEY AROUND THE WORLD*

IN THE ANNALS of American presidential history, there is no more pecu-
liar tale than the eerie similarities between President Donald J. Trump
and three novels now referred to as *The Baron Trump Collection,* penned
by the seemingly prophetic hand of American lawyer and novelist Ingersoll
Lockwood in the late 1800s.

At the heart of this mysterious story is Little Baron Trump, the protagonist in two of the three novels in the collection, whose image on the cover of
the book resembles Trump's son, eighteen-year-old Barron Trump.

In two of the novels, Baron Trump, a wealthy boy with a "very active"
brain who lives in Castle Trump, embarks on fantastical traveling adventures.
His adventures take him to Russia, guided by a manuscript written by Don
Fum, the "great master of all masters," to find a portal to a magical world,
which some believe is a code for time travel.[1]

The eerie parallels between these fictional tales and the real-life Trump
family, particularly Donald Trump and his youngest son, Barron, have led to
a resurgence of interest in the books, with YouTube and TikTok videos about
the sensational story garnering millions of views and media outlets such as
Newsweek, Politico, and the *Daily Mail* penning stories about growing public
interest in this puzzling phenomenon.

*The Trump Code: Exploring Time Travel, Nikola Tesla, the Trump Lineage,
and America's Future* delves into the connections between the novels and the
enigmatic Trump family legacy, asking whether this nineteenth-century novelist foresaw the future of not only Trump but America and the world.

The Trump Code uncovers a web of historical events and divine providence.
Drawing from passages about biblical figures who foresaw the future, or may
have even traveled through time, along with an exploration of mind-blowing,

top-secret government programs and the research of Albert Einstein, Nikola Tesla, and others into time travel, *The Trump Code* explores these mysteries, posing the question of whether "truth is stranger than fiction," as Mark Twain famously said.[2]

What makes *The Trump Code* remarkable are the uncanny connections between the novels Lockwood wrote over a century ago and the Trump family. Central to this enigma is the figure of John G. Trump, a distinguished Massachusetts Institute of Technology professor and uncle to President Trump.

The Trump Code uncovers John G. Trump's involvement with the remnants of Tesla's groundbreaking research on time travel and other hidden scientific secrets. Through a mysterious turn of events involving the Federal Bureau of Investigation, John Trump was granted access to examine sixty to eighty trunks of Tesla's research—including a black notebook of several hundred pages, some of which were marked "Government"—following the inventor's death in 1943. The government ultimately returned most of the papers to Tesla's nephew, Sava Kosanovich, which are now housed at the Nikola Tesla Museum in Belgrade, Serbia, but allegedly retained some trunks that are missing.[3]

The intrigue doesn't end there. Lockwood also wrote *1900: or, The Last President*, a book about an unlikely candidate for president who is elected, followed by political upheaval and societal discord. The novel portrays the East Side of New York City "in a state of uproar" after the election. As the presidential inauguration neared, "it was only too apparent that from a dozen different points in the South and North West '...Armies' were forming for an advance on Washington."[4]

Could this fictional novel hold clues to the 2024 presidential election, with all its division and chaos? Were Lockwood's novels prophetic? Does God speak this way to humanity?

Even more intriguing: Has Trump, born in 1946, three years after Tesla's death in New York City, traveled through time, as some have posited, helping explain his vast wealth and rise to political power? *The Trump Code* confronts the darker undercurrents of speculation and conspiracy surrounding the Trump family's ties to prophecy and time travel.

Interestingly enough, a recent Freedom of Information Act request from *The Sun*, Britain's largest newspaper, unearthed documents from the Pentagon's secretive UFO program, the Advanced Aerospace Threat

Identification Program (AATIP), revealing that time travel may be possible. One report explores how to use antigravity technologies, noting the "effects can be implemented by manipulating spacetime." In looking at different ways of "controlling gravity," the report states, "It might be possible to produce exotic phenomena such as faster-than-light travel…and time machines."[5]

From scientific theories to secret government programs, *The Trump Code* navigates through a maze of intrigue and speculation. As we peel back the layers of history, *The Trump Code* confronts questions that defy easy answers.

Is there a divine hand guiding the course of human events, as suggested by the parallels between fiction in these novels and reality? Or are we witnessing the machinations of darker forces, hinted at by the curious numerology surrounding Lockwood's name?

In the search for truth, *The Trump Code* confronts uncomfortable possibilities. Could the Trump family's ties to time travel and esoteric knowledge hold clues to unlocking the mysteries of our past and future? And what implications does this have for the legacy of Trump and the future of America?

Join us on a journey of investigation and revelation as we unravel *The Trump Code,* a saga of prophecy, intrigue, and the enduring legacy of one of America's most popular, beloved, and polarizing figures.

Prepare to confront the unknown and challenge your perceptions of reality, for the truth may lie in the most unexpected of places.

PART ONE

TRUMP'S TIME MACHINE

CHAPTER ONE

RED OR BLUE PILL?

Truth is what is true, and it's not necessarily factual. Truth and fact are not the same thing. Truth does not contradict or deny facts, but it goes through and beyond facts. This is something that it is very difficult for some people to understand. Truth can be dangerous.

—MADELEINE L'ENGLE, AUTHOR OF *A WRINKLE IN TIME*

IN THE NOW infamous scene from *The Matrix*, Morpheus offers Thomas Anderson, alias Neo, a red pill and a blue pill. The red pill would reveal the harsh reality, while the blue pill would allow Neo to remain in the delusional world of the Matrix. Neo chooses the red pill.

If you are reading this book, you have either taken the red pill and want to delve deeper into reality or are just beginning your journey out of the Matrix.

Donald Trump's presidency has exposed the depths of the deep-state rabbit hole, revealing an elite ruling class in America, widespread corruption, and a deluge of deceptions. Despite attempts to suppress the truth, it is now out in the open, never to be hidden again.

Mark Twain and Madeleine L'Engle said truth can be stranger than fiction and dangerous. Yet Jesus declared, "And you will know the truth, and the truth will make you free" (John 8:32, NRSVUE).

Since 2015, Trump has upended politics, media, and other cultural institutions, acting as "God's chaos candidate."[1] He has exposed the global deep-state system that threatens to enslave humanity in a one-world artificial intelligence–controlled system.

Many elites once considered Trump one of their own. Michelle Fields wrote in *Time* in 2016 that Trump, like France's King Louis XIV, represented an elite class disconnected from the governed.[2] However, Trump's actions suggest a different plan, possibly divinely inspired, for America and the world.

Here are some facts about Trump's stance on God and faith that are compelling:

- He is the first president to issue an official proclamation for a day of national repentance since Abraham Lincoln.[3]

- His appointment of conservative judges to the Supreme Court paved the way for the answer to millions of prayers with the overturning of Roe v. Wade.[4]

- During Easter 2020, amid the devastating COVID-19 pandemic, he issued a statement and asked God to "hold all Americans in the palm of His hand," encouraging people to "rejoice in knowing that Christ has risen."[5]

WHAT IS TRUTH?

However, the forces of evil are relentless. Amid fake news and AI-generated deceptions, Pontius Pilate's question to Christ resonates: "What is truth?" (John 18:38).

Solomon wrote that there's "nothing new under the sun" (Eccles. 1:9). Isaiah prophesied about the deceit and injustice of his time, which mirrors today's world. (See Isaiah 5:20–23.) Evil is now called good, darkness is preferred over light, and justice is denied the innocent.

The Enlightenment's questioning of God, truth, and morality led to the deconstructionist views of the late twentieth century, dissolving reality into today's age of deception foreseen by authors such as George Orwell, Ray Bradbury, and Aldous Huxley.

God is not surprised by what's happening. He knows the end from the beginning. Isaiah 46:10 tells us: "I make known the end from the beginning, from ancient times, what is still to come. I say, 'My purpose will stand, and I will do all that I please.'"

God holds our lives and times in His hands. David, in Psalm 31:15, said, "My times are in your hands; deliver me from the hands of my enemies, from those who pursue me." And God often lets us know what He is doing. "Surely the Sovereign Lord does nothing without revealing his plan to his servants the prophets" (Amos 3:7).

Is The Baron Trump Collection Prophetic?

So should it surprise us that God seems to have used an obscure lawyer and veteran of the US consular service turned author in the late 1800s to reveal to us what He is doing today?

In his series of enigmatic books published from 1890 to 1896, now known as the Baron Trump Collection—consisting of *Travels and Adventures of Little Baron Trump and His Wonderful Dog Bulger, Baron Trump's Marvellous Underground Journey,* and *1900: or, The Last President*—Ingersoll Lockwood penned a seemingly prophetic collection of tales.

As I mentioned in the introduction, Little Baron Trump is the protagonist in two of Lockwood's novels, and his image on the frontispiece of *Baron Trump's Marvellous Underground Journey* resembles Trump's son Barron, the target of TikTokers who say he and his father may be time travelers. In the novels, Baron Trump, a wealthy boy who lives in "Castle Trump" and comes from "one of the most ancient and honorable families of North Germany—famous for its valor and love of adventure," embarks on fantastical traveling adventures.[6] His adventures take him to Russia, guided by a manuscript by the "great master of all masters," a Spaniard named Don Fum.[7]

The parallels between the novels and the Trump family legacy are startling.

Most notable is the third book, ominously titled *The Last President.* In the story, an unlikely candidate for president, a businessman, is elected, and political upheaval and societal discord follow. The night of the election, "mobs of vast size...under the lead of Anarchists and Socialists" converge on the "Fifth Avenue Hotel"—where Trump Tower now stands in New York City—chanting, "Death to the rich man!"[8]

Could this fictional novel hold clues to the 2024 presidential election? Were Lockwood's novels prophetic?

"What are the odds statistically of this author writing the book where... the main characters are [Don Fum] and Baron Trump, and the character in [another] book is a wealthy guy who becomes president?" said Paul McGuire, former host of the nationally syndicated *Paul McGuire Show* and an internationally recognized prophecy expert. "There are so many stranger-than-real coincidences in that book....It's as if somebody did go back in time, get some information, and went back to the future because the similarities between the real Donald Trump of today and the so-called fictional character are just amazing."[9]

Is it possible that God speaks to humanity through fictional books?

"Well, prophetically this has happened to people," said Pastor Paul Begley, host of the syndicated television show *The Coming Apocalypse*. "George Orwell, [in his novel] *Nineteen Eighty-Four*, basically writes what he sees is coming and in his creative mind and within him; he begins to write things that have come to pass.

"So I believe that…the Spirit of prophecy [Rev. 19:10] can come upon people when they're writing, especially when they're writing of future events. Prophetically, God will speak to people, and they will write it not knowing that what they're writing is actually going to take place. So yeah, I do believe [Lockwood] was inspired to write it. I don't think he had any idea.…Donald Trump wasn't born yet. He has a son named Barron. He…ended up being president. You can't make that up. I mean, the guy published this in the late 1800s. So he was writing creatively, and then prophecy was coming to him, [without] him even knowing it."[10]

WHAT DO MODERN-DAY PROPHETS SAY?

Lockwood's novels seem to suggest prophecy was coming to him, even if he didn't realize it, and many of the events he wrote about line up with what modern-day prophets have declared about Trump.

For example, the late South African prophet Kim Clement, as far back as 2007, pronounced God was handpicking Trump to be His "trumpet" in government.[11]

"'Trump shall become a trumpet,' says the Lord," Clement prophesied in 2007. "'There will be a praying president, not a religious one, for I will fool the people,' says the Lord.…God says, 'The one that is chosen shall go in, and they shall say, "He has hot blood," for the Spirit of God says, "Yes, he may have hot blood, but he will bring the walls of protection on this country in a greater way, and the economy of this country shall change rapidly,"' says the Lord of Hosts. Listen to the word of the Lord. God says, 'I will put at your helm for two terms a president that will pray, but he will not be a praying president when he starts. I will put him in office, and then I will baptize him with the Holy Spirit and My power,' says the Lord of Hosts."[12]

Lance Wallnau wrote in *God's Chaos Candidate: Donald J. Trump and the*

American Unraveling, released shortly before the 2016 election, that Trump was called to be "a wrecking ball to the spirit of political correctness."[13]

"I believe Trump is the chaos candidate who has been set apart by God to navigate us through the chaos coming to America," Wallnau wrote. "Trump has come to the amazing and underpublicized conclusion that, 'America's been lifted out of many of its most difficult hours through the miracle of faith. Now, in these hard times for our country, let us turn again to our Christian heritage to lift up the soul of our nation.'"[14]

In 2011 retired Orlando firefighter Mark Taylor said he received a prophetic word from the Lord, indicating Trump would become president. "The Spirit of God says: I have chosen this man, Donald Trump, for such a time as this," Taylor wrote on April 28, 2011. "For I will use this man to bring honor, respect and restoration to America. America will be respected once again as the most powerful and prosperous nation on earth, (other than Israel). The dollar will be the strongest it has ever been in the history of the United States, and will once again be the currency by which all others are judged….They [the enemy] will even quake and shake when he announces he is running for president, it will be like the shot heard across the world. The enemy will say what shall we do now? This man knows all our tricks and schemes. We have been robbing America for decades, what shall we do to stop this?"[15]

In light of these predictions regarding Trump, and the public attention Lockwood's novels have attracted, the question that remains in many people's minds is this: How did Lockwood seemingly foresee what was going to happen in the future? Did God give him a prophetic vision that he included in his novels? Is it possible that he traveled through time? And what are his ties to the Trump family, if any?

Is Time Travel Possible?

The fascination with time travel spans from *The Time Machine* by H. G. Wells to the film *Back to the Future*. Albert Einstein's theories on time travel, as well as a much-rumored US Navy experiment in 1943—the Philadelphia Experiment, in which a US Navy destroyer was reportedly "made invisible and teleported from Philadelphia, Pennsylvania, to Norfolk, Virginia"—have raised questions about the possibility of time travel.[16]

Famous inventor Nikola Tesla's missing documents supposedly had experiments with bending time. Around the time of his death in 1943, Tesla's research had gained attention from reporters whose editors were "uncertain how seriously his futuristic prophecies should be regarded." At the time, "caustic criticism greeted his speculations concerning communication with other planets, his assertions that he could split the Earth like an apple, and his claim of having invented a death ray capable of destroying 10,000 airplanes at a distance of 400 km (250 miles)."[17]

"When Albert Einstein was asked by a reporter, 'What's it like being a genius?' you know what he said? 'I wouldn't know. Ask Nikola Tesla.' Nikola Tesla was probably the great genius of the twentieth century," Dr. Steven Greer, founder of the Center for the Study of Extraterrestrial Intelligence (CSETI), told Patrick Bet-David on his podcast, noting Tesla's inventions involved "forbidden science," including teleportation and antigravity technologies and free energy that could solve global energy problems and end pollution but remain suppressed due to vested interests in maintaining current energy paradigms that generate trillions of dollars annually. "[Tesla] died a poor man, a bitter man. Most of his huge breakthroughs never saw the light of day. He had one of these sort of electromagnetic generators that was free energy. J. P. Morgan famously told him if we can't put a meter on it and charge, like the utilities, it's not coming out."[18]

Eventually the government returned most of the papers to Tesla's family, and they are now housed at the Nikola Tesla Museum in Belgrade, Serbia, as I mentioned, but many of the papers are still missing. In a History Channel series *The Tesla Files*, researcher Marc J. Seifer and others helped to unravel the mystery of Tesla's missing files:

> Why were trunks belonging to genius inventor Nikola Tesla confiscated in 1943? Did they contain the plans for nearly free worldwide electricity, massive death rays, and other inventions out of the future? A new investigation driven by declassified CIA documents suggests a secret history of bitter rivalries, government conspiracies, Cold War and WW2 spycraft, extra-terrestrial communication, and amazing achievements of a truly gifted man—Nikola Tesla.[19]

Seifer, author of *Wizard: The Life and Times of Nikola Tesla*, said John G. Trump was hired to look through Tesla's research papers following his death, raising many questions about how Tesla's research may have been used over the decades.

"There were probably fifty of the big wooden trunks, but he had eighty or a hundred other things, just boxes with all that stuff," Seifer said. "It was a vehicle for the television show that maybe the government kept some of the trunks....I think it's certainly within the realm of possibility that the government did keep certain key papers for one reason or another. There's a theory that there is a way to trigger earthquakes at a distance, maybe what happened in Haiti or what happened in Japan. It's using Tesla as the tele-geodynamics [a scientific field involving the idea of transmitting strong pulses through the earth using ultrasound] mechanisms for sending certain impulses from one side of the planet to the other. So it is a potential...weapon. So it's possible that the government did keep some of the trunks and didn't release all of them to [the museum in] Belgrade. However, they did release the particle beam weapon paper to Belgrade....It's still a mystery, and it's kind of fun to speculate if indeed they did keep some of that information and they're still sitting on it."[20]

As far as the intrigue surrounding the papers, Paul McGuire said Tesla reportedly invented time travel technologies. "Our government, the Russian government, other governments, the Nazi German government, they've all been working on time-travel technology secretly, even if they publicly deny Tesla," McGuire said. "People need to know that part of the secret of the CERN [European Organization for Nuclear Research particle physics laboratory in Switzerland] project is opening up time-travel technology."[21]

Some of the most prestigious scientific institutions and largest militaries in the world are experimenting secretly with time-travel technologies and remote viewing, the practice of using the mind to sense and gain impressions about a subject that is distant or unseen, McGuire said.

"But remote viewing that can locate something that's not, let's say a secret missile base in Syria...[but] remote viewing that theoretically can go back into time or go forward into the future," McGuire said. "The discoveries of quantum physics, the discoveries of...Tesla, all in the last hundred years or so, have proven that according to quantum physics, everything in this physical reality is a product...of specific numerical electromagnetic frequencies.... And each one of us has a specific numerical number attached to the electromagnetic frequency.

"So once we know that all of our reality is nothing more than electromagnetic frequencies—sickness is an electromagnetic frequency, health is an electromagnetic frequency...we don't have to be a quantum physicist to...entertain the possibility that via the discoveries...it may be possible, to whatever degree, to go back in time or to go forward in time. We don't know how far they've developed these sciences and technologies."[22]

Based on what he's learned in his decades of research, McGuire said he believes scientists and militaries are now experimenting with various forms of time travel.

"By that I mean, can they look at a distorted black and white picture of something in the past for a couple of seconds and it [fades] away, or can they look at something in the future for a couple of seconds in black and white, and then the signal interrupts?" McGuire said. "It's very primitive, but it's still workable going to the future, going into the past. Or has the technology been developed up until the point that we can see clearly into the past—to what extent, I don't know—or see clearly into the future?"

For instance, how much information can be obtained with a GPS-type satellite system coupled with time-travel technologies? "Let's say with the drone, you use a powerful telescope and you read the cover of a newspaper or a magazine—'Trump Wins the Presidency' or whatever," McGuire said. "Now it's very possible that our time-travel technology is up to that extent. So if it is...there is the potential that somebody as sophisticated and wealthy as Donald Trump with an uncle who was one of the top premier scientists for MIT, Dr. John Trump, who the US government hired to look through all the secret scientific papers of Nikola Tesla—well, Trump's relative, Dr. John Trump, had to know a ton of classified information about time travel and infinite energy and all kinds of things. So I can't say conclusively, but I wouldn't be surprised."[23]

A recent article in the *Scientific American* explored the possibility of time travel. The author of the article "Is Time Travel Possible?" wrote that the popular conception of time travel as depicted in movies, where time travelers step inside a machine, disappear, and reappear in another time, isn't "likely in the real world, but [scientists] also don't relegate time travel to the crackpot realm. In fact, the laws of physics might allow chronological hopping, but the devil is in the details....Science began to take time travel seriously in the 1980s. In 1990, for instance, Russian physicist Igor Novikov and American physicist Kip Thorne collaborated on a research paper about closed time-like curves. 'They started to study not only how one could try to build a time machine but also how it would work.'...Since the 1990s, [Fabio Costa, a physicist at the Nordic Institute for Theoretical Physics] says, there's been on-and-off interest in the topic yet no big breakthrough."[24]

IS TIME TRAVEL BIBLICAL?

Scripturally, the Bible doesn't seem to provide a definitive answer as to whether time travel is possible, noting every person has an appointed time for their death (Heb. 9:27), our lives were "ordained" and "written in [God's] book before one of them came to be" (Ps. 139:16), and that God is outside of time and space, "declaring the end from the beginning" (Isa. 46:10, NKJV). The Bible says every event happens according to God's plans and timing (Gen. 21:1; John 7:8; 1 Tim. 2:6), so even if people could travel through time, the events would adhere to God's timing and be under His control.

Throughout Scripture, God often gave people visions, allowing them to witness future events, including the prophet Daniel (Dan. 7:13–14) and the apostle John (Rev. 1:9–19). The argument can be made that what they and other biblical prophets experienced was a form of time travel.

"Did you know there are examples of a strange form of time travel in the Bible?" Josh Peck, a biblical researcher and documentary filmmaker, asked in his *Prophecy Watchers* magazine article, "Biblical Time Travel and the Two Witnesses." "It's not what we typically think of when it comes to time travel. No one in the Bible jumps into a high-tech machine and travels to the past or the future. However, it seems that God Himself has initiated a type of time travel for His prophets in the past."[25]

In the Bible, we find Moses and Elijah traveling forward in time, Peck argued, to see Jesus on the Mount of Transfiguration (Matt. 17:1–13; Luke 9:28–36); Philip was whisked away by the Holy Spirit from the Ethiopian eunuch's side to a different city in a blink of an eye (Acts 8:39–40); and we find Ezekiel carried away by the Spirit of God, one moment sitting in his house, and the next inside the temple (Ezek. 8:1–4).

Some have even claimed that Trump is a time traveler, helping explain his vast wealth and rise to the political pinnacle of power. Even though some of the information about the connection between the Lockwood novels and the Trump family is incorrect (for example, Don Fum is a fifteenth-century Spaniard, so he doesn't live on Fifth Avenue in New York or travel with Baron

Trump, who also doesn't live in New York), videos and other posts on the subject have gotten millions of hits. In a recent *Newsweek* article, Benjamin Lynch noted Ingersoll's novels feature the character Baron Trump and his enigmatic guide Don, reigniting conspiracy theories about Trump and his youngest son, Barron Trump.

"Time travel talk was reignited after a viral TikTok...since viewed more than 5.9 million times, discussed Ingersoll Lockwood's [books]," Lynch wrote. "Lockwood's stories became a hot topic of conspiracy theorists, some of whom claim the Trump family has a time machine, after the Republican entered the White House in 2016. In the new video post, user mattyicer-ants said: 'I've thought about this every day for the past two years: In 1888, a man named Ingersoll Lockwood wrote a book called *Baron Trump's Marvellous Underground Journey*, where a 10-year-old boy named Baron Trump who has a mentor named Don, who is a rich man who lives on Fifth Avenue in New York City. He and Don travel to Russia to find a portal to a magical underground world.' The TikTok user pointed out the books' author lived in New York City at the same time as Serbian-American scientist Nikola Tesla, who some conspiracy theorists often suggest was a time traveler. The name of the book's character, Baron, which is short for the Germanic name 'Wilhelm Heinrich Sebastian Von Troomp,' is further evidence of time travel, according to some. In real life, ex-President Trump descends from German immigrants to the U.S."[26]

In YouTube videos that have garnered millions of views, many have posited dark undercurrents of speculation and conspiracy surrounding the Trump family's ties to prophecies and time travel.

PREDICTING OR CREATING THE FUTURE

Humanity longs to know what is going to happen in the future. From the famous sixteenth-century French seer Nostradamus to the oracles of Greece to the Hebrew prophets, attempting to peer into the future is one of humanity's greatest fascinations and deep-seated needs.

The Lockwood novels are "just mind blowing to me," said Rabbi Jonathan Bernis, host of the syndicated television show *Jewish Voice With Jonathan Bernis*. "They're unexplainable without...prophetic insight that looks to the future. There are two kinds of prophecy as I see it. One is revealing the present, a prophetic word that looks into a person's heart and actually sees the condition of a person or the need of a person, whatever it is. And there is edification that's brought, or truth that's brought, or healing that is brought, or whatever through a contemporary prophetic word.

"But there is also throughout Scripture, in both the Old and New Testaments, a dimension of prophecy that's futuristic. For example, the Messianic prophecies contained both in the Torah and the Prophets were describing things that would happen hundreds of years or thousands of years later in great detail. Isaiah 53, for example, is absolutely stunning. It's clearly talking about the Messiah, that He would be despised, rejected, that He would be bruised for our transgressions, and that the sin of the world would be placed upon Him. He would be led as a lamb to the slaughter. We have predictive prophecy in Micah that the Messiah would be born in Bethlehem. At the time it was written, Bethlehem was just a tiny little village of no significance....There are so many prophecies that speak of the second coming of the Messiah, that spoke about His first coming hundreds of years before He was born....and then many, many prophecies that talk about the end of days, the last days, [and that] we'd see some very specific things happening, [a] crescendo of immorality, of violence, the time of Noah. We would see a return to the time of Noah, the political unrest, the economic upheaval, rampant sin, and on and on. These are all clearly prophesied in the Scriptures [and] are yet to come. This is a prophecy, in a sense...time travel....I don't know about the scientific dimensions of that with H. G. Wells and so on, but it's certainly uncanny. It's amazing to me when we see things like the Lockwood novels....It's stunning."[27]

The drive for prescient knowledge involves a complex set of psychological motivations. Some want to predict the future for good and noble reasons: to know how to prepare for catastrophes, to know what to do with their lives, or to warn others of what is on the horizon in terms of God's plan for humanity.

Enoch, Noah, Moses, Samuel, Elijah, Isaiah, Jeremiah, Ezekiel, Daniel, and others were true prophets whose predictions came "to pass" (Jer. 28:9, NKJV). For example, Moses predicted the Israelites would successfully conquer the Promised Land under Joshua (Deut. 31:23), Samuel foresaw the failure of Saul's kingdom (1 Sam. 15:28), Elijah prophesied the deaths of Ahab and Jezebel (1 Kings 21:19–23), Isaiah foresaw that Jerusalem would be delivered from the Assyrian King Sennacherib's invasion (2 Kings 19:34–37), and Jeremiah predicted the seventy-year captivity of the Jews in Babylon (Jer. 25:9–13).

You may wonder whether prophets still exist today. We know the gift is still active because Acts 2:17–18 tells us, "In the last days, God says, I will pour out my Spirit on all people. Your sons and daughters will prophesy, your young men will see visions, your old men will dream dreams. Even on my servants, both men and women, I will pour out my Spirit in those days, and they will prophesy." Romans 12:6 says, "We have different gifts, according to the grace given to each of us. If your gift is prophesying, then prophesy in accordance with your faith."

But amid the mix of true prophets today, just as in biblical times, there are the false prophets. Jesus said, "Watch out for false prophets. They come to you in sheep's clothing, but inwardly they are ferocious wolves," and, "For false messiahs and false prophets will appear and perform signs and wonders to deceive, if possible, even the elect" (Matt. 7:15; Mark 13:22).

Today there are false prophets promoting fake visions and prophetic words, deceitful ideologies, and even occult beliefs, some concealed behind the mask of Marxism, socialism, or globalism.

James Lindsay, a critic of woke ideology and coauthor of the bestseller *Cynical Theories: How Activist Scholarship Made Everything About Race, Gender, and Identity—and Why This Harms Everybody*, documents the progress and tactics of these modern false prophets—many who have invaded the American church—in an ongoing series of articles about the Marxism "cult" that has taken over much of the academic, media, and political worlds.[28] He says they do three things:

1. They tell people what is going to happen.

2. They create the chaos needed to destroy the current conditions.

3. Then they come in with the answers they prepared to make the prophecy a reality.

In light of this, the question is, Was Lockwood accurately predicting the future? Did God indeed show him the future?

Whatever the answer is, anchoring our lives to the truth of God's Word; learning to walk in the supernatural power, protection, and provision of the Holy Spirit; and a lifestyle of repentance and holiness are key to navigating this tumultuous time in history.

BILLY GRAHAM AND THE RETURN: NATIONAL AND GLOBAL DAY OF PRAYER AND REPENTANCE

In 2013, I did an interview with world-renowned evangelist Billy Graham for a seven-part series of articles about the possibility of an end-times "great spiritual awakening." One of the articles, "Billy Graham Sounds Alarm for 2nd Coming," went viral after my friend, *New York Times* bestselling author Rabbi Jonathan Cahn, sent it to actor Pat Boone's wife, who sent it out to her entire email list.[29]

I included the interview in my first book, *The Babylon Code*, which I coauthored with McGuire. It is an investigative exposé of globalism and exploration of "Mystery, Babylon" in Revelation 17–18. In early 2016, a prominent pastor, inspired by the book, decided to deliver a box of copies of *The Babylon Code* to the Trump campaign. Two months later, Trump announced "Americanism, not globalism, will be our credo" as his platform for president.[30] I don't know if there is a connection, but I've always been curious.

In my interview with Graham, he told me that in Jonah's day, Nineveh was the lone world superpower—wealthy, unconcerned, and self-centered. When the prophet Jonah traveled to Nineveh and proclaimed God's warning of impending judgment, the people heard and repented. He said he believed the same thing could happen once again, this time in America—that America could have its own Nineveh moment.

> We need to turn around, repent of sin, turn to God and take the narrow road that Jesus talks about in the Bible. The narrow road means that you forsake sin and you obey God, that you live up to the Ten Commandments and that you live up to the Sermon on the Mount desiring to please God in everything. The narrow road is hard and it is difficult; you can't do that yourself. You need God's help and that's the reason we ask people to come to receive Christ because when you receive Him, the Holy Spirit comes to live within to help us live the life. Our world is desperately seeking answers to the deepest questions of life—answers that can only be found in the Gospel. That is the reason for my hope, that there can be changed hearts and a changed society as we yield ourselves to Christ.[31]

I was so inspired by that interview that McGuire and I called for a day of national repentance in our bestseller *Trumpocalypse*. The last chapter featured an interview with our friend Rev. Kevin Jessip, who later became cochair of The Return. Jessip is a descendant of "Pilgrim Fathers" pastor John Robinson, who provided spiritual guidance to the Pilgrims before their 1620 journey to America aboard the Mayflower, and I met him when I was executive editor of *Charisma* magazine and Charisma Media a decade ago. At the time, Jessip told me he felt called to lead a national repentance movement.

He told me that President Abraham Lincoln was the last president to call for such an event. At the height of the Civil War, on March 30, 1863, Lincoln proclaimed "a day of National Humiliation, Fasting and Prayer."[32] He later credited it with the North winning the Civil War, saving America, and ending slavery. George Washington credited a similar event with the colonial forces beating the British in the Revolutionary War and the birth of America. Throughout America's early history, many presidents called for these sacred solemn assemblies, modeled after the ones the ancient Israelites would hold at times of national crisis.[33]

After the release of *Trumpocalypse* in early 2018, Jessip began networking with a who's who of major faith, political, and business leaders. He asked McGuire and me to write the White House executive summary for the event and persuaded Cahn to be the spokesman, and by a miracle of the Holy Spirit, it went forward. It was called The Return: National and Global Day of Prayer and Repentance. It was held September 26, 2020, on the National Mall in Washington, DC. Thousands of people attended, and over forty-two million people watched it on television or online. On that day, Trump issued a proclamation for a "National Day of Prayer and Return" and also flew over the National Mall in Marine One.[34]

I later learned by reading *A Prophet with Honor: The Billy Graham Story* that Graham asked presidents from Dwight D. Eisenhower to George W. Bush to call for such an event, but none did until Trump did so.

IS THIS AMERICA'S NINEVEH MOMENT?

As Jesus' followers, are we being called to action? Is the destiny of America and the world in our hands? If we truly repent, turn away from our sins, and devote our lives to serving in God's army of warriors, could we witness one last great revival before Jesus' return?

Many people believe that we are now in a Nineveh moment. Has God put the ball in our court?

How does Trump fit into unfolding end-times prophecies? As the first president to issue a proclamation for a day of prayer and return since Lincoln, is he tied to the Nineveh moment? Did The Return and Trump's proclamation affect God's deliberations regarding our future?

After The Return, many prophetic leaders predicted that Trump would win the 2020 presidential election, but he didn't.

Trump and many others have claimed the 2020 election was rigged, and a recent Monmouth University poll found 30 percent of Americans—including 68 percent of Republicans—"believe that Joe Biden only won the presidency because of voter fraud."[35]

But regardless of what really happened, did God use the outcome of the election to humble Trump, widely known for his hubris, and has He used the last four years to awaken much of the United States and the world to the shocking level of evil and corruption in government, media, education, and society?

Will the pockets of revival that seemed to have started with the release of Pastor Greg Laurie's hit movie *Jesus Revolution*, along with the Asbury Revival and similar ones, continue and grow?

Many people believe we are at a crossroads in time and wonder if America could still have a promising future, despite its many challenges.

VOTING AND PRAYER: CIVIC AND BIBLICAL DUTIES

Given Lockwood's seemingly prophetic warnings, how should America respond? With so many people questioning the legitimacy of the 2020 presidential election, many may be discouraged, wondering if their vote will count in the 2024 presidential election.

However, following the first presidential debate between Trump and Biden in late June 2024, a CNN poll found most voters say they have no real confidence in Biden's ability to lead the country, with 67 percent saying Trump beat Biden in the debate.[36] "It was clear a political disaster was about to unfold as soon as the 81-year-old commander in chief stiffly shuffled on stage in Atlanta to stand eight feet from ex-President Donald Trump at what may turn into the most fateful presidential debate in history," CNN analyst Stephen Collinson wrote.[37]

Then, on July 21, 2024, amid mounting pressure, Biden announced that he was dropping out of the race and ending his presidential campaign but planned to serve out the remainder of his term. He endorsed Vice President Kamala Harris for the presidential nomination. "My very first decision as the party nominee in 2020 was to pick Kamala Harris as my Vice President," Biden wrote on social media. "And it's been the best decision I've made. Today I want to offer my full support and endorsement for Kamala to be the nominee of our party this year. Democrats—it's time to come together and beat Trump. Let's do this."[38]

In response, US Rep. Elise Stefanik (R-NY) questioned whether Biden was capable of serving out the remainder of his term given his cognitive decline. "If Joe Biden can't run for re-election, he is unable and unfit to serve as President of the United States. He must immediately resign," she said. "The Democrat Party is in absolute free fall for their blatantly corrupt and desperate attempt to cover up the fact that Joe Biden is unfit for office. Every elected Democrat in America owns Joe Biden's failed and feckless record causing the border crisis, Bidenflation, and chaos and weakness around the world. President Trump will win this November to save America."[39]

Given this development, as I was making final changes to *The Trump Code* in mid-July 2024, it was unclear who Trump would face on the ballot in November, although Harris was widely seen as the Democrat most likely to take Biden's place. Shortly after Biden's announcement, Bill and Hillary Clinton and other prominent Democrats endorsed Harris.[40]

Biden's announcement upended the election process several months before Election Day. Initially, Trump's lead in the polls soared while Democrats fought internally.[41] But by July 30, 2024, a Reuters/Ipsos poll found Trump and Harris were essentially tied in the polls, with 43 percent of registered voters supporting Harris and 42 percent supporting Trump, within the poll's 3.5 percentage point margin of error.[42]

And although there was speculation why former President Barack Obama didn't initiallly endorse Harris, with pundits asking whether Harris might name Obama's wife, Michelle, as her vice president, Obama endorsed Harris later in the month, saying, "We called to say Michelle and I couldn't be prouder to endorse you and do everything we can to get you through this election and into the Oval Office."[43]

In light of this election chaos, how should believers respond? As God's sons and daughters, we know we are to pray for our leaders, vote biblical values in elections, be active in our communities and cities, participate in our government and schools, and take a stand for the truth of Jesus Christ.

From all the indications this is the presidential election of all elections. Whether this is about the last president of the United States or not, for all intents and purposes, this is the most crucial election this country—and possibly the world—has ever seen. The importance of voting and prayer cannot be overstated. If we, the free people of America, sit back and let things go along as they are, we are finished as a nation.

"[The Biden administration has] obviously been devastating in a lot of ways, economically, spiritually; it's unleashed a whole realm of demonic influence in the US federal government," said Christian worship leader Sean Feucht, who ran for Congress in 2020. "It's normalized perversion....I think that we're kind of in a place now where...it's not even the choice of trying to choose the lesser [of] two evils. It's the choice of choosing survival for American Western civilization. That's how strongly I feel about it.

"Of course, there's a lot of policies and things I appreciate about Trump being strong on. One of the biggest ones, obviously, is the open borders in the situation we have in America right now. We don't know who is coming into our country [or the number] of deaths that have happened from illegal immigrants that are part of gangs, the [number] of terrorists that have probably made their way...into the nation. The amount of drugs that have poured in from the borders, it's just incredible. I mean, we've never seen anything so horrible, and that's just one aspect....We're just in a really crucial place right now in America where we are praying and believing and standing and doing our best....So that's obviously why we want to see Trump elected in November. And we're praying that God would give us a chance in America, although we don't deserve it. We're praying that God would give us His grace and would help stop some of the insanity that's happening."[44]

If we all get to work, pray, and have faith, could what Pastor Begley calls the "great harvest revival" be just around the corner? As Jesus, the biblical prophets, and Graham have said, it will only come through repentance and holiness.

This is truly America's Nineveh moment.

CHAPTER TWO

AGE OF DECEPTION

The simple step of a simple courageous man is not to partake in falsehood, not to support false actions!...One word of truth shall outweigh the whole world.
—ALEKSANDR SOLZHENITSYN, RUSSIAN NOVELIST AND DISSIDENT, NOBEL LECTURE

E VERY GENERATION FACES trying times. Today we confront global famine, collapsing economies, fake news, and rampant depravity. But this era seems very different, marked by an unprecedented age of deception.

Consider the following two scandals, both uncorked during the last four years:

THE COVID-19 SCANDAL

In an interview on Epoch TV, *New York Times* bestselling author and journalist Lee Smith talked to Dr. Robert Malone, the inventor of mRNA and DNA vaccination technologies, about his book *Lies My Gov't Told Me.* In the book, Dr. Malone "tells the unknown story about the real origins of the pandemic." While Malone says there is nearly a complete media blackout on this topic, the US House of Representatives Committee on Oversight and Accountability revealed on its website that "mounting evidence points to the virus originating from a leak at the Wuhan Institute of Virology (WIV). EcoHealth Alliance, a U.S. National Institutes of Health (NIH) grantee, awarded taxpayer funds to the WIV to conduct gain of function research on bat coronaviruses—research that may have started the pandemic. Committee Republicans have unearthed emails revealing that top virologists warned Dr. Anthony Fauci, the Director of the National Institute of Allergy and Infectious Diseases, that the virus appeared to be genetically engineered and pointed to a lab leak in Wuhan. However, these emails reveal that Dr. Fauci and former NIH Director Dr. Francis Collins may have colluded with scientists to downplay the lab leak theory for their preferred narrative of natural origin."[1] As it turns out, "COVID wasn't just a public health disaster—it's also a national security scandal of the first order."[2]

The COVID-19 vaccine scandal

Even though the COVID vaccines were labeled safe and effective, the truth about the mRNA vaccines is pouring out. On the Children's Health Defense Fund website, Michael Nevradakis, PhD, wrote:

> U.S. Food and Drug Administration (FDA) officials Dr. Janet Woodcock, principal deputy commissioner of food and drugs and Peter Marks, M.D., Ph.D., director of the FDA's Center for Biologics Evaluation and Research, knew about COVID-19 vaccine injuries in early 2021, according to documents obtained by Children's Health Defense (CHD). The same documents revealed that Dr. Anthony Fauci knew COVID-19 vaccines were causing serious injuries within days of their rollout in December 2020. The latest documents show vaccine-injured individuals emailed Woodcock and Marks several times throughout 2021 and 2022 with pleas for help regarding their injuries—when they claimed the vaccines were "safe and effective."[3]

This scandal reveals a disturbing trend where public health decisions are influenced more by political and financial interests than by genuine concern for public welfare. The consequences of such deception are far-reaching, impacting public trust and the overall health system.

AN UPSIDE-DOWN WORLD

Lies and deception are not new weapons against mankind. After all, what was Satan's first weapon in the Garden of Eden? Genesis 3:1–5 tells the story:

> Now the serpent was more crafty than any of the wild animals the LORD God had made. He said to the woman, "Did God really say, 'You must not eat from any tree in the garden'?"
> The woman said to the serpent, "We may eat fruit from the trees in the garden, but God did say, 'You must not eat fruit from the tree that is in the middle of the garden, and you must not touch it, or you will die.'"
> "You will not certainly die," the serpent said to the woman. "For

God knows that when you eat from it your eyes will be opened, and you will be like God, knowing good and evil."

Throughout history, the father of lies has used deception as a primary tactic in his war against humanity and God. In John 8:44, Jesus told us that the devil was "a murderer from the beginning, not holding to the truth, for there is no truth in him. When he lies, he speaks his native language, for he is a liar and the father of lies."

It is not an overstatement to say that Satan's "wiles" (Eph. 6:11, NKJV)—the tricks and deceptions he employs to harm, trouble, and deceive people, especially believers who are serving God—have accelerated dramatically in recent decades and years.

Today Satan's deceptions have accelerated, eroding reality aggressively.

Jack Hibbs, senior pastor at Calvary Chapel Chino Hills in Southern California, said the world stage is being set for the coming of a global dictator who will gain power through deceit, as detailed in Revelation 13 and other parts of Scripture.

"He's going to be the Antichrist, the coming of the lawless one," Hibbs said. "It means that he's going to make up the rules, and people will love him. He's going to bring demonically energized ideas to the forefront, and people will swoon over his demonic genius."[4]

The effort to prepare the world for the arrival of Antichrist is waging in the media and on social media, and it is all about reality and who gets to define it. It has only begun.

THE GREAT RESET AND GLOBAL CONTROL

James Poulos, executive editor of *The American Mind*, a publication of the Claremont Institute think tank dedicated to restoring the principles of the American Founding Fathers, wrote, "One of the deepest sources of confusion about the course of the present struggle is whether the online ferment better favors a recovery of the republic or a radical departure toward more futuristic or atavistic arrangements. Disillusionment with the bipartisan and global elite, and the sprawling apparatus of communication and criticism through which they wield control, is not just heady stuff. It acts, in the parlance of online culture, like one of the pills from *The Matrix*, after which the consumer is awakened to the vastness of true reality and will never be the same."[5]

Not long after the outbreak of the COVID-19 pandemic, World Economic Forum Executive Chairman Klaus Schwab announced the "Great Reset" of capitalism, a plan critics say calls on nations to surrender their sovereignty to an international body amid the disappearance of middle-class lifestyles and a reset of the financial system before the introduction of digital currencies and IDs. In the article Schwab wrote:

> To achieve a better outcome, the world must act jointly and swiftly to revamp all aspects of our societies and economies, from education to social contracts and working conditions. Every country, from the United States to China, must participate, and every industry, from oil and gas to tech, must be transformed. In short, we need a "Great Reset" of capitalism.[6]

They want to strip us of our freedom of speech, freedom of religion, and other rights detailed in the Bill of Rights. Though it was quickly paused and then disbanded, the Disinformation Governance Board set up by the Biden administration was intended to coordinate "activities related to disinformation aimed at the US population and infrastructure."[7] It was shut down months after being chartered due to an outcry of censorship.

Meanwhile the growing popularity of artificial intelligence and virtual assistant programs like OpenAI software ChatGPT is going to massively disrupt the lives of tens of millions of people. The investment bank Goldman Sachs estimates three hundred million jobs in the United States and Europe "could be lost or diminished by this fast-growing technology."[8] Replacing human workers with artificial intelligence will save big business, government, education, the entertainment industry, and the media time, money, and hassle.

What are we to do? How do we navigate this world drowning in a tsunami of lies, cancel culture, wokeism, artificial intelligence, loss of freedoms, the Great Reset, and push for digital currencies and IDs? And why is this happening so fast, especially after President Trump's inauguration in January 2017?

NAVIGATING THE LIES AROUND PRESIDENT DONALD J. TRUMP

The fake news onslaught didn't begin with President Trump's inauguration, but it certainly hit a fever pitch once he entered office. According to mainstream media and elite pundits, President Trump was going to destroy America and our way of life. *The Guardian*'s headline after Trump's stunning victory in 2016 read: "Donald Trump Wins Presidential Election, Plunging US Into Uncertain Future: Trump Rides Wave of Anti-Establishment Sentiment to One of the Most Improbable Political Victories in Modern US History."[9]

While no president makes it through a term unscathed, the attacks on Trump before, during, and after his term are unprecedented in American history. Rumors, lies, and innuendos spouted by FBI agents, CIA directors, heads of major government departments, representatives, senators, and presidential candidates swirled around Trump from day one. These deceptions were published, aired, posted, and blogged twenty-four hours a day, seven days a week, all four years of his presidency—and ever since.

The question is why those in power have overwhelmed the airwaves, internet, and every other vehicle of information delivery, all to confuse and deceive us about who Trump is and what he wants.

One of the most virulent attacks launched against the president has come to be known as Spygate, the name of the scandal referring to Trump's claim that the FBI implanted officials for political purposes inside his 2016 presidential campaign. "Reports are there was indeed at least one FBI representative implanted, for political purposes, into my campaign for president. It took place very early on, and long before the phony Russia Hoax became a 'hot' Fake News story," Trump tweeted. "If true—all time biggest political scandal!"[10]

Newsmax offered this explanation, putting the Spygate scandal in the larger context of the constant political attacks Trump sustained during his first term in office:

> Not since 1776, has this nation ever been in the worst throes of a national unraveling. Not even the Civil War the nation experienced caused so much loathing and uncivil discourse as the Democrat Party's attempt to influence the 2016 presidential election. The alleged collusion by President Trump with Russia and/or

intimidation of Ukraine is the Democrat's creation. This creation should be titled as "The Pelosi-Schiff Legislative Fairytale: The Impeachment of President Trump." Unfortunately, a Democrat-controlled U.S. House of Representatives voted the fairytale into reality. This present impeachment try will haunt the Democrats in November 2020—and beyond.[11]

Alongside the Spygate scandal, there were two impeachments (both failed), declarations of his incompetency to lead, assertions that his stand against countries like China would send us into another world war, and defaming accusations of mental illness.

He is now embroiled in lawfare over stored declassified documents at his Mar-a-Lago Club in Palm Beach, Florida, his claims that the 2020 elections were rigged, assaults on his private businesses in New York City, as well as personal attacks on his wife and children.

On May 30, 2024, he became the first former president to be convicted of felony crimes after a New York jury found him guilty of falsifying business records to cover up hush money payments to a porn actor who alleged she had sex with Trump in 2006. Trump maintained throughout the trial that he did nothing wrong, and the case should never have been brought. In addition, he denied the sexual encounter, with his lawyers arguing during the trial "that his celebrity status…made him a target for extortion."[12]

In a Charisma News article—"After Guilty Verdict, Can Christians Still Support Donald Trump?"—Shane Idleman, founder and lead pastor of Westside Christian Fellowship in Southern California, wrote the better, biblical question to ask is what direction the country is heading. "The short answer to the original question is 'Absolutely, especially after a sham trial that resembles Venezuela more than America,'" Idleman wrote. "If a leader lacks Christian character but is pointing the nation back to God, is that a bad thing? If they are being a terror to terrorists and making America secure, is that a bad thing? If they are honoring hard work and minimizing free handouts, is that a bad thing? If they are fighting the global agenda to enslave America, is that a bad thing? God doesn't judge a nation based on the character of one man; He judges it based on the spiritual health of its people—from corrupt Balaam to ungodly kings in the Old Testament—if they direct the people back to God, it can be a good thing."

Idleman continued, "Not voting for Trump is a vote against what needs to happen in this nation. We can't allow personal pain or flawed character to have national consequences. We're not playing games anymore—serious things are on the line that have massive consequences. We need to wake up. There is no plan B."[13]

"THEY ARE AFTER YOU. I'M JUST IN THE WAY."

These assaults on freedom and rights, integrity and beliefs are not confined to Trump and his family. In fact, he has tweeted out images numerous times, saying, "In reality they're not after me. They are after you. I'm just in the way."[14]

He's not wrong. Take the case of the parents who stood up to school board policies they felt were damaging their children—like mask and vaccine mandates—who were investigated by the FBI.

In a May 12, 2022, article Jeremiah Poff of the *Washington Examiner* wrote:

> The FBI has opened multiple investigations into parents protesting education policies, including a father who was upset over mask mandates, according to new whistleblower revelations. The FBI's activities were publicly revealed in a letter Wednesday from Republicans on the House Judiciary Committee to Attorney General Merrick Garland. The specifics of the FBI's investigations were disclosed to lawmakers by whistleblowers. Garland directed the FBI and the Department of Justice to form a joint task force in October 2021 to investigate threats against school board members after the National School Boards Association asked the Biden administration in a September 2021 letter to investigate parents protesting at school board meetings as domestic terrorists under the Patriot Act.[15]

During the pandemic, people who didn't want to take the COVID-19 vaccine were vilified as haters, killers, and villains. Many people lost their jobs for wanting bodily autonomy.

An NPR article headline from October 24, 2021, stated, "Thousands of Workers Are Opting to Get Fired, Rather Than Take the Vaccine." Andrea Hsu wrote in the article,

Across the country, employers are firing workers for refusing to comply with vaccine mandates. Some people are opting to quit their jobs rather than take the shot. These workers represent only a tiny fraction of overall employees, not even 1% in some workplaces. But it can add up to thousands of people in many states.[16]

She also quoted Karl Bohnak, who "worked at his dream job delivering weather forecasts on TV for what he considers one of the most challenging but beautiful spots in the United States—Michigan's Upper Peninsula." He said, "I just did not want to take the shot. I felt it was my right as a human being and a citizen of the U.S. to decide what I put in my body."[17]

IS AMERICA UNDERGOING A COVERT MARXIST REVOLUTION?

All of this is happening in America—not the People's Republic of China, not the former Soviet Union, but in America, the land of the free and home of the brave.

Is America, under the Biden administration, undergoing what amounts to a covert socialist or communist takeover? That's the opinion of many people I know, including many conservatives and Christians who write for various media outlets. After all, in 2019, nearly two-thirds of Democrats and Democratic leaners (65 percent) had a positive view of socialism, dropping to 57 percent in 2022. In comparison, only 15 percent of Republicans and Republican-leaning independents had a positive impression of socialism in 2019, with the percentage remaining almost the same, at 14 percent, in 2022, according to the Pew Research Center.[18]

In a *New York Post* article titled, "Four Communist Escapees Warn: 'America Is Becoming Authoritarian Nation,'" Rikki Schlott wrote that four people who escaped communist regimes to come to America believe the United States is now heading in the same direction. "Having survived authoritarianism, they see ominous signs here—groupthink, cancel culture and young Americans favoring socialism just as much as capitalism," Schlott wrote. "Four foreign-born Americans shared their concerns as a warning to fellow citizens. 'Hear our voices,' said Amy Phan West, an émigré from Vietnam. 'We are speaking the truth because we experienced it....I'm especially concerned about censorship....If we don't follow the status quo, we get censored and silenced. As long as people can speak their minds, they can't be controlled....With the rise of socialism, our country is in the beginning stage of communism....It doesn't happen overnight. First, they say they'll take care of you. But I don't think people understand what a slippery slope this is. You guys want socialism? Are you kidding me?"[19]

These people understand the extreme brutal nature of totalitarian communist and socialist regimes. Since 1900, the world has witnessed numerous communist and socialist revolutions, resulting in wholesale death, suffering, and deprivation, including the Russian Revolution led by leftist revolutionary Vladimir Lenin in 1917 that propelled the Bolsheviks to power, the rise of the National Socialist German Workers' Party (Nazi Party) under Adolf Hitler, and the 1949 Chinese Revolution under Chinese Communist leader Mao Tse-tung, leading to the creation of the People's Republic of China.

During the twentieth century, governments, primarily communist and fascist ones, murdered over two hundred million people, not counting battle deaths from wars. "Communist regimes are far away the most murderous," David Kopel wrote in his *Reason* magazine article "Data on Mass Murder by Government in the 20th Century." "Overall, the communists murdered approximately 168,759,000 from 1900 to 1987. On the whole, the most-murderous fascist regimes proved to be less durable than their communist counterparts, so their killing sprees did not last as long. The 1900–87 murder count by fascist regimes was 27,848,000....All these figures are rough midpoint estimates. They come from a scholar who dedicated his outstanding career to quantifying mass murder by government and examining it[s] causes."[20]

Could this happen in America?

"Christians in America need to read their history books," said Paul McGuire. "We will either have a biblical revival and a reprieve...[or we will have what] history guarantees...we will have totalitarianism on the level of Hitlerian dictatorship, a holocaust where thirty to thirty-five million people were killed, or something along the lines of the death camps of Chairman Mao or a communist revolution. Do not think for a moment that it can't happen in America. It could happen in America in the blink of an eye. The only thing that's standing between us and total murderous totalitarianism is the power of God and the fact that we need to be stewards over our nation and have proper discernment regarding who we're voting for and be righteous in our voting. I believe that, energized by a biblical third Great Awakening, [we] can turn the tide of the spiritual battle."[21]

THE GOD FACTOR AND DEEP STATE

What is the truth of what God did through Trump during his first term in office? Here is some information showing that good, not evil, was coming out of the leadership God set up (see Daniel 2:21) in the White House:

- His Supreme Court justice picks—Neil Gorsuch, Brett Kavanaugh, and Amy Coney Barrett—were appointed, allowing the prayers of millions of people to be answered as the justices bravely took on the *Roe v. Wade* ruling in 1973 that legalized abortion. In June 2022, the high court reversed *Roe v. Wade*, declaring that the constitutional right to abortion no longer exists.

- He stood with people of faith—Protestant, Catholic, and Jewish—and signed a "'religious liberty' executive order allowing for broad exemptions," which eased "the ban on tax-exempt organizations such as churches engaging in political speech. 'We are giving our churches their voices back,' Trump said."[22]

These are just a few of the many ways that morality and righteousness were restored to America under Trump. His willingness to boldly stand up and speak out about the dangers of socialism, communism, globalism, and the deep state gave a voice to millions of people in this country who share his concerns.

McGuire said globalism is an "evil organizational structure."

"Globalism by its very nature is Luciferian," McGuire said. "That's why in ancient Babylon at the time of the Tower of Babel…they used that Luciferian organizational structure. They were globalists; they spoke a common language. So globalism…by its very DNA, has to eventually morph into a digital totalitarian state.…The media [and] globalists have been brainwashing people for centuries…telling them that, well, if we all unite as one like the John Lennon song 'Imagine'…then the [world's] problems will be healed and everything will be great. We'll have paradise on earth. That's a total lie. Every time you see a push for globalism, you always see totalitarianism."[23]

During Trump's term in office, a Monmouth University Poll found a large bipartisan majority of Americans "feel national policy is being manipulated or directed by a 'Deep State.'" A total of 60 percent of Americans "feel that unelected or appointed government officials have too much influence in determining federal policy....Democrats (59%), Republicans (59%) and independents (62%) agree that appointed officials hold too much sway in the federal government."[24]

"We usually expect opinions on the operation of government to shift depending on which party is in charge. But there's an ominous feeling by Democrats and Republicans alike that a 'Deep State' of unelected operatives are pulling the levers of power," said Patrick Murray, director of the independent Monmouth University Polling Institute.[25]

When the term *deep state* is "described as a group of unelected government and military officials who secretly manipulate or direct national policy, nearly 3-in-4 (74 %) say they believe this type of apparatus exists in Washington. This includes 27% who say it definitely exists and 47% who say it probably exists."[26]

Inspired by Trump's shoot-from-the-hip style, his success as a billionaire real estate and resort developer, and his belief that America can be great again, many Americans have become courageous to stand up to the progressive and woke ideologies they view as harmful and detrimental to their families and the nation. As the apostle James explained, describing a key strategy in achieving victory over Satan's schemes, "Therefore submit to God. Resist the devil and he will flee from you" (Jas. 4:7, NKJV).

It all began with Trump's inaugural address on January 20, 2017, coming only two months after his election on November 8, 2016. Just Trump's election sent shock waves around the world, inspiring Billy Graham Evangelistic Association President Franklin Graham to ask whether the "God-factor" was behind Trump's unexpected election.[27] On Inauguration Day, President Trump famously declared:

> We, the citizens of America, are now joined in a great national effort
> to rebuild our country and restore its promise for all of our people.
> Together, we will determine the course of America and the world for

many, many years to come. We will face challenges. We will confront hardships. But we will get the job done....

Today's ceremony, however, has very special meaning. Because today we are not merely transferring power from one Administration to another, or from one party to another—but we are transferring power from Washington, D.C. and giving it back to you, the people.

For too long, a small group in our nation's Capital has reaped the rewards of government while the people have borne the cost. Washington flourished—but the people did not share in its wealth. Politicians prospered—but the jobs left, and the factories closed. The establishment protected itself, but not the citizens of our country. Their victories have not been your victories; their triumphs have not been your triumphs; and while they celebrated in our nation's Capital, there was little to celebrate for struggling families all across our land.

That all changes—starting right here, and right now, because this moment is your moment: it belongs to you. It belongs to everyone gathered here today and everyone watching all across America. This is your day. This is your celebration. And this, the United States of America, is your country.

What truly matters is not which party controls our government, but whether our government is controlled by the people. January 20th, 2017, will be remembered as the day the people became the rulers of this nation again. The forgotten men and women of our country will be forgotten no longer.[28]

NAVIGATING FAKE NEWS AND ARTIFICIAL INTELLIGENCE

While Americans like former Defense Department official Kash Patel, who has been touted as a possible acting attorney general under Trump, and former congressman Devin Nunes did the American people and the world a tremendous service by exposing the reality behind Spygate, they had access to sources of information that everyday Americans will never gain access to.

What does the everyday American do to steer his or her way through the sea of accusations, misdirects, and deepfakes involving Trump and today's political system?

Further muddying the waters is the release of artificial intelligence (AI) into the public. What once was hypothetical and academic now sits in the palms of our hands, giving us the power to create photographic scenes that never happened, videos of people doing things they have never done, and write entire books on subjects we've never studied, all in the blink of an eye.

While we'll go into more depth later, AI needs to be mentioned due to the fact that countries are in a race for supremacy in using AI to control all aspects of life—even our beliefs.

As James Poulos wrote, "Technological and theological issues intersect." He argued that the present conflicts and crises we see in our world are due to a covert war raging on the internet. He posited that it has been going on for a long time and is rooted, in turn, "in the scramble to reestablish sovereign political authority necessitated by the meteoric rise of digital technology."[29]

Why? Because the globalist elite want to rule the world through digital technology—with AI at the core.

> In the digital age, he who is not the leader appears destined to be not the master but a servant or slave. Accordingly, each digital super-power is compelled to reason that the only path to world mastery runs through digital world war—a conflagration without precedent or parallel on earth, a wager of incalculable risk with outcomes impossible, even for the most advanced AI itself, to predict....The answer... appears to turn on the way in which many Gentile and Jewish elites of the Western ruling class have abandoned their inherited religions in favor of a new project to construct a new religion around the worship of technology. This endeavor itself appears sharply divided: on one side, superhumanists promising individualist emancipation from the constraints of merely human life; on the other, transhumanists invoking a new and utopian collectivity through our merger with our machines....If both Jews and Gentiles fail to muster spiritual alternatives sufficient to overcome the massive temptation to worship technology and the logic of absolute and unbounded technological "progress," "Judeo-Christian values" will swiftly prove unable to stop the transformation of the West's "rules-based" regional order into a cyborg theocracy bent on planetary domination and transformation.[30]

In an interview with Charisma News titled "5 Ways AI Is Summoning the Antichrist Agenda," author and international prophetic voice Joseph Z said AI will be at the forefront of the end times struggles people will face in the future. The uses of AI "could range from autonomous weapons systems used in warfare to AI algorithms that perpetuate biases and discrimination" against believers. AI is already being used by innovators like SpaceX and Tesla founder Elon Musk to create brain chips for mind-control based products.

"AI itself is not bad coming out of the gate; it's who programs it," Z said. "When we're talking about Elon Musk and AI, on the one hand, he's kind of a white knight of liberty and freedom of speech. And on the other hand, he says, you know they're summoning demons....When you look at medical tyranny, and then you look at technological tyrannies, such as AI, or what could begin to rise from it, I see the mark of the beast scenario coming into play. When you look at digital currency being a programmable issue, you look at AI, the technology that can run everything....They're even predicting the next few years that the wars we would supposedly get into would be fought AI to AI, by China, by other nations, by us... that AI would actually step up and people would step away from it. AI, I believe, is the system that the beast will use to rule the world when his time comes."[31]

THE WORD OF GOD AND REALITY

Amid the rise of AI, the deep state, and massive levels of deception today, millions of people are asking the same question: How can we know what is true?

This book is about how to discern what is true about Trump, prophecy, and the future of America and the world.

It seems like a simple question. But with the never-ending outpouring of opinions and the overwhelming invasion of the internet and media into our lives, discovering what the truth is on a very basic level can be quite daunting.

God has not left us to ourselves, however. We have a way forward in the dark. The Word of God is the light we need at this moment, and it leads us to Jesus Christ. Why? Because Jesus wants us to come into a living, vibrant, life-changing relationship with truth Himself, our Lord and Savior Jesus Christ. "I am the way and the truth and the life," Jesus said in John 14:6.

John 16:13 (ESV) says, "When the Spirit of truth comes, he will guide you into all the truth, for he will not speak on his own authority, but whatever he hears he will speak, and he will declare to you the things that are to come."

John 8:31–32 (ESV) says, "So Jesus said to the Jews who had believed him,

'If you abide in my word, you are truly my disciples, and you will know the truth, and the truth will set you free.'"

The truth first reveals Himself through general revelation: what God has revealed about Himself through reality, life, nature, and inside our hearts. The apostle Paul wrote in Romans 1:18–21:

> The wrath of God is being revealed from heaven against all the god-lessness and wickedness of people, who suppress the truth by their wickedness, since what may be known about God is plain to them, because God has made it plain to them. For since the creation of the world God's invisible qualities—his eternal power and divine nature—have been clearly seen, being understood from what has been made, so that people are without excuse. For although they knew God, they neither glorified him as God nor gave thanks to him, but their thinking became futile and their foolish hearts were darkened.

Truth also reveals Himself through special revelation in His Word: "All Scripture is God-breathed and is useful for teaching, rebuking, correcting and training in righteousness, so that the servant of God may be thoroughly equipped for every good work" (2 Tim. 3:16–17).

In a talk given to the Association of Christian Character Development in 2012, the late Dr. Dallas Willard, theologian and professor of philosophy at the University of Southern California, said that the world can only produce "second-level theories" about knowledge, belief, ideas, and concepts. These second-level theories are weak and point to human wisdom as the only wisdom available to us. Because of this, "reality and truth are scorned as something human beings have no access to."[32]

Where does this leave us? According to Dr. Willard, it leaves us floating in a sea of opinions pushed on us by social, political, or even governmental forces. He pointed out that relativism, postmodernism, and deconstructionism undermine traditional values and teachings.

Continuing, Dr. Willard said that the vanishing of moral knowledge from our society, a bedrock of what is real in our world, has left us at the mercy of those in power, driven by their desires to rule and reign.

Multitudes are already ruined by habits of thought, feeling, and action by the time they are beyond elementary grades, or even before that. "Home" often is little more than hell for the little ones. Then they go on to perpetrate what they have experienced. There is no alternative reality and knowledge available for them as they mature.[33]

The answer? The Word of God. Relativism and other isms may make people think they are free, but they are actually enslaved by ideas that lead eventually to destruction. True freedom, true wisdom, and true grace are found only in Jesus. As Dr. Willard said, "Let us present this as public knowledge of moral truth and reality. Let this be our constant vision and intention as we live as students and apprentices of Jesus in Kingdom Living in all aspects of life."[34]

Underscoring Dr. Willard's words, Dr. James Lindsay, author, mathematician, and founder of New Discourses, said, "It's not enough to say the truth; it's not enough for us to tell the truth....You must love the truth, and you must love the truth with all of your heart and all of your mind and all of your soul and all of your strength, and then you must tell the truth to your neighbor as you would have him tell the truth to you."[35]

CHAPTER THREE
THROUGH THE LOOKING GLASS

The broad face is full of intelligence, and the large gray eyes are lighted up
with a good-natured but quizzical look that invariably attracts attention.
—INGERSOLL LOCKWOOD, *BARON TRUMP'S MARVELLOUS UNDERGROUND JOURNEY*

FICTION HAS BEEN said to be an artist (a writer or creator) going out into the world, seeing what is coming, and coming back to tell others what they have seen.

Fox's famed animated show *The Simpsons*, described by Entertainment Weekly as "TV seers," and "eerily (or at least semi-) prophetic," has a track record of doing just that. They predicted smartphones, Lady Gaga flying over the audience attached to cables like she did at the 2017 Super Bowl, and even Disney buying Fox, around nineteen years before it actually happened, in the episode "When You Dish Upon a Star."[1]

In the case of Donald J. Trump, the show has often poked fun at him, but it accurately predicted his run and election in an episode of the show in 2000. The seventeenth episode of season 11, "Bart to the Future," has Bart exploring the future. He is able to go thirty years forward, and while he is there, Bart finds out that Trump had previously run the country.[2] Another episode has a banner showing Trump running in 2024.[3]

There are a dozen other examples of this in the show's past, but the main question is, How are they doing it? Do they have a tap into the psychic world? Is God speaking to them?

While no one knows for sure, some of the show's writers credit it to being immersed in the news, discussing things they think are outlandish, and coming up with plots that might take place.[4] The author, essayist, and Christian apologist G. K. Chesterton also offered an answer:

> Every true artist does feel, consciously or unconsciously, that he
> is touching transcendental truths; that his images are shadows of
> things seen through the veil. In other words, the natural mystic does

know that there is something *there*; something behind the clouds or within the trees; but he believes that the pursuit of beauty is the way to find it; that imagination is a sort of incantation that can call it up.[5]

It's undeniable that something unique has happened when a cartoon for adults accurately predicts the election of a man many did not take seriously as a political figure—despite his repeated claims he would run for president one day.

It seems that they were confirming words spoken by Kim Clement and others that Trump will have a second term and win in 2024.

This phenomenon of fiction seeing into the future and telling us what might happen is not unique to *The Simpsons* or Trump.

Mission: Impossible 7 and Artificial Intelligence

The Simpsons aren't alone as a fictional work predicting the real-world future:

- Jules Verne predicted the lunar landing in his book *From the Earth to the Moon* in 1865.

- In 1953, Ray Bradbury wrote about wireless technology in his book *Fahrenheit 451*.

- *Nineteen Eighty-Four* by George Orwell foresaw the surveillance state the world now lives in, with cameras on every street corner, watching all we do.[6]

- In 1909 E. M. Forster wrote in *The Machine Stops* about a time when people would live and work from their own rooms. The book also proposed people would be communicating with each other entirely through electronic means.[7]

- More recently, Sarah Pinsker's novel *Song for a New Day*, published on September 10, 2019, deals with a culture battling the combination of domestic terrorism and a deadly pandemic.[8]

Also startling is the film *Mission: Impossible—Dead Reckoning Part One*. It has brought to mind the question: What does the most recent *Mission: Impossible* movie, starring Tom Cruise, have to tell us about artificial intelligence and its intrusion into reality? Is it predicting the future or preparing us to accept it?

In the movie, we are thrown into a world that is stalked by a villain never seen before: an artificially intelligent creation that knows the future. But we don't really know what it wants and why it wants it. The AI villain is known as the Entity, and it presents frightening problems and hits very close to home.

The Entity can hack any system, change reality at any time, and impact everyone's decisions in a blink of an eye. The Entity has taken on a life of its own and is out of control.

While the intent of the Entity is not known in part one of the film, it is obvious that it wants to control the world and use it for its own gain. It has become a god, and it wants its wishes fulfilled.

While the ability to hack any database, gather data, and store it in an ultimate manner is not new to us, the ability for the Entity to see the future is new for AI. Throughout the movie, as the good guys attempt to thwart its plans, the Entity predicts people's motives, moves, and deaths.[9]

In the minds of many, *Mission: Impossible* is presenting AI as the threat that it really is for mankind. An article in HuffPost depicted the film as showing the stark reality of the dangers of the rapid and currently uncurbed development of AI, as it is

> among the first major studio blockbusters to directly engage with the threat of AI this year amid our real-life reckoning with it....
>
> Numerous articles have emerged since organizations...have begun co-opting human performance for AI technology....
>
> Many have rightfully asked pressing questions such as, how might this impact people's livelihoods? How could AI possibly take the place of nuance or human emotion? From a legal standpoint, could it potentially exploit people's work—or spark new copyright concerns?[10]

On the opposite end of the spectrum, *Wired* called the film the "perfect AI panic movie." Villains are needed in action movies, so could *Mission:*

Impossible be tapping into the fear of many, and putting out there a "paranoia litmus test, capturing a snapshot of the particular anxieties plaguing the country and its citizens at any given time"?[11]

A lot of action films in the past have made Russians, North Koreans, communists, terrorists, cyber warriors, rogue spies, and more the people to fear.

> Maybe *Mission: Impossible*'s Entity is just the harbinger of the future for action movie baddies....Humanity will no doubt prevail and endure in...*Dead Reckoning*—at their core, action movies are feel-good romps, after all—but in the meantime, millions of moviegoers can come together, bonded by their fear of what's to come.[12]

Or is the film trying to tell us something, something deeper than we see right now? Could the world be on the verge of a human-created intelligence that can control all of life at any moment it wishes?

Could AI be connected to the image of the beast described in Revelation 13? In the famous chapter in the Bible that talks about the beast, or the Antichrist, and the mark of the beast, Revelation 13:15 raises an intriguing question about the second beast, or the false prophet, potentially employing AI: "The second beast was given power to give breath to the image of the first beast, so that the image could speak and cause all who refused to worship the image to be killed."

Whether *M:I 7* is predictive or preparatory, AI is deeply impacting our lives right now: socially, morally, and electorally.

DAYS OF THE AI DEEPFAKE AND THE "SON OF DESTRUCTION"

Pastor Paul Begley said we are now living in the "day of [AI] deepfake [and] deep-state propaganda like we've never seen."

> Now propaganda has always been used in kingdoms trying to take over other kingdoms, especially once the printing press came and publications were being done. Then we had a lot of propaganda. Hitler, of course, was the one who used propaganda probably better than anybody, using publications and radio to really deceive a nation with propaganda. Today, it's unbelievable with the political ads that

are flowing everywhere, TV, the internet, what have you. So people have to take all of it in with a grain of salt.

Whatever you see, don't believe everything you see. Don't believe everything you hear....You know, somebody said, basically digest it all, pray, and use good common sense to start to understand really the agendas. And mainly they are big agendas by two or three great big factions that are trying to control the world, and the puppets are the political pundits a lot of times. So really this is the era of AI and the deep state and the deepfake.[13]

In 2 Thessalonians, the apostle Paul warned that a "falling away" from the true tenets of Christianity would occur in the last days before the "man of sin is revealed, the son of destruction....[His] coming is in accordance with the working of Satan with all power and signs and false wonders.... Therefore God will send them a strong delusion, that they should believe the lie: that they all might be condemned who did not believe the truth but had pleasure in unrighteousness" (vv. 3, 9, 11–12, MEV).

Given the rise of the internet, AI, the surveillance state, smartphones, and the global push for digital currencies, for the first time in history, we can now see how the man of sin, or the Antichrist, could preside over a one-world government in which people can't buy or sell unless they take the mark of the beast (Rev. 13:17).

"It's called a strong delusion in 2 Thessalonians 2," Begley said. "Paul is writing to the Thessalonians, and he's telling them that, look, there's a day coming in the last days, there's going to be this son of perdition, which is the son of hell, the wicked one with a capital W, the lawless one, talking about the Antichrist, and that he will finally reveal himself when he walks into the temple of God and shows himself and declares himself to be God in front of the worshippers of God. And he takes control of the world...and he uses deception, strong delusion. And now also, if you go to the Book of Revelation...chapter 13, it tells you that they...the Antichrist and his sidekick of false prophet, will use...signs and wonders, so much that they could call fire down from heaven and deceive people. So they're going to use all kinds of deepfake trickery and technologies that we don't even know about to help enhance the propaganda that he is this special one, the chosen one....We're talking about somebody who can literally deceive the world to worship him like he's God. And yeah, we're going to see a lot of delusion."[14]

HOW AI IS INFLUENCING SOCIETY AND BELIEFS

Fear and excitement swirl around all things AI. The idea of creating a machine that operates like humans seems terrifying to most and a miraculous wonder to behold to others.

AI has been "a standard part of the industrial repertoire since at least the 1980s."[15] From checking circuit boards to detecting credit-card fraud to machines learning via algorithms to scheduling, AI has been developing for a long time.

Now it is at the center of the most successful companies in the world: Apple, Microsoft, Google, and Amazon. It is making everything easier, giving people a chance to gain unimaginable knowledge, have access to credit they couldn't before, as well as other benefits of contemporary society.[16]

Despite the good that is being done, academics, technologists, and the public have raised concerns that constraints may need to be placed on the growth of AI soon.

As early as 2014, Stephen Hawking, an English theoretical physicist and author, said, "The development of full artificial intelligence could spell the end of the human race....It would take off on its own, and re-design itself at an ever increasing rate."[17]

Elon Musk also warned that AI holds a dark potential. "With artificial intelligence, we are summoning the demon," Musk said at an MIT symposium in 2014. "You know all those stories where there's the guy with the pentagram and the holy water and he's like...yeah, he's sure he can control the demon, [but] it doesn't work out."[18]

AI experts say artificial intelligence already exceeds the human brain, processing information more than one hundred thousand times faster. Developers have also learned that AI accesses available data and teaches itself new skills without being prompted by developers, which they say is mysterious.[19]

In a Goldman Sachs report, economists predicted 18 percent of work globally could be computerized by AI.[20]

AI technology is expanding and being employed at a rate that seems unprecedented. It's changing how we live, work, think, interact, and believe. Though many experts, innovators, and thought leaders are pushing AI research forward, social implications, as we have just looked at, have arisen, and on the tail end of them are the ethical and spiritual implications. .

A Charisma News article entitled "Is Explosion of Artificial Intelligence a Threat to the Bible, Morality?" brings up the emergence of AI and the intense debates around it and its place in our lives as believers. The article reported that a survey by the American Bible Society—which asked respondents if they thought "AI could be relied on for moral reasoning," would they be against their pastors using AI to help prepare sermons or teachings, and do people believe that AI "goes against Biblical teaching"—found that people who were reading Scripture on a regular basis were skeptical of AI; these people had keyed in on the moral hazards coming from how we think about machines and ourselves.

> Scripture-engaged respondents were less optimistic about AI's future benefits, less likely to believe it aids in moral reasoning, and less likely to see it as enriching spiritual practices or promoting "spiritual health."
>
> It's not just Christians who are cautious, though. The general public seems overwhelmingly unsure of what the future holds and appears to be more driven by fear than excitement over what's to come.
>
> The results found 68% of the public disagreed with the idea AI could "promote spiritual health" and 58% also disagreed when asked if it could "aid in moral reasoning."[21]

Jason Jimenez, a Christian apologist and worldview expert, said that AI is very impressive and could be used to improve the lives of people and maybe advance education, but he also warned that AI could wind up as a controlling agent of our lives.

And he noted it could be sooner than we all guess. The faith leader addressed several major concerns he has with AI: "We need to be discussing...[the] many legal and ethical concerns that other people in different professions and expertise are having. And I find myself having them as well."[22] Leading his list of issues is the extinction of human jobs, which would lead to an explosive wave of unemployment.

That will be a crisis that we probably have never seen. Now, on one hand, with AI, with that intelligence, it's going to produce more jobs...to maintain certain aspects, if you will, of AI in that infrastructure. But the vast majority of the jobs that people are currently holding...logistics statisticians, analysts, you name it, marketers, web development, all of these types of things will be replaced.[23]

Jimenez believes that Christians and church leaders need to be aware that the technology is advancing so fast that it will become smarter than us and control and manipulate us.

This will deeply impact our faith walks.

AI: TODAY'S TOWER OF BABEL—"NOTHING WILL BE IMPOSSIBLE FOR THEM"

Perry Stone, founder of Voice of Evangelism Outreach Ministries, in his book *Artificial Intelligence Versus God: The Final Battle for Humanity*, noted that tens of billions of dollars are being invested into AI technology systems that are designed to "turn machines into humans and humans into machines."[24]

As you will see, people once again are attempting to build a Tower of Babel where nothing will be impossible for them. They desire to become like God. This goal will be achieved, they believe, through AI....There is a small but powerful group of people in the world who believe that, if they can increase their knowledge and build technology based on that knowledge, one day they can create a new world and a utopian society. This will be a place with no barriers to tolerance and acceptance, so long as everybody thinks and acts in a government-approved manner. They desire a world where the planet is saved because nobody owns cows or cars, and fossil fuels stay underground where they belong. It will be a world where knowledge is limitless, and where they will live forever without aging, even if they must depopulate the earth and give up their own humanity to achieve these goals. The spirit that motivates this group is the same spirit that tempts people with the desire to gain knowledge and abilities that surpass those of God Himself.[25]

The prophet Daniel predicted that the last days would be characterized by an explosion in knowledge. Daniel 12:4 (NKJV) says, "But you, Daniel, shut up the words, and seal the book until the time of the end; many shall run to and fro, and knowledge shall increase."

From World Economic Forum speaker Yuval Noah Harari's call to have AI rewrite the Bible the "correct" way, to having an actual church service in Germany led by a ChatGPT preacher, to the extreme where someone is working with an AI-generated Ouija board to help people talk to their deceased loved ones, if we aren't careful, discerning, and filled with the mind of Christ, even the elect will be swept away by the intense deception being unleashed.[26]

And it's going to be unleashed because humanity has always wanted to create an entity in our image without divine assistance. Consider the words of transhumanist Dr. Hugo de Garis, known for his work on artificial intelligence and his controversial prediction that "a major war between the supporters and opponents of intelligent machines, resulting in billions of deaths, is almost inevitable before the end of the 21st century."[27]

"The prospect of building godlike creatures fills me with a sense of religious awe that goes to the very depth of my soul and motivates me powerfully to continue, despite the possible horrible negative consequences," de Garis wrote in his book *The Artilect War*.[28]

Repeatedly the Bible warns of the dangers of creating idols and worshipping the works of our hands. (See Exodus 20:4–5; Leviticus 19:4; and Leviticus 26:1.)

Literature throughout history demonstrates humanity's desire to create beings in our own image, with or without God's help. From the Greek story of Pygmalion, who finds himself in love with a statue he created, to the Jewish Golem brought to life through an incantation, to Mary Shelley's warning in *Frankenstein* about the dangers of trying to create a living being from dead things, humanity wants to create something that can come to life and be on its own.[29]

"Therefore, my beloved, flee from idolatry," the apostle Paul warned in 1 Corinthians 10:14 (NKJV).

"In recent years, astonishing developments have pushed the frontiers of science and technology toward far-reaching morphological transformation that promises in the very near future to redefine what 'intelligence' even means, as well as consciousness, autonomous warfare, and evolving opinions on being human," wrote the late SkyWatch TV founder Dr. Thomas Horn, Joe Horn, and Allie Anderson in their book, *Summoning the Demon: Artificial Intelligence and the Image of the Beast.* "Much of this is set to rapidly unfold following the 'technological Singularity'—a hypothetical future point when technological growth 'becomes uncontrollable and irreversible, resulting in unforeseeable changes to human civilization by an upgradable artificial intelligence [AI] agent that enters a 'runaway reaction' of self-improvement cycles, each new and more intelligent generation appearing more and more rapidly, causing an 'explosion' in intelligence and resulting in a powerful superintelligence that qualitatively far surpasses all human intelligence.'"[30]

A recent Reuters/Ipsos poll found that more than two-thirds of Americans believe the swift growth of AI technology could put the future of humanity at risk, with 61 percent saying AI could threaten civilization.[31]

"Some highly qualified experts, including the 'godfathers' of artificial intelligence, agree and have become very outspoken on the dangers," the Horns and Anderson wrote in *Summoning the Demon.* "Some are now claiming we could reach the Singularity by 2024–2025 (the same time frame the ancient Essenes of Dead Sea Scroll fame predicted the world will enter its final age...) and quickly thereafter, an autonomous, godlike artificial mind will come online with an 'I Am that I Am' moment, leaving all bets off the table regarding what this synthetic deity will decide for the fate of humanity and the world. Will it be benevolent or a violent, anthropomorphic, unstoppable sociopath?"[32]

How Is AI Influencing the 2024 Presidential Election?

Another big question looms in the not-too-distant future: How will AI impact the US elections in November 2024 and Donald Trump's run at his second term?

Can AI predict the future like *The Simpsons* or even Ingersoll Lockwood?

Currently there are organizations trying to use AI to forecast future events, basing their predictions on the GPT-4 language model. They have found that it can predict future events better than people.[33]

Kira Radinsky, cofounder and chief technology officer at Diagnostic Robots, "a health care artificial intelligence system with predictive analytics," believes AI's ability to predict future events is only going to increase. She is a member of the United Nations Secretary-General's high-level panel on digital cooperation, and she created an AI system that predicted "a cholera outbreak in Cuba, riots, the pricing of electronic products, and more high-impact global events."

> When asked if AI can predict the future, Radinsky replied, "I think the best way to predict the future is to create it. One of the things that we are doing right now is identifying the patterns, and when the patterns start, try to predict the next step. So, it can predict things that have a pattern. Random things? It's a philosophical question. Do we even have random things? Or is it part of a pattern that we don't have data for? So, if you believe there is no random thing and everything has a pattern, then AI can predict the future. We just need more data for that."[34]

Please pause for a moment and read her startling statement once again. She said to predict the future, one needs to create it. Sounds like the people we mentioned in the last chapter.

And they are doing it right now in our election cycle. Currently there are growing concerns that "AI will make it cheaper and easier to spread misinformation and run disinformation campaigns" in upcoming elections, especially with the use of deepfakes—videos, photos, and audio recordings that seem real but have been manipulated with AI.[35]

"Deepfakes already have affected other elections around the globe," wrote Rehan Mirza, a research associate on the Democracy & Internet Governance Initiative. "In recent elections in Slovakia, for example, AI-generated audio recordings circulated on Facebook, impersonating a liberal candidate discussing plans to raise alcohol prices and rig the election. During the February 2023 Nigerian elections, an AI-manipulated audio clip falsely implicated a presidential candidate in plans to manipulate ballots. With elections this year in over 50 countries involving half the globe's population, there are fears deepfakes could seriously undermine their integrity."[36]

In response to robocalls impersonating President Joe Biden that went out to New Hampshire voters in January 2024, advising them not to vote in the state's presidential primary election, the Federal Communications Commission (FCC) issued a ruling making it illegal to use AI-generated voices in robocalls. The increase in robocalls has escalated during the last few years, and the AI technology has the potential to confuse people with mis-information by imitating the voices of celebrities and political candidates.[37]

Politics is all about persuasion, and it has always been marked by propaganda. Exaggerations and outright lies are not uncommon in the political world.

"Because people are not angels, elections have never been free from falsehoods and mistaken beliefs," said an article in *The Economist*. "But as the world contemplates a series of votes in 2024, something new is causing a lot of worry. In the past, disinformation has always been created by humans. Advances in generative artificial intelligence (AI)—with models that can spit out sophisticated essays and create realistic images from text prompts—make synthetic propaganda possible. The fear is that disinformation campaigns may be supercharged in 2024, just as countries with a collective population of some 4 [billion]—including America, Britain, India, Indonesia, Mexico and Taiwan—prepare to vote."[38]

As the country races toward the presidential election, the idea of lies being created by only people is out the window. Now the lies can be supercharged and made to look so real that no one can tell reality from a lie.

ONE IN THREE EVANGELICAL CHRISTIANS DON'T VOTE CONSISTENTLY

Meanwhile, as AI, deepfakes, and robocalls further call into question the integrity of elections and the information prospective voters receive, Jason Yates—the CEO of My Faith Votes, a ministry committed to mobilizing Christians to engage in every election—said one of the key reasons he left his career at a Fortune 100 company in 2015 to join My Faith Votes is that he learned a statistic that "kind of blew us away."[39]

In the 2012 presidential election, twenty-five million evangelical Christians who were registered to vote didn't vote. "The difference in that election was less than five million votes," Yates said. "In fact, if you look back on the recent history of presidential elections, the average difference between presidential elections is not more than five million votes. So the point is that if Christians were involved, they would change the outcome of every election if they were fully committed."[40]

Today one in three evangelical Christians doesn't vote consistently.[41]

According to a recent national survey, 6 out of 10 evangelicals said their faith did not influence their vote in the 2022 midterm elections. Pair that with recent Barna research that found only 4% of Americans hold a biblical worldview and see that Christians are in desperate need of Biblical clarity on issues that matter, now, before secularism fills the void Christians left in politics and culture.[42]

The reason why many Christians don't vote boils down to two reasons. They're either deceived or uninformed. Of those who are deceived, the majority falls into two camps.

"They fall into the camp that says, 'I can't vote for either of them,' that they don't buy into the idea of a lesser of two evils," Yates said. "Well, the fact of the matter is, and maybe you've heard it said this way, but Jesus isn't on the ballot. And so...whether you're Christian or not, you are always faced with a choice between two flawed people, people who have sin in their lives, people who have done things wrong, and they've done things right. And I know it's not the greatest way to think about it, but in some sense, you've got to think, 'OK, who's the best, or maybe who's the least worst of my choices, the one that's going to make the choice to best restrain evil and promote good?' And you just have to be willing to make that choice."[43]

As far as deception of voters, Yates said people hear a lot about the separation of church and state. and many Christians believe in this.

In fact, the phrase "separation of church and state" isn't found in the US Constitution. Rather, President Thomas Jefferson used a similar phrase in response to a letter from the Danbury Baptist Association in 1802. The association had written a letter to Jefferson, voicing their concern that their state constitution lacked specific protections to ensure their religious freedom. Jefferson responded by referencing the Establishment and Free Exercise clauses of the First Amendment. "I contemplate with sovereign reverence that act of the whole American people which declared that their legislature should 'make no law respecting an establishment of religion, or prohibiting the free exercise thereof,' thus building a wall of separation between Church & State," Jefferson wrote.[44] The phrase "wall of separation" was not intended to mean that religion shouldn't influence people's opinions on government matters. Rather, Jefferson used it to affirm that citizens are free to practice their faith. But the quote stuck, and in the mid-twentieth century,

US Supreme Court justices began using it as proof that the Founding Fathers endorsed strict church-state separation. Unfortunately, as a result, many Americans now believe that religion and politics are two separate entities that can't intersect. As believers we should be alarmed by this misinterpretation because our faith in God is the foundation of who we are, our nation and its founding documents were inspired by the Bible, and our faith should influence every aspect of our lives, including our politics.[45]

Then, in 1954, Congress approved an amendment by Senator Lyndon Johnson to prohibit nonprofit organizations, including charities and churches, from engaging in any political campaign activity. It's known as the Johnson Amendment.

"I think the Johnson Amendment established by President Johnson...was really an attempt to silence churches," Yates said. "It was using the tax code to say...we really don't want pastors speaking up into these issues. And so we want to put a restriction and say, 'You know what? If you play nice and you don't say anything, then we'll help you keep your tax code and tax benefits, but otherwise you won't have those same benefits.' And as a result, pastors, staff, elders of churches across this nation have conceded, they've obeyed, and as a result, pastors aren't speaking about issues, let alone encouraging people to vote or even encouraging them of what they should look for in candidates....As a result...[Christians] have also then bought into this lie that maybe they too shouldn't care about politics, that they too shouldn't be involved, and yes, even voting. And so those are just two really slippery slopes. And so we can't be self-righteous, can't be deceived, but we also can't be uninformed. And I think there is a contingent of Christians out there that...would vote if they had the right information, if they had the right tools and the reminders."[46]

SHOWDOWN FOR AMERICA: GOOD VERSUS EVIL

My coauthor of *Revelation 911*, Paul Begley, predicted in a September 6, 2016, episode of *The Coming Apocalypse* that Trump would win the presidency two months later.[47]

"I was in Jerusalem doing an interview with a man named Avi Lipkin on my television show, *The Coming Apocalypse*, and we start talking about Brexit and things that were going on in the election," Begley said. "He mentioned that Trump was sort of like a King Cyrus....He asked me, 'Do you think Trump is going to win?' And I said, '…I've been praying about this and what the Lord showed me is if you [see] UK United Kingdom Brexit, then Trump will be elected.'… And that's exactly what happened…. That didn't happen in [2020], but the Lord never told me that he was going to win….I wanted Trump to win [in 2020]. I heard a lot of people…prophesying it, but it never came to me. So I never prophesied he would win. I just said, 'I don't know. I just don't know.'"[48]

I also thought Trump would win in 2016, but as the 2020 presidential election approached, I told my wife and others that I didn't think Trump was going to win.

I didn't believe Trump was going to win reelection in 2020 even though Paul McGuire and I had called for a day of national repentance in our book *Trumpocalypse*, and even though The Return took place on September 26, 2020, on the National Mall in Washington, DC.

At the time, many faith leaders predicted Trump was going to win. But I believed that God, in allowing Joe Biden to win the presidential election (see Daniel 2:21), was working a bigger plan—setting the stage for the possibility of an end-times revival. First, I believe God wanted to humble Trump; second, He wanted to reveal to the world just how evil and corrupt our governments and the world have become; and third, He wanted to show us just how close we are to the end-times events described in the Book of Revelation.

"I really believe if God wanted Trump to win 2020, Trump would've won," Begley said. "Trump accomplished great things for America as well as for Israel [during his presidency], but God also knew…Trump would have to not have that second term in 2020, that there would be another man [Biden]." The current race is good against evil," he said. "One's pushing righteousness; the other one's pushing wickedness….

"I think that this is the showdown for America, good versus evil, [and it feels] like good, that right, is going to win….I've seen that same indication of that right wing movement in Europe. Europe is tired of the taxation, migration, the frustration of everything that they've gone through with all the different immigrants coming out of the Middle East that won't assimilate within their culture. America's seeing the exact same thing with the southern border frustration. The taxes are outrageous; the inflation's incredible….People are swinging to the right because they know that you got to fix this. And [the Democrats] can't fix it, won't fix it. [Their] platform will not allow that even to be thought about. And Trump's will fix it. He'll work toward it, turn toward righteousness, and it could be...the spark of the last days' revival is a Trump presidency. That may be how it comes about, or unfortunately, it could come about from great woes...sorrow on the earth....As a Christian, [you're] a winner either way....Either way, you just got to hold to your faith. Either way, I pray for America, and I pray the right thing happens."[49]

Paul McGuire believes that America and the world are at a pivotal moment in history.

"We are literally at—I believe this passionately—...the most important sector in all of human history," McGuire said. "The decisions we make, the choices we make, especially those of us who are part of the body of Christ, will literally determine irreversibly the fate of mankind. And anybody who doesn't get that yet...I pray that they will, and I pray that [*The Trump Code*] will help open their eyes to that fact."[50]

Following news that President Joe Biden had dropped out of the race, Harris initially faced an uphill battle to secure the nearly thirty-eight hundred delegates that pledged support to Biden in the primary. However, by early August she had enough votes to become the Democratic nominee.[51]

Despite the tumult in the election, the presidential race is poised to be decided by six toss-up states—Arizona, Georgia, Michigan, Nevada, Pennsylvania, and Wisconsin—in addition to one congressional district in Nebraska, which has its own electoral vote.[52]

Meanwhile, Allan Lichtman, a professor of history at American University who correctly predicted the winner of nine out of the ten most recent presidential elections, offered his reaction to Biden's announcement that he would not seek reelection. Lichtman developed the metrics for his predictions in the early 1980s. He uses thirteen historical "keys" to determine the winner of presidential races. Four of those keys are based on politics, seven on performance, and two on the personality of the candidate.[53]

"With Biden dropping out, they [Democrats] lose one more key: the incumbency key," Lichtman told Fox 5. "But they can still preserve another key: the contest key if, finally, the Democrats get smart and unite behind Kamala Harris as the consensus nominee, they keep that key in line....There are four shaky keys that I haven't decided and I haven't made a final prediction yet. They are third party, social unrest and foreign/military failure and success. Provided Harris becomes the consensus nominee, three of those four keys would have to fall to predict the Democrat's defeat. If she doesn't become the consensus nominee, only two would have to fall."[54]

MISSION: IMPOSSIBLE 7 AND THE ANSWER

When revisited, the film *Mission: Impossible 7* holds a unique, and not often discussed, key to destroying the Entity and freeing humanity of demonic, tyrannical control.

In fact, in the film, it is a literal key, one that every major world leader is willing to kill for. The key is made of gold and has two halves. When the two halves are put together, the key can be used to shut off the Entity.

The key is in the shape of a cross.

How amazing is God? Deep in the heart of a Hollywood film—in fact, the central object of the film—is a cruciform key that will bring about the end of an all-enslaving digital god unleashed by evil men.

While some may dismiss this symbology, it seems that God is speaking once again through the arts and a fictional story. He is giving us a key, the weapon that will overcome the lies of the enemy, the threats of AI, the discouragement, and the despair many people—Christians and non-Christians—face as the future of this country, and possibly the world, hangs in the balance.

The cross of Christ is the answer to all the issues we face—natural or mental, digital or spiritual. And because the filmmakers chose to use a cruciform key, we need to take a moment to see why this is important.

Cruciform (cross shaped) points to the apostle Paul's writings, especially in 1 Corinthians, and calls us all to a life of *cruciformity*, a word derived from *cruciform* and *conformity*. *Cruciformity* is defined simply as conformity to Jesus, the crucified Messiah.[55]

The cruciform key in the film, if we allow it, will remind us that the way forward for our families, our cities, our nation, and our world is not through the power of men, through the amazing technology we create, through data, or even through the predictions of stories. The saving grace, the only thing that will save, is but the "foolishness" of the cross of Christ, which is "the power of God and the wisdom of God," as it can "nullify the things that are" (1 Cor. 1:23–24, 28).

The cross of Jesus Christ has the power to dismantle and destroy all the weapons of the enemy, even AI and its toxic impacts.

While we pray for our leaders and that God's will is done in the presidential election, it is vital to keep hold of this main fact: the way forward through the lies bombarding our world night and day is Jesus and His sacrifice.

His life and death, His miracles and His cross, His Word and His wisdom are the root of all truth and the root of all discernment we need moving forward.

CHAPTER FOUR
TRUTH IN FICTION

Why may it not be the famous Wilhelm Heinrich Sebastian von Troomp,
commonly called "Little Baron Trump," and his wonderful dog Bulger?
—INGERSOLL LOCKWOOD, *BARON TRUMP'S MARVELLOUS UNDERGROUND JOURNEY*

O FTEN GOD SENDS people who know Him well to warn and
encourage His children to stay the course, to follow Him, to love
Him, and to trust Him.

Jeremiah 7:25 says, "From the time your ancestors left Egypt until now,
day after day, again and again I sent you my servants the prophets." Jeremiah
25:4 adds, "And though the LORD has sent all his servants the prophets to
you again and again, you have not listened or paid any attention."

Other times, the Lord has sent His prophets to nations or people who
do not know Him to deliver words of judgment or to warn His people to
spur them to humble themselves and pray and seek His face. (See Judges 3.)
Sometimes He has used stories, songs, and art to confirm what He has been
saying or doing in our midst. (See Ezekiel 4:1–2 and 2 Samuel 12.)

It seems that God began to confirm what His prophets were saying to the
church regarding President Donald J. Trump in the summer of 2017.

Around this time, articles popped up in mainstream and Christian news
outlets, highlighting an obscure collection of novels written by a relatively
unknown author in the 1890s. These articles highlighted the overwhelming
interest in the online research community regarding American political
writer, lawyer, and novelist Ingersoll Lockwood and his Baron Trump novels,
as well as *The Last President*.

In a July 31, 2017, article, *Newsweek's* Chris Riotta wrote, "Trump, an aris-
tocratically wealthy young man living in Castle Trump, is the protagonist of
Lockwood's first two fictional novels, *The Travels and Adventures of Little
Baron Trump and His Wonderful Dog Bulger* and *Baron Trump's Marvellous
Underground Journey*....There are some incredible connections to be made to

the first family of the United States and Lockwood's novels from the turn of the 19th century."[1]

The next day, on August 1, 2017, HuffPost released an article entitled, "Internet Freaks Over 19th-Century Books Featuring Boy Named 'Baron Trump.'" In the article, the author wrote, "The internet tends to trump things up, but even this boggles the mind: A series of books from the late 1800s depicts a character named Baron Trump. Oh, and the boy is aided in his quest by a man named Don."[2]

Charisma News reported on the story as well in an article titled, "Did a Novelist From the 1800s Warn Us Donald Trump Would Be 'The Last President'?"[3] *The Daily Mail's* article said about *The Last President*:

> The story opens in a New York City in turmoil. It's early November right after the election of an enormously opposed candidate. The East Side of the city, which is where the Women's March began the day after Donald Trump's inauguration, is in a "state of uproar." The 19th-century book says police officers shouted through the streets as "Mobs of vast size are organizing under the lead of anarchists and socialists, and threaten to plunder and despoil the houses of the rich who have wronged and oppressed them for so many years."
>
> "The Fifth Avenue Hotel will be the first to feel the fury of the mob," the novel continues. "Would the troops be in time to save it?"
>
> The Women's March concluded just two blocks short of Trump Tower International on 5th Ave.[4]

Snopes, which bills itself as "the definitive Internet reference source for researching urban legends, folklore, myths, rumors, and misinformation," even got in on the action.[5] In an August 1, 2017, article titled, "Is *'Baron Trump's Marvellous Underground Journey'* a Real Book From the 1890s," the author wrote:

> A pressing matter, largely ignored by the mainstream media has come up: Is Donald Trump a time traveler?
>
> The question has been circulating on conspiracy theory web sites for several months and is backed by various pieces of "evidence" (such as Donald Trump's uncle John Trump's purported relationship with Nikola Tesla). Now a series of books published over [a] century ago

is receiving attention for their seemingly all-too-eerie connections to the Trump family. The books, one of which is titled *Baron Trump's Marvellous Underground Journey*, have been discussed on both reddit and 4chan.

Baron Trump's Marvellous Underground Journey, and *1900: or, The Last President*, are indeed real books by writer Ingersoll Lockwood. (We haven't been able to uncover any evidence proving that Donald Trump and his family have access to a time machine, however)....Although these books contain some seemingly bizarre coincidences, they are not evidence that Donald Trump has access to a time machine.[6]

In *The 1896 Prophecies: 10 Predictions of America's Last Days*, authors Liz Martin and Brandon Vallorani compared Lockwood's literary works to the famous dystopian novels *Nineteen Eighty-Four* by George Orwell, *Brave New World* by Aldous Huxley, and *Fahrenheit 451* by Ray Bradbury.

"The ideas, the issues, and the warnings written in [*1900: or, The Last President*] more than one hundred years ago are suddenly very much alive again and have been thrown back into national debate," Martin and Vallorani wrote. "We think of Orwell and Huxley as being, in a sense, *prophetic* because of how they described the ways in which totalitarians would control the people either through fear or through entertainment and distraction. We see how dystopian writers predicted a world in which nothing we did would be hidden from the watchful eyes of the state. We saw how science would be weaponized against our own humanity, and language would be weaponized against our ability to think independently. Ray Bradbury wrote of book burnings, predicting thought control and cancel culture. Nonconformists would be the enemy. But these weren't prophecies, really. They were just an extrapolation of known trends being carried forward into a foreseeable future."[7]

The interest in the books and Lockwood has not waned since the first round of news stories during Trump's first term in office. In fact, on January 25, 2024, *Newsweek* published another article about the novels and the resurfacing theories about Trump and his son Barron: "'Baron Trump' Book Theories Resurface About Donald Trump's Son." The author wrote Lockwood's novels became a "hot topic of conspiracy theorists, some of whom claim the Trump family has a time machine."[8]

We will explore the time-travel theory later in the book, but for now, what we can say is that people aren't letting go of this story, and in the pages of these books, it does appear that God was shining a light on future events through a very unlikely source.

WHO WAS INGERSOLL LOCKWOOD?

Very little is known about Ingersoll Lockwood, yet his long forgotten but seemingly prophetic books about little Baron Trump have created quite a stir.

Lockwood, an American lawyer and writer, was born on August 2, 1841, in Ossining, New York, the second son of state militia Brigadier General Munson Ingersoll and Sarah Lewis (Smith) Lockwood. His father, Munson, and two of his uncles were lawyers. His father seems to have achieved fame during his military career with the New York National Guard and then in the civic arena, collecting money for Hungarian statesman and freedom fighter Lajos Kossuth.[9]

Like his father and uncles, Lockwood became a lawyer, eventually setting up a legal practice in New York City with his older brother Henry. *The New York Times* described him as "well known as a lawyer of this city."[10] Before practicing law, however, he served as the consul to the Kingdom of Hanover. When he was appointed by Abraham Lincoln in 1862, he was the youngest member of the US consular force. After four years in Hanover, he set up his law practice, and by the 1880s, Lockwood was also lecturing and writing. In 1884, he married Winifred Wallace Tinker, but their marriage did not last long, and they were divorced by 1892.[11]

We know almost nothing as to what motivated him to do so, but Lockwood wrote children's fantasy novels that have now garnered the attention of online researchers, Christian leaders, and the mainstream press. The Baron Trump series of children's novels were published in 1890 and 1893, followed by the dystopian novel titled *1900: or, The Last President* in 1896.

His last book, *In Varying Mood: or, Jetsam, Flotsam and Ligan,* a book of poetry, was published in 1912. He died in 1918 in Saratoga, New York, at the age of seventy-seven.

There is not much else we know about him. Yet what he seems to have foreseen and put into novels for children has now stoked the flames of inquisitive minds all across the world who want to know how he knew about Trump and what he was trying to tell us.

UNLOCKING WHAT LOCKWOOD SAW

What did Lockwood see and put into his novels, and how do the novels parallel the journey of Trump? What can we find in his books that has drawn the attention of Christians and non-Christians alike? What is God saying to us about the past and what might be in the future for America and Trump?

The "biographical notice of Wilhelm Heinrich Sebastian Von Troomp, commonly called little Baron Trump," in *Baron Trump's Marvellous Underground Journey* sets the stage:

> As doubting Thomases seem to take particular pleasure in popping up on all occasions, Jack-in-the-Box-like, it may be well to head them off in this particular instance by proving that Baron Trump was a real baron, and not a mere baron of the mind. The family was originally French Huguenot—De la Trompe—which, upon the revocation of the Edict of Nantes in 1685, took refuge in Holland, where its head assumed the name of Van der Troomp, just as many other of the French Protestants rendered their names into Dutch. Some years later, upon the invitation of the Elector of Brandenburg, Niklas Van der Troomp became a subject of that prince, and purchased a large estate in the province of Pomerania, again changing his name, this time to Von Troomp.
>
> The "Little Baron," so called from his diminutive stature, was born sometime in the latter part of the seventeenth century. He was the last of his race in the direct line, although cousins of his are to-day well-known Pomeranian gentry. He began his travels at an incredibly early age, and filled his castle with such strange objects picked up here and there in the far away corners of the world, that the simple-minded peasantry came to look upon him as half bigwig and half magician—hence the growth of the many myths and fanciful stories concerning this indefatigable globe-trotter. The date of his death cannot be fixed with any certainty; but this much may be said: Among the portraits of Pomeranian notables hanging in the Rathhaus at Stettin, there is one picturing a man of low stature, and with a head much too large for his body. He is dressed in some outlandish costume, and holds in his left hand a grotesque image in ivory, most elaborately carved. The broad face is full of intelligence, and the large gray eyes are lighted up with a good-natured

but quizzical look that invariably attracts attention. The man's right hand rests upon the back of a dog sitting on a table and looking straight out with an air of dignity that shows that he knew he was sitting for his portrait.

If a visitor asks the guide who this man is, he always gets for answer: —

"Oh, that's the Little Baron!"

But little Baron who, that's the question?

Why may it not be the famous Wilhelm Heinrich Sebastian von Troomp, commonly called "Little Baron Trump," and his wonderful dog Bulger?[12]

In chapter one of *Baron Trump's Marvellous Underground Journey*, we discover that Baron Trump's mentor is a man named Don Fum, the author of ancient manuscripts that lead him to start traveling the world looking for portals to hidden worlds:

Possibly I might have discovered at an earlier day what it was all about, had it not been that just at this time I was very busy, too busy, in fact, to pay much attention to any one, even to my dear four-footed foster brother. As you may remember, dear friends, my brain is a very active one; and when once I become interested in a subject, Castle Trump itself might take fire and burn until the legs of my chair had become charred before I would hear the noise and confusion, or even smell the smoke.

It so happened at the time of Bulger's low spirits that the elder baron had, through the kindness of an old school friend, come into possession of a fifteenth-century manuscript from the pen of a no less celebrated thinker and philosopher than the learned Spaniard, Don Constantino Bartolomeo Strepholofidgeguaneriusfum, commonly known among scholars as Don Fum, entitled "A World within a World." In this work Don Fum advanced the wonderful theory that there is every reason to believe that the interior of our world is inhabited; that, as is well known, this vast earth ball is not solid, on the contrary, being in many places quite hollow; that ages and ages ago terrible disturbances had taken place on its surface and had driven the inhabitants to seek refuge in these vast underground chambers, so vast, in fact, as well to merit the name of "World within a World."[13]

Before he sets out on his travels, the elder baron, Baron Trump's father, bestows a blessing and a familiar slogan on him:

> The elder baron was silent for a moment, and then added: "Little baron, much as thy mother and I shall dread to think of thy being again out from under the safe protection of this venerable roof, the moss-grown tiles of which have sheltered so many generations of the Trumps, yet must we not be selfish in this matter. Heaven forbid that such a thought should move our souls to stay thee! The honor of our family, thy fame as an explorer of strange lands in far-away corners of the globe, call unto us to be strong hearted. Therefore, my dear boy, make ready and go forth once more in search of new marvels. The learned Don Fum's chart will stand thee by like a safe and trusty counsellor. *Remember, little baron, the motto of the Trumps, Per Ardua ad Astra—the pathway to glory is strewn with pitfalls and dangers...*[14]

Then we quickly find little Baron Trump traveling to Russia and having influence and favor bestowed on him by the Russian government.

> According to the learned Don Fum's manuscript, the portals to the World within a World were situated somewhere in Northern Russia, possibly, so he thought, from all indications, somewhere on the westerly slope of the upper Urals. But the great thinker could not locate them with any accuracy. "The people will tell thee" was the mysterious phrase that occurred again and again on the mildewed pages of this wonderful writing. "The people will tell thee." Ah, but what people will be learned enough to tell me that? was the brain-racking question which I asked myself, sleeping and waking, at sunrise, at high noon, and at sunset; at the crowing of the cock, and in the silent hours of the night.
> "The people will tell thee," said learned Don Fum.
> "Ah, but what people will tell me where to find the portals to the World within a World?"
> Hitherto on my travels I had made choice of a semi-Oriental garb, both on account of its picturesqueness and its lightness and

warmth, but now as I was about to pass quite across Russia for a number of months, I resolved to don the Russian national costume; for speaking Russian fluently, as I did a score or more of languages living and dead, I would thus be enabled to come and go without everlastingly displaying my passport, or having my trains of thought constantly disturbed by inquisitive travelling companions....

It was about the middle of February when I set out from the Castle Trump, and I journeyed night and day in order to reach Petersburg by the first of March, for I knew that the government trains would leave that city for the White Sea during the first week of that month. Bulger and I were both in the best of health and spirits, and the fatigue of the journey didn't tell upon us in the least. The moment I arrived at the Russian capital I applied to the emperor for permission to join one of the government trains, which was most graciously accorded. Our route lay almost directly to the northward for several days....We proceeded in a straight line over the snow fields to Archangel, an important trading-post on the White Sea.

As this was the destination of the government train, I parted with its commandant after a few days' pleasant sojourn at the government house, and set out, attended only by my faithful Bulger and two servants, who had been assigned to me by the imperial commissioner.[15]

In Lockwood's dystopian novel titled *1900; or, The Last President*, the story begins on a Tuesday in November, as an unexpected candidate wins the presidential election:

That was a terrible night for the great City of New York—the night of Tuesday, November 3rd, 1896. The city staggered under the blow like a huge ocean liner which plunges, full speed, with terrific crash into a mighty iceberg, and recoils shattered and trembling like an aspen.

The people were gathered, light-hearted and confident, at the evening meal, when the news burst upon them. It was like a thunder bolt out of an azure sky: "Altgeld holds Illinois hard and fast in the Democratic line. This elects Bryan President of the United States!"...

In less than half an hour, mounted policemen dashed through the streets calling out: "Keep within your houses; close your doors and barricade them. The entire East side is in a state of uproar. Mobs of vast size are organizing under the lead of Anarchists and Socialists, and threaten to plunder and despoil the houses of the rich who have wronged and oppressed them for so many years. Keep within doors. Extinguish all lights."[16]

Elsewhere in the book we get other glimpses into the future, like the location of a hotel and a man with the last name of Pence being put into the new president's cabinet:

The police force was now almost helpless. The men still used their sticks, but the blows were ineffectual, and only served to increase the rage of the vast hordes now advancing upon Madison Square.

The Fifth Avenue Hotel will be the first to feel the fury of the mob. Would the troops be in time to save it?...

The young President stood firm and fast on the platform of the parties which had raised him to his proud eminence. And what better proof of his thorough belief in himself and in his mission could he have given than the following:

...Secretary Agriculture—Lafe Pence, of Colorado.[17]

Lastly, and even more prophetically, we get the following passage from *The Last President*, seemingly undergirding the words of modern-day prophets:

And yet, at this moment when the night air quivered with the mad vociferations of the "common people," that the Lord had been good to them; that the wicked money-changers had been driven from the temple, that the stony-hearted usurers were beaten at last, that the "People's William" was at the helm now, that peace and plenty would in a few moons come back to the poor man's cottage, that Silver was King, aye, King at last, the world still went wondering why red-eyed anarchy, as she stood in Haymarket Square, with thin arms aloft, with wild mien and wilder gesticulation, drew no bomb of dynamite from her bosom, to hurl at the hated minions of the law who were silent spectators of this delirium of popular joy.

Why was it thus? Look and you shall know why white robed peace kept step with this turbulent band and turned its thought from red handed pillage. He was there. The master spirit to hold them in leash. He, and he alone, had lifted Bryan to his great eminence. Without these twenty-four electoral votes, Bryan had been doomed, hopelessly doomed. He, and he alone, held the great Commonwealth of the West hard and fast in the Democratic line; hence he came as conqueror, as King-maker, and the very walls of the sky-touching edifices trembled as he was dragged through the crowded streets by this orderly mob, and ten times ten thousand of his creatures bellowed his name and shook their hats aloft in mad exultation:

"You're our Saviour, you've cleaned the Temple of Liberty of its foul horde of usurers. We salute you. We call you King-maker. Bryan shall call you Master too. You shall have your reward. You shall stand behind the throne. Your wisdom shall make us whole. You shall purge the land of this unlawful crowd of money lenders. You shall save the Republic. You are greater than Washington. You're a better friend of ours than Lincoln. You'll do more for us than Grant. We're your slaves. We salute you. We thank you. We bless you. Hurrah! Hurrah! Hurrah!"[18]

PARALLELS TO PRESIDENT TRUMP

In each of these examples, we can see parallels to President Trump:

- Baron Trump is pictured as a boy of uncommon intelligence that wasn't easily recognized and is the master of a palace-like structure called Castle Trump; President Trump's son is named Barron Trump, and Trump has vast holdings, some looking like modern-day castles.

- Baron Trump is shown unusual favor by the government of Russia; President Trump was shown unusual favor by leaders of China, Saudi Arabia, and Russia in 2017 and 2018.[19]

- The riots in *The Last President* are set in New York City.

- The Trump family's business seat has been New York City, and there has been great upheaval in the city over Trump and his business dealings, including his recent conviction on falsification of business records and the riots of 2020.

Heading into the 2024 presidential election, many expect all manner of chaos to unfold.

- The new president in *The Last President* put a man named Pence into his cabinet.

- The common people crying out that Bryan—the unexpected president of *The Last President*—was the answer from the Lord they had sought and that he would cleanse the government of those abusing the people.

- The people claiming that the unexpected president was like Abraham Lincoln mirrors the comparisons of Trump's term to Lincoln's. In fact, *New York Times* bestselling author Dinesh D'Souza compared Trump to Lincoln in his 2018 film, *Death of a Nation: Can We Save America a Second Time?*[20]

The stage seems to be set for an uprising if President Trump is elected again in 2024, possibly leading to major cities rioting, similar to *The Last President*. In a Charisma News article about the Lockwood books, the author wrote:

> To me, that is rather remarkable, but once again many are pointing out that this could potentially be "just a coincidence."
>
> When it comes to Trump, there seems to be so many of these "coincidences." For instance, on his first full day in office Trump was 70 years, 7 months and 7 days old, and that just happened to take place in year 5777 on the Hebrew calendar.
>
> And here are some more extremely strange numbers...:

- Israel was 77 days old exactly 777 days after Trump was born.

- Israel's 70th birthday will come exactly 700 days after Trump's 70th birthday.

- Trump won the election on Israeli Prime Minister Benjamin Netanyahu's 7th year, 7th month and 7th day in office.[21]

When do coincidences become fact?

Amidst all of this, there arises the significance of the names Lockwood included in his books: New York City, Fifth Avenue, Baron Trump, the Don, and Pence all show up in these tales. It makes the ties to Donald Trump and the possible future of America seem even more than chance or coincidence and even possibly divinely inspired.

How Does God Use Names?

To even the casual reader of the Bible, it's obvious that names matter to God.

From the creation of the earth, we recognize that names signify origin. When God named the first man Adam, the word was closely tied to the word *ground* in the Hebrew language and calls to mind the fact that Adam was created from the dust (Gen. 2:7). Adam, drawing on God's example, named Eve, and her name means "life" or "life-giver," pointing to the fact that her role would be mothering all the living (Gen. 3:20).[22]

Reading through the Bible's many genealogies and lists of towns and nations (read 1 and 2 Chronicles if you love lists), we can see that God loves names. They are important to Him.

Names carry meanings, and for people, they carry mental frameworks that shape their lives. This is why Solomon wrote in Proverbs 22:1, "A good name is more desirable than great riches; to be esteemed is better than silver or gold." This verse is about more than a person's reputation or status; it is about the identity and purpose God has designed for their life from the "foundation of the world" (Eph. 1:4, NKJV).

This is why God chose to highlight what names meant or give people new names when He was ready for them to do something for Him. The choices He made are never random; they are significant, meaningful, and full of life-changing power.

Does this apply to Lockwood and Trump?

What's in the meaning of their names that could tie them together prophetically and speak to the destiny God might have for America?

Donald Trump's name is very fascinating. Donald comes from Scottish origins and holds in it the meaning of "world leader." Ancestry.com explains:

> It can be traced back to the early medieval period when it was associated with the powerful clans and ruling families of Scotland....
> In early Scottish history, Donald I, better known as Domnall mac

Ailpn or Donald II, became one of the first kings of Scotland in the 9th century. He played a crucial role in consolidating the kingdom and establishing the Scottish royalty.[23]

His last name, Trump, is an English name rooted in an occupation: a trumpeter. It can literally mean "trumpet horn."[24]

Prophet Kim Clement declared very boldly that Trump would live up to his surname:

> "Trump shall become a trumpet" says the Lord. "I will raise up the trump to become a trumpet..." says the Lord.... "It shall come to pass that the man that I place in the highest office shall go in whispering My name, but," God said, "when he enters into the office, he will be shouting out by the power of the Spirit. For I shall fill him with My Spirit when he goes into office, and there will be a praying man in the highest seat in your land.[25]

Ingersoll is an English name, drawn from two Old English words: *limper* and *hill*. Lockwood is also English in origin and made up of two Old English words: *loc*, which means "lock enclosure fold," and *wudu*, which means "wood."[26]

It's not a stretch to see in the life of Ingersoll Lockwood a path of humility—limping about this world with no acclaim for his writings and alone in the end, yet a position of some height where he could see what was coming for at least one family, the Trumps.

His last name could signify something even more powerful. What if his name, a combination of a "lock enclosure fold" and "wood," represents God's desire to enclose this country with the divine presence of Jesus, empowered by a new revelation of the cross, or wood, that Jesus willingly died on for us?

Taking the prophetic significance of both men's names deeper and turning to a Hebrew tool called a Gematria calculator, an even brighter light seems to illuminate what God is saying to us through these two men.

Gematria, which comes from the same Greek word as *geometry*, "refers to a process by which numerical values are ascribed to the letters of the Hebrew alphabet." Each letter has been given a numerical value, from Aleph, the first Hebrew letter, given the value of one, to the last Hebrew letter, Tav, being given the value of four hundred.[27]

The Gematria calculator gives Donald Trump's name a 589. The phrase "a storm is coming" also has a value of 589.[28] Ingersoll Lockwood's name is given the number 1,408, as is the phrase "we caught them all."[29]

If we look ahead and consider some of the things Lockwood wrote about, especially in *The Last President*, we can see that a storm is coming, and it could possibly result in Trump's repeated statements that "We will demolish the deep state" and "drain the swamp"—a reference to his remarks to "make every executive branch employee fireable by the president of the United States" and to "remove rogue bureaucrats."[30]

Russ Vought, director of the Office of Management and Budget under Trump, explained in an interview why Trump wants to "drain the swamp." Vought discussed dismantling or remaking the Department of Justice, the Federal Bureau of Investigation, and the Environmental Protection Agency, among other federal agencies.

"This is not Bill Clinton's big government," Vought said. "It's not Jimmy Carter big government. It's a Barack Obama, Joe Biden infused, hybrid, militant, woke and weaponized government that makes every decision on the basis of climate change extremism and on the basis of woke militancy where you're effectively trying to divide the country into oppressors and the oppressed."[31]

While the Gematria connections of Trump's and Lockwood's names are intriguing, the fact is that names in the Bible have prophetic meanings, often communicating a person's destiny. Take Abraham for example. In God's perfect timing, He stepped into Abram's world and changed his name, calling him Abraham, a prophetic sign of the Lord's promise to him: he would be blessed and be the father of many nations (Gen. 12). Abram went from being "exalted father" to the "father of a multitude" (Gen. 17:5).[32]

CAN GOD SPEAK THROUGH AN UNBELIEVER?

There is no claim by Lockwood that he heard from God. In fact, a book he wrote just before his death points to his disbelief in God. In the book, he proposed to start a new religion. As an elderly man in 1910, Lockwood wrote a book titled *Laconics of Cult* in which he attempted to construct his own religion, dismantling the Christian religion among others, claiming all religions are the same, created by humans.

There is but one form of human enslavement more villainous and more detestable than the chains of the tyrant or the shackles of the despot, and that is the enslavement of the human mind under ecclesiastical tyranny, whose cowering and crouching victims at the crack of the priestly lash are driven from the cultivation of their own intelligence, from the custody of their own thoughts, from the guardianship of their own souls, and who, like whipt dogs, trembling and whining in abject submission at the feet of the oppressor, lick the very hand that wields the lash. I'm well aware what a thankless task it is to attack the established order of things, theological, political or ethical.[33]

On an episode of the *Sunday Cool* show, host Josh Hooper said the book "seemed like a step-by-step guide to reaching immortality."[34]

What was it that influenced Lockwood to write such a book? It could be that he was heavily influenced by the esoteric, false religious cults brewing in Europe when he was the American representative to the Kingdom of Hanover.[35] Or was it trauma he experienced early in life that turned him away from Jesus Christ? We'll never really know the root, but by 1910, he had turned away from Christ and sought to dismantle faith, much like Karl Marx and other radicals of the age.

What we do know is that it is not uncommon for people to fall away from the faith. Many prominent men and women—even those who called themselves prophets and healers—have fallen away from the faith in God and Jesus. Here are some examples:

- Judas, a disciple of Christ—The single greatest example of this type of change in a person's life is Judas Iscariot, one of the twelve original disciples of Christ. He walked and talked and spent countless days and nights with Jesus. He was even given the role of being the treasurer of the ministry. Yet, in the end, he betrayed Christ for money and, well, you know the rest of his story.

- Karl Marx—As a university student, Karl Marx wrote a paper titled, "The Union of Believers With Christ," in which he wrote, "Indeed, the greatest sage of antiquity, the divine Plato, expresses in more than one passage a profound longing for

a higher being, whose appearance would fulfill the unsatis-
fied striving for truth and light. Thus the history of peoples
teaches us the necessity of union with Christ."[36] But after
that, he abandoned his faith in Jesus, and he eventually wrote
poetry and plays dedicated to Satan himself.[37]

Despite Lockwood's writing of *Laconics of Cult*, it still appears that God
spoke through him regarding Trump. Likewise, we can see prophetic messages in popular television shows such as *South Park* and *The Simpsons* (which
we will look at further in the book). And in the Bible, God sometimes used
secular voices to get His message across:

- After Cyrus, the Persian emperor, captured Babylon, God led
  him to issue the decree that permitted the captive Jews to
  return to their homeland and rebuild the temple (Isa. 44:28;
  2 Chron. 36:22–23; Ezra 1:1–4). We will look more at him, as
  Trump was linked to King Cyrus by Lance Wallnau as well
  as Israeli Prime Minister Benjamin Netanyahu.

- In Matthew 27 we find Pilate's wife warning her husband of
  Jesus' innocence—she seems to be trying to help the Lord.
  She said, "Don't have anything to do with that innocent man,
  for I have suffered a great deal today in a dream because of
  him" (Matt. 27:19).

In fact, many modern-day prophets—men such as Kim Clement, Lance
Wallnau, and Mark Taylor, to name a few—heard from God regarding
Trump's election and presidency, much like Lockwood potentially did.

And they were right for the most part.

CHAPTER FIVE

TIME TRAVEL

He has made everything beautiful in its time. He has also set eternity in the human heart; yet no one can fathom what God has done from beginning to end.
—ECCLESIASTES 3:11

According to the learned Don Fum's manuscript, the portals to the World within a World were situated somewhere in Northern Russia, possibly, so he thought, from all indications, somewhere on the westerly slope of the upper Urals.
—INGERSOLL LOCKWOOD, BARON TRUMP'S MARVELLOUS UNDERGROUND JOURNEY

DEEP IN MAN'S heart is the desire to know what is going to happen before it does. We don't like mystery much, especially when it comes to the future. We want to see ahead of us in time and know if our families will be well, if our businesses will survive, and if our country will make it.

People are looking for hope and certainty at a time when so little of it seems present. Hence the theory of time travel appeals to everyone at some level.

From novels like H. G. Wells' *The Time Machine* to film franchises like *Back to the Future* to the massively popular and expansive British TV show *Dr. Who*, time travel has not only captivated our imaginations but also become a significant part of our cultural narrative.

But let's delve deeper into this concept. Is there a reality to what the theory propounds: that we can go into the past and the future, see why things happened or what will happen, and maybe change both? Could time travel be more than just a figment of our imaginations?

These questions have fueled the resurgence of interest in Ingersoll Lockwood's books. Was time travel involved, allowing him to see Donald Trump and Barron Trump in the future?

Intrigued by Lockwood's books, many have wondered if Trump has traveled through time to see what was coming and, therefore, has incredibly accurate answers to problems we have faced and will face.

For disciples of Jesus Christ this question goes deeper: Is time travel biblically supported, and is it something God has allowed or does allow today?

BIBLICAL PERSPECTIVES ON TIME TRAVEL: MYTH OR REALITY?

Throughout the Bible, miraculous events happen that defy facts and logic. This isn't shocking; the Bible is a book about Yahweh (the Hebrew name of God revealed to Moses in the Book of Exodus), the triune God, the source of all supernatural activity.

Supernatural things are common in the text He gave us to guide and regulate our lives.

The Bible, while not addressing time travel directly, presents a framework of God's sovereignty over time and His ability to manipulate it according to His will. Stories of miraculous events involving changes to the natural order of time, prophetic visions of future events, and discussions on the timeless nature of God help us understand the Bible's perspective on time.

We don't know much about Enoch outside of the passages in Genesis, Hebrews, and Jude. But what we do know makes one stop and think about time travel in a new way.

In Genesis 5:21–24, we read:

> When Enoch had lived 65 years, he became the father of Methuselah. After he became the father of Methuselah, Enoch walked faithfully with God 300 years and had other sons and daughters. Altogether, Enoch lived a total of 365 years. Enoch walked faithfully with God; then he was no more, because God took him away.

Hebrews 11:5–6 expands on what we know of Enoch:

> By faith Enoch was taken from this life, so that he did not experience death: "He could not be found, because God had taken him away." For before he was taken, he was commended as one who pleased God. And without faith it is impossible to please God,

because anyone who comes to him must believe that he exists and that he rewards those who earnestly seek him.

Enoch was taken by God after walking faithfully with Him for three hundred years, believing that God exists and that He rewards the people who seek Him passionately. He simply passed from this time into eternity.

"Enoch was in such close fellowship with God that he was able—literally—to step through the dimensional wall," wrote Gary Stearman, host of the *Prophecy Watchers* television show. "As we have already seen, by definition, this means that he was a time traveler. From the other side of that dimensional barrier, he could travel in the Spirit of the Lord to any point along the timeline of redemption. Furthermore, we have biblical proof of his future vision: 'And Enoch also, the seventh from Adam, prophesied of these, saying, Behold, the Lord cometh with ten thousands of his saints' (Jude 14). Enoch actually witnessed the Second Coming of Christ! Was he actually there? Yes... the Lord took him. You may ask, 'Was he there bodily, or only in his spirit?' We must answer that from our perspective; it doesn't really matter. He was there. And, of course in Enoch's case, he was, in fact, taken bodily into the Lord's dimension, where time travel is a matter of simple fact."[1]

In an article on Charisma News, a question was posed: Does the First Book of Enoch, written mainly by Enoch before he was taken, offer insights into God's prophetic calendar? What information can be gleaned by studying this man who so pleased God that he didn't die?[2]

While the First Book of Enoch is not included in the Bible, the biblical writers quoted, paraphrased, or referenced it, including a direct quote in Jude, and it "influenced the writers of the Bible as few [other books] have."[3]

"The best evidence we have for the undisputed authenticity of Enoch is not the connection to Genesis, but the faith Jesus and the Apostles had in the Book of Enoch, demonstrated by various references and quotes," wrote Joseph B. Lumpkin in *The Books of Enoch*. "It is hard to avoid the evidence that Jesus not only studied the book, but also respected it highly enough to allude to its doctrine and content. Enoch is replete with mentions of the coming kingdom and other holy themes. It was not only Jesus who used phrases or ideas from Enoch, there are over 100 comments in the New Testament which find precedence in the Book of Enoch."[4]

In Jude 14–15, we get an expanded glimpse into what Enoch saw during his three hundred years of walking with God—and it's startling:

> Enoch, the seventh from Adam, prophesied…: "See, the Lord is coming with thousands upon thousands of his holy ones to judge everyone, and to convict all of them of all the ungodly acts they have committed in their ungodliness, and of all the defiant words ungodly sinners have spoken against him."

While this picture shows massive judgment coming, it is also a ray of hope, warning us of how we should live our lives: like Enoch, faithfully walking with God, pleasing Him because we live every day believing He exists, and that He rewards those who seek Him earnestly.

ELIJAH AND THE CHARIOT OF FIRE

Enoch wasn't the only man in the Bible to not die physically; Elijah was taken up to heaven by a chariot of fire. We read about this fantastic event in 2 Kings 2. Elijah and Elisha were traveling to various cities because the Lord had already revealed to Elijah, Elisha, and the prophets of the land that He would take him up in a whirlwind (2 Kings 2:1, 3, 7). When they crossed the Jordan River:

> As they were walking along and talking together, suddenly a chariot of fire and horses of fire appeared and separated the two of them, and Elijah went up to heaven in a whirlwind. Elisha saw this and cried out, "My father! My father! The chariots and horsemen of Israel!" And Elisha saw him no more. Then he took hold of his garment and tore it in two.
>
> —2 KINGS 2:11–12

What a story! What a reversal! Elijah went from running from Jezebel to being so pleasing to God with his life that he didn't see death. He was taken up in a whirlwind of fire that astounds the mind and stretches the imagination.

"Like Enoch, Elijah walked in such communion with the Lord that he was taken—alive—into heaven," Stearman wrote in *Time Travelers of the Bible*.

"Elijah was gone, but not forgotten. In the fifth century BC, Malachi prophesied that Elijah would return to his people: 'Behold, I will send you Elijah the prophet before the coming of the great and dreadful day of the LORD: And he shall turn the heart of the fathers to the children, and the heart of the children to their fathers, lest I come and smite the earth with a curse' (Malachi 4:5, 6). Here, in the closing words of the Old Testament, Elijah is seen as the forerunner of faith in the grim days of the Tribulation....Then, in the far future, Elijah appears as one of the two witnesses in Revelation. As he once did in the days of Ahab, he withholds the rain for three and a half years. Furthermore, just as he once stood against the priests of Baal, he will stand against the same evil spirits who are the power behind the throne of Antichrist. But in the most vivid sense, Elijah became a time traveler the moment he stepped aboard that fiery chariot. Entering the dimension of the heavens, he had access to the entire timeline, available for God's service as his destiny called."[5]

Although we may think this idea is confined to the Old Testament, several stories in the New Testament indicate that traveling through time is possible.

JESUS AND HIS DISCIPLES: THE BOAT

In John 6, we learn the story of Jesus walking on water amid a tremendous storm. Tucked inside this story is a verse we miss if we don't look closely. In a moment of great fear, the disciples, who couldn't make out whether Jesus was a ghost, suddenly had a moment of clarity:

> Then they were willing to take him into the boat, and immediately
> the boat reached the shore where they were heading.
>
> —JOHN 6:21

Read that again. The text says when they were willing to have Jesus get on the boat—Jesus hadn't even gotten on the boat yet—they were immediately on the other shore, where they were heading.

JESUS AND HIS DISCIPLES: THE LOCKED ROOM

> On the evening of that first day of the week, when the disciples were
> together, with the doors locked for fear of the Jewish leaders, Jesus

came and stood among them and said, "Peace be with you!" After he said this, he showed them his hands and side. The disciples were overjoyed when they saw the Lord.

—JOHN 20:19–20

The doors were locked, and Jesus showed up in the middle of the room. He didn't knock, He didn't bust the door down, He just showed up. Miraculous.

PHILIP AND THE SPIRIT

In the Book of Acts, we read about Philip teaching an Ethiopian eunuch the gospel of Jesus from the Book of Isaiah, which the eunuch read on his own.

When they came upon a body of water, the eunuch wanted to be baptized. So Philip baptized him, and "when they came up out of the water, the Spirit of the Lord suddenly took Philip away, and the eunuch did not see him again, but went on his way rejoicing. Philip, however, appeared at Azotus and traveled about, preaching the gospel in all the towns until he reached Caesarea" (Acts 8:39–40).

One moment he was with the eunuch, and the next he was in Azotus, traveling about and preaching the gospel.

THE FOLDING OF TIME

In her influential young adult novel *A Wrinkle in Time*, Madeleine L'Engle brought into the imagination of young readers the idea of a wrinkle, or tesseract, to travel through space and time. An article about the film version of the novel notes that "characters rely on a weird, real-world theoretical physics-influenced concept with a *very* familiar name."[6] Phil Hornshaw wrote:

> Mrs. Whatsit explains that if we understand space to be three-dimensional, and time represents a fourth dimension, then the tesseract is a fifth-dimensional bridge between two points in time and space....A tesseract is the literal "wrinkle in time."...The idea is that you use your mind to fold the fabric of space together to bridge two faraway points. In other words, tessering creates a so-called Einstein-Rosen Bridge.[7]

The Einstein-Rosen bridge, commonly known as a wormhole or a cosmic tunnel, is part of Einstein's theory of relativity and also a science fiction standard, but could it allow real-world humans to time travel? In an article in *Discover* magazine, Paul M. Sutter explored whether wormholes could allow people to travel back in time:

> Wormholes also have the somewhat mystical ability to allow backwards time travel. If you take one end of the wormhole and accelerate it to a speed close to that of light, it will experience time dilation— its internal "clock" will run slower than the rest of the universe.
>
> That will cause the two ends of the wormhole to no longer be synchronized in time. Then you could walk in one end and end up in your own past. Voilà: time travel.[8]

Sutter also pointed out, however, that the entrances to wormholes are behind the black hole horizon, and things that go into black holes never come out.[9]

MOUNT OF TRANSFIGURATION

Possible evidence for the idea of folding time to travel through it is found in the remarkable but mysterious event in Jesus' life known as the transfiguration. During the event, Jesus took Peter, James, and John up a high mountain where Moses and Elijah appeared and Jesus was transfigured, His face and clothes becoming dazzlingly white. The transfiguration, recorded in Matthew 17:1–13, Mark 9:2–13, and Luke 9:28–36, is "understood to have been the revelation of the eternal glory of the second person of the Trinity, which was normally veiled during Christ's life on earth."[10]

The question has long been asked, Why were Moses and Elijah there? One commentator noted, "This crucial episode draws heavily on Jewish tradition, yet adapts it to a uniquely Christian message. For starters, in rabbinic literature, Moses and Elijah often appear in the same passage, and are frequently compared. Elijah also appears at times with the Messiah."[11]

But how did they get there? Could it be that Moses was on Mount Sinai and saw Jesus at the same time as Elijah was in the cave hiding from Jezebel, and both were brought through time to be with Jesus, hundreds of years later on the Mount of Transfiguration? Josh Peck, a biblical researcher and author of *Quantum Creation: Does the Supernatural Lurk in the Fourth Dimension?*, believes that may be what happened.

"So we know that on the Mount of Transfiguration, Jesus is transfigured," Peck says. "We see Him in a glorified state basically for a few seconds. And who's present there? It's Moses, and it's Elijah. Well, what's really interesting is for the longest time I always thought...Moses and Elijah are dead, so they were in heaven, and they're called out. But now when we look at especially Moses, that's like the strongest case. Moses has an encounter with God [on Mount Sinai in the Book of Exodus] where when he's done with this encounter, he comes down and his face is shining and the people can't even be around him. They're so freaked out by it [that] he's got to wear a veil over his face [because] his face is shining. We get that same description of Jesus in the transfiguration. So what I think is actually happening is Jesus Himself in a sense brought two points of time together into one...really three because I think this happened with Elijah too because Elijah had a somewhat similar encounter. We don't have as much detail about his, but it's similar, and it still seems to fit.

"But in Moses' time, he actually got to see the future Messiah, the future Jesus. So he was brought there by Jesus through time, or there was an opening in time or however it worked, but where Moses was actually seeing the transfigured Jesus. To Jesus that would've been present time. To Moses that would've been way in the future....[It's the] same thing with Elijah. And of course Elijah and Moses were in different times too. So you have these three points in time all converging. But the important thing is that it's Jesus doing it because Jesus [is] God in the flesh. And God, of course, He created time. He's the master of time. He can manipulate it as He sees fit. We don't have that ability, but He does."[12]

Did Einstein and physicist Nathan Rosen, who used the theory of general relativity to propose the existence of bridges through space-time, have it right? Can time be folded and passed through?

WHAT DOES SCIENCE SAY CURRENTLY?

Theories and fiction are fun, but what has science—especially physics—discovered about time travel? Could Ingersoll Lockwood and later Donald Trump have passed through the veils of time to see what was going to happen?

Michael Marshall of the BBC wrote an article titled, "Is Time Travel Really Possible? Here's What Physics Says":

> Answering this question requires understanding how time actually works—something physicists are far from certain about. So far, what we can say with confidence is that travelling into the future is achievable, but travelling into the past is either wildly difficult or absolutely impossible.[13]

Starting out with Einstein's theories of relativity, in which he described space, time, mass and gravity, a key result is that time doesn't flow constantly. It speeds up, slows down, and is influenced by different circumstances. Marshall pointed out that if you travel at the speed of light or are in an intense gravitational field, time will slow down, especially if the gravitational field is a black hole.

So, according to what Einstein proposed, we can travel into time by going the speed of light or getting sucked into a black hole. Both would slow time down in the traveler's world, while speeding time up in the "normal" universe. To see what will happen hundreds of years from now by traveling physically through time, that is how you would do it.

Setting aside traveling at the speed of light, Marshall continued with the idea of wormholes.

> There is another phenomenon that is seemingly allowed by relativity: wormholes. In theory, it is possible for space-time to be folded like a piece of paper, allowing a tunnel to be punched through to create a shortcut between two widely-separated points. "Wormholes are theoretically possible in general relativity."[14]

Scientists have discovered they are mathematically possible, but do we have evidence they can exist?

Looking back at the stories of Philip, Jesus, Enoch, Moses, and Elijah, we can see that "with God all things are possible" (Matt. 19:26), and He is the only One who can create them because "real wormholes would also be microscopically tiny. You couldn't fit a person, or even a bacterium, through one."[15] And to make one large enough to pass through would require an immense amount of energy—like God-sized energy.

Despite the seeming impossibility of manufacturing time travel or folding time on our own, there are a few cases of military and intelligence agencies reportedly trying to break through the space-time barrier. One of them involves a long-denied experiment with a United States naval ship during World War II.

THE FAMED PHILADELPHIA EXPERIMENT

The subject of a television movie, a few TV show episodes on the History Channel, hundreds of internet postings, and a few books, the Philadelphia Experiment is a well-chased-after story.

The "infamous World War II conspiracy theory" goes as such: Following the release of his book *The Case for the UFO*, Morris Ketchum Jessup was contacted by a man named Carl M. Allen, who went by the pseudonym Carlos Miguel Allende. In a series of letters to Jessup, Allende claimed he could prove Einstein's unified field theory based on what he witnessed in 1943 at the Philadelphia Naval Yard. At the time, as the story goes, the US Navy began toying with parts of unified field theory, a theory by Einstein and others in which electromagnetism and gravity would be united into a single fundamental field.[16]

Allende claimed he was present when the navy "was conducting top-secret experiments designed to win command of the oceans against the Axis powers. The rumor was that the government was creating technology that would render naval ships invisible to enemy radar."[17] During the test, according to Allende, the *USS Eldridge* vanished from Philadelphia, briefly appeared in Norfolk, Virginia, and then returned to the Philadelphia Naval Yard. Allende claimed he was on board another ship, the *USS Andrew Furuseth*, observing the experiment when he saw this happen. He wrote that he watched "the air all around the ship turn slightly, ever so slightly, darker than all the other air. I saw, after a few minutes, a foggy green mist arise like a cloud. I watched as thereafter the [*USS Eldridge*] became rapidly invisible to human eyes."[18]

This is where things get even more otherworldly. Allende claimed that "while the experiment worked—in terms of achieving both teleportation and invisibility—it had terrible effects on the crew." He claimed some sailors were fused to the metal structures of the ship once it reappeared, some disappeared from sight and were never seen again, and others later went insane and were committed to asylums.[19]

Jessup confirmed that Allende was actually on the *Andrew Furuseth* at the time. Later, he was contacted by the navy's Office of Naval Research, which had received a package with Jessup's book filled with handwritten messages about the events that allegedly occurred at the Philadelphia Naval Yard, including "annotations claiming that extraterrestrial technology allowed the U.S. government to make breakthroughs in unified field theory."[20]

Then, in 1959, Jessup was found dead in his car in a Florida park, the victim of a purported suicide, but UFO buffs suggested "he was murdered to silence some secret knowledge connected with the Bermuda Triangle or the 'Philadelphia Experiment.'"[21] Then, in 1979, Bill Moore and Charles Berlitz wrote the book *The Philadelphia Experiment: Project Invisibility*, claiming that "the 'impossible' experiment actually took place," but the navy subsequently covered it up.[22] Ultimately, Allende, or Allen, confessed that he had made up the story and gave ufologist Jim Lorenzen a signed statement to that effect.[23]

The Office of Naval Research denied that such an experiment ever took place, offering this explanation:

> Personnel at the Fourth Naval District believe that the questions surrounding the so-called "Philadelphia Experiment" arise from quite routine research which occurred during World War II at the Philadelphia Naval Shipyard. Until recently, it was believed that the foundation for the apocryphal stories arose from degaussing experiments which have the effect of making a ship undetectable or "invisible" to magnetic mines. Another likely genesis of the bizarre stories about levitation, teleportation and effects on human crew members might be attributed to experiments with the generating plant of a destroyer, the *USS Timmerman*. In the 1950's this ship was part of an experiment to test the effects of a small, high-frequency generator providing 1,000hz instead of the standard 400hz. The higher frequency generator produced corona discharges, and other well-known phenomena associated with high frequency generators. None of the crew suffered effects from the experiment.
>
> ONR has never conducted any investigations on invisibility, either in 1943 or at any other time (ONR was established in 1946.) In view of present scientific knowledge, ONR scientists do not

believe that such an experiment could be possible except in the realm of science fiction.[24]

Yet, despite Allende's purported confession that he made up the story and the Office of Naval Research's denial that the Philadelphia Experiment took place, many researchers believe it did take place and the government covered it up.

ATOMIC BOMBS, UFOS/UAPS, NIKOLA TELSA, AND TELEPORTATION

On May 9, 2001, physician Steven Greer spoke at the National Press Club in Washington, DC, claiming the federal government had long withheld information from the public about UFOs and extraterrestrial visitations.

Greer, considered "the world's leading authority on the subject of UFOs/ UAPs [unidentified aerial (or anomalous) phenomena], advanced energy and propulsion systems," presented twenty speakers at the 2001 press conference, along with a 492-page "Disclosure Project Briefing Document," outlining what he claimed was the greatest secret in human history. The twenty former government workers, including military and security personnel, said they had witnessed UFOs/UAPs hovering over nuclear weapons bases, in some cases rendering inert the nuclear capabilities of those weapons. They called for congressional hearings into the matter.[25]

"Over several decades, according to Greer, untold numbers of alien craft had been observed in our planet's airspace; they were able to reach extreme velocities with no visible means of lift or propulsion, and to perform stunning maneuvers at g-forces that would turn a human pilot to soup," Gideon Lewis-Kraus wrote in *The New Yorker*. "Some of these extraterrestrial spaceships had been 'downed, retrieved and studied since at least the 1940s and possibly as early as the 1930s.' Efforts to reverse engineer such extraordinary machines had led to 'significant technological breakthroughs in energy generation.' These operations had mostly been classified as 'cosmic top secret,' a tier of clearance 'thirty-eight levels' above that typically granted to the Commander-in-Chief. Why, Greer asked, had such transformative technologies been hidden for so long? This was obvious. The 'social, economic and geo-political order of the world' was at stake."[26]

In a recent interview Greer said the testing of atomic bombs in the 1940s and 1950s ripped the "fabric of inter- or trans-dimensional space-time, which disrupts extraterrestrial communications and transport systems."[27]

Greer said, "So when we detonated the first atomic bomb...all of a sudden there were ET [extraterrestrial] vehicles investigating everything we were doing on this planet because it wasn't just that we were on a path where we could kill ourselves; we were disrupting other operations that are extraterrestrial."[28]

At the time, Greer noted, Tesla's research into scalar waves helped the government develop faster than the speed of light scalar electromagnetic weapons that were used to knock the UFOs/UAPs down so scientists could begin reverse engineering their technologies.

"They knew these ET craft were all around our nuclear facilities," Greer said. "Roswell was the only nuclear bomb squadron in the world, or atomic bomb squadron technically....And so they were trying to track and knock these [UAPs] down....It's not like you're hitting them with a missile or a laser. It's these weird directional energy weapons that...cross over into this scalar area. And to this day, when I was over a black site [recently]...there [were] these massive electromagnetic pulse generators....So you can target an object with that, hit it, but you also have the scalar, and that can cause these ET craft to get stunned or lose control and crash. So some of the people I'm working with currently have been on those retrieval teams that are actively still doing this. In fact, one of the sites I went over, and I'll show you this video, that one or two ET craft per year are knocked down there, and it's very worrisome."[29]

The interviewer, Patrick Bet-David, then asked Greer about "zero-point energy teleporting, like the concept of teleporting." "Do we have access to it?" Bet-David asked. "How long have we had it? Who invented it? Is it being used? What's the worry with that? Why are they not releasing it if they have access?"

Greer said the government doesn't want people to know about its teleporting technologies:

> But if you look at the testimony of one of our witnesses...[in] 1953
> he was at a Canadian air force base, and they were experimenting
> with that so-called teleportation. And he said it was so funny...
> everyone smoked back then, [they had] these big ashtrays, and it

would be...an electromagnetic system here, and on the other end of the base, another one. And this ashtray would go, boom, teleport. Now Einstein, when he said the same particle could be in two places at once, he called it the "spooky effect." But really what it is, is what's called quantum entanglement, where every point in space and time is connected to the other. And if you look up quantum entanglement, that's what this is. But imagine doing that not just with a particle, but a whole object or spacecraft. So those experiments were going on also [in the] thirties, forties, fifties, but when they began to unpack and really have some of the most brilliant minds—I mean, I will tell you the smartest people I've ever met...have been working on these projects...underground.[30]

Bet-David asked Greer if he's convinced "teleportation is a real thing."

"Oh, it certainly can be done," Greer said. "Teleportation is the theoretical transfer of matter or energy from one point to another without traversing the physical space between them. It is a common subject in science fiction, fantasy, literature, film, video games, and television. In some situations, teleporting is presented as time traveling across space."[31]

An early example of scientific teleportation is found in an 1897 novel, *To Venus in Five Seconds* by Fred Jane. Jane's protagonist is transported via strange machinery on earth to Venus. A common fictional device for teleportation is a wormhole.

"In video games, the instant teleportation of a player character may be referred to as a warp," Greer said. "How are you going to go from one star system to another?...In order to traverse interstellar space, and this was concluded early on by the fact [UAPs] were here and we downed some of them...you're basically bending space-time. So visualize this like a piece of paper....You have a star system here, and we're here. Instead of going in a straight line...through these very high voltage electromagnetic systems that also create gravitational waves, you can bend space-time....Actually that's where you get into this whole non-locality and physics and quantum entanglement in an applied setting. So the fact that it is relegated to science fiction is fine. It doesn't mean that it isn't being done, because it has to be. You're not going to be able to travel through interstellar distances in any way during any species' lifespan without obliterating, as it were, linear space-time. And it doesn't mean you're not traversing, but you're moving trans-dimensionally."[32]

Greer said the government's teleportation technologies are "forbidden" technologies that are "highly classified," and "they were standing on the shoulders of great people—Nikola Tesla discovered many of these phenomena."

As far as the UFOs/UAPs, Greer said it appears that spacecraft, both ones operated by extraterrestrials and those designed and operated by what he calls the "parallel illegal black government system," are using these technologies.

"So [it's] called electromagnetic gravitic, where certain voltages cause objects to float and change their structure," Greer said. "I think it has more to do with the magnetic spin....It causes a magnetic field flux that alters the mass...of an object, and then it can float and go up...against gravity and that's also how you control it....We had one case when I was in France... we attempt[ed] to make contact with these objects and these civilizations— and the object was moving over us at two hundred thousand kilometers per hour. It was tracked by the French Ministry of Defense....It could make a righthand turn or stop. Now, if you were in a normal vehicle...your brains would come out of your nose. The g-forces would kill you immediately....So you're really in an electromagnetic space-time bubble when you're moving like that."[33]

It should be noted here that while Greer and many other ufologists believe governments are in contact with extraterrestrial races and have reverse engineered their technologies, Christian experts on this phenomenon, including Christian astrophysicist Dr. Hugh Ross, founder of Reasons to Believe, believe "we're dealing with...interdimensional phenomena" that is "consistent with [what] the Bible teaches about angels."[34]

Ross said many of his fellow astrophysicists don't believe it's possible—even if intelligent life exists in the universe—for aliens to survive a trip to earth through the vast expanse of space from planets many light-years away, and so instead Ross believes these entities are demons posing as extraterrestrials.

"I've written a book on UFOs, *Lights in the Sky & Little Green Men*, where I say the vast majority of what people report as UFOs can be naturally explained," Ross said. "They could be hoaxes or secret military activity, but there's about a 1 percent residual. And the 1 percent residual is phenomena as brought about by humans dabbling in the occult. Take the occult out, that's the end of their close encounters with UFOs. Bring the occult in, don't be surprised if these things start happening to you and you see the correlations. I mean the incidence is much higher in equatorial Brazil and in France than here in the United States, but that's because the percentage of people involved in the occult is much higher in those places than [it] is here in the United States. There is a direct correlation."

Governments around the world are releasing classified data on reports of UFOs/UAPs, and Ross said he's examined the data, and it basically demonstrates that, "Hey, something real is going on, but it's not physical."

"And so its pilots documenting that they see phenomena where apparent craft are making sharp right-angle turns at thousands of miles per hour, g-forces that would destroy any physical craft, and yet they witness this," Ross said. "And as we document in *Lights in the Sky & Little Green Men,* there are at least two thousand reported cases where UFOs are observed going through the atmosphere at thousands of miles per hour, and the human observers never report a sonic boom. They don't report heat friction in the trail behind the UFO.

"It's going through our atmosphere without heat friction, no sonic boom. It crashes into the earth, and when you go to the crash site, you can see a shallow depression. If there's snow, the snow is melted. The vegetation is damaged. When you go to the crater, there's no artifacts, there's no debris. If this was a physical phenomenon, you would hear sonic booms, you'd see heat friction, there would be debris at the crash site. None of that is there, but the fact that you get a crater and melted snow and damaged vegetation tells us something real is going on. And again, in my collection of books here, I've got six books written by physicists on the UFO phenomena. I think I'm the only one that's a follower of Jesus Christ; the others are not. But they all say that we're dealing with something interdimensional, phenomena that are not subject to the laws of physics or the space-time dimensions of the universe, which is consistent with [what] the Bible teaches about angels [and demons]. These are beings that are not constrained by the physics of our universe, but they can come into our realm and leave our realm at will."[35]

At a time when a recent Pew Research Center poll found 65 percent of Americans now believe intelligent life exists on other planets and 51 percent say UFOs reported by the military are likely evidence of this,[36] Ross and others are concerned the growing popularity of UFOs/UAPs could be setting the world up for what the apostle Paul warned would involve a "powerful delusion" accompanied by "signs and lying wonders" in the end times—what's known as the "great deception" that could help persuade humanity to worship the Antichrist as God.

> Let no man deceive you by any means: for that day shall not come, except there come a falling away first, and that man of sin be revealed, the son of perdition....And then shall that Wicked be revealed, whom the Lord shall consume with the spirit of his mouth, and shall destroy with the brightness of his coming: Even him, whose coming is after the working of Satan with all power and signs and lying wonders....And for this cause God shall send them strong delusion, that they should believe a lie: that they all might be damned who believed not the truth, but had pleasure in unrighteousness.
>
> —2 THESSALONIANS 2:3, 8–9, 11–12, KJV

CIA EXPERIMENTS WITH TIME TRAVEL

Lest we think the military is the only organization to attempt time travel, a declassified document from the Central Intelligence Agency describes their attempt to escape the boundaries of time and space, and provides a workbook for doing just that.[37]

Known as the "Gateway Experience," this technique was something the CIA was looking to use to escape the boundaries of space-time through altering the consciousness. In an article titled "How to Escape the Confines of Time and Space According to the CIA," Thobey Campion wrote that the declassified document shows that the CIA developed the Gateway Experience as a "training system designed to focus brainwave output to alter consciousness and ultimately escape the restrictions of time and space. The CIA was interested in all sorts of psychic research at the time, including the theory and applications of remote viewing, which is when someone views real events with only the power of their mind."[38]

The article goes into depth on the timeline of the research—it began in the 1950s—and states that in the 1970s our military and intelligence agencies were reading a report about the Soviet Union "pouring money into research involving ESP and psychokinesis for espionage purposes." The CIA wrote a report, "Analysis and Assessment of The Gateway Process," in 1983; it provided "a scientific framework for understanding and expanding human consciousness, out-of-body experiments, and other altered states of mind." In 2003, the CIA released the paper, and then, in 2017, they declassified "12 million pages of records revealing previously unknown details about the program, which would eventually become known as Project Stargate."[39]

In all, the procedure claims to have helped people "access the intuitive knowledge of the universe, as well as travel in time and commune with other-dimensional beings." They claim successes, but those were limited. Author Susan Lahey wrote that an army colonel working for the CIA "packaged the document in physical science lingo to avoid any unwanted connections to the occult. He leaned on quantum mechanics sources to 'describe the nature and functioning of human consciousness,' and on theoretical physics to explain the character of the time-space dimension and the means by which expanded human consciousness transcends it."[40]

Why hide the connections to the occult unless they are trying to go around the Lord God Almighty and do something that only He can do?

NIKOLA TESLA'S RESEARCH AND TRUMP

This still leaves us with the question: What if God gave a man the knowledge needed to travel through time?

Internet researchers, major magazines, and media networks have asked whether Nikola Tesla had discovered or been given this knowledge. A *Publishers Weekly* review of a book about Tesla says the author credits Tesla "with the invention of the induction motor, long-distance electrical power distribution, fluorescent and neon lights, the first true radio tube and remote control, besides making vital contributions to the technology underlying television, wireless communication, robotics, lasers, the facsimile machine and particle-beam weaponry anticipating the space-based 'Star Wars' defensive shield."[41]

Did Tesla come up with a time travel machine too, as many have postulated? What happened to the infamous Tesla missing documents? Further, is his research connected to Donald Trump through Trump's uncle John G. Trump?

Tesla's list of inventions is immense, with around three hundred patents registered in his name.[42] One of them is rumored to be a device that allowed him to see or travel into the future: how else could some of his predictions

of the future have been so spot on? Among his futuristic insights, he predicted the creation of the Environmental Protection Agency, the emergence of
robotics—he experimented with a robotic boat in the 1890s—cheaper energy,
the management of natural resources, and the rise of scientific research taking
a preeminence in the minds of humanity.[43]

It's well documented that shortly after the famous inventor's death the
government "confiscated Tesla's property and kept it for 10 years, citing war-
time national safety."[44] If he did find a way to see things like the establishment of the EPA, decades before it happened, it would then make sense
why the United States government confiscated most of his research, although
they eventually returned all but several trunks.

Writing for *Popular Mechanics*, Jessica Coulon stated that the FBI obviously didn't trust Tesla's nephew, who also happened to be the Yugoslavian
ambassador to the US, with Tesla's research, which is why the research was
confiscated.

> At the time it was rumored that Tesla may have made some incred-
> ibly powerful and life-changing discoveries. On September 22, 1940,
> the *New York Times* reported that Tesla had created a "death ray"
> that could melt airplane motors from 250 miles away, called the
> "teleforce."...If true, such a weapon would be critical to national
> security.[45]

It's here that Donald Trump is connected. After Tesla's belongings were
collected, Dr. John G. Trump, an electrical engineer with the National
Defense Research Committee, was assigned the job of investigating Tesla's
papers for anything that might be of importance to the government.

After reviewing the materials, Dr. Trump told the chief of the Division of
Investigation and Research in Washington, DC, that Tesla's papers "contain
nothing of value for the war effort, and nothing which would be helpful to
the enemy if it fell into enemy hands."[46]

However, in Dr. Trump's report, he described articles, interviews, and
scientific treatises, including "The New Art of Projecting Concentrated
Non-Dispersive Energy Through the Natural Media." "This article, in con-
tradiction to Trump's statement, contained explicit information which had
never been published describing the actual workings of a particle-beam

weapon for destroying tanks and planes and for igniting explosives," Marc J. Seifer wrote in *Wizard: The Life and Times of Nikola Tesla*. "Written virtually as a patent application, the Tesla article presents in clear and straightforward terms the mathematical equations and schematics of his death ray.... Although Trump downplayed the importance of this paper, it is, to the present day, classified top secret by the U.S. military, with copies at the time going to naval intelligence, the FBI, the OAP, the NDRC, Wright-Patterson Air Force Base, MIT, and most likely, the White House....A few days after viewing the estate, Trump went to Governor Clinton to view the actual death ray held in their vault."[47]

Sava Kosanovich received his uncle's possessions in 1952. But even then, many of Tesla's belongings were not returned. "Reportedly, his family only received 60 trunks full of his research out of the eighty Tesla had said he'd had," Coulon wrote.[48]

The question remains though: Did Dr. Trump and the government return all of Tesla's research? And if not, why not?

What did Dr. Trump find in the trunks he was tasked with searching?

Though the FBI appointed him to search for evidence that Tesla's death ray was real and viable, did Dr. Trump find something else in the research that warranted further research, hence the still-missing files and trunks of research never returned to the Tesla family?

"Despite John G. Trump's dismissive assessment of Tesla's ideas immediately after his death, the military did try and incorporate particle-beam weaponry in the decades following World War II, Seifer says," Sarah Pruitt wrote in a History Channel article. "Notably, the inspiration of the 'Death Ray' fueled Ronald Reagan's Strategic Defense Initiative, or 'Star Wars' program, in the 1980s. If the government is still using Tesla's ideas to power its technology, Seifer explains, that could explain why some files related to the inventor still remain classified."[49]

CHAPTER SIX

PREDICTING OR CREATING THE FUTURE?

It was about the middle of February when I set out from the Castle Trump, and I journeyed night and day in order to reach Petersburg by the first of March, for I knew that the government trains would leave that city for the White Sea during the first week of that month. Bulger and I were both in the best of health and spirits, and the fatigue of the journey didn't tell upon us in the least. The moment I arrived at the Russian capital I applied to the emperor for permission to join one of the government trains, which was most graciously accorded.

—INGERSOLL LOCKWOOD, *BARON TRUMP'S MARVELLOUS UNDERGROUND JOURNEY*

WHEN INGERSOLL LOCKWOOD wrote about Baron Trump traveling to Russia from Castle Trump and having extreme favor in the foreign country, was he seeing over one hundred thirty years into the future—a future when Donald J. Trump would travel the world and do things no other sitting president had done before?

In a 2017 CNN article, "Trump to Become First Foreign Leader to Dine in Forbidden City Since Founding of Modern China," James Griffiths wrote:

> Donald Trump will receive an honor in Beijing not granted to any US President since the founding of the People's Republic of China: official dinner inside the Forbidden City....
>
> Trump will be the first foreign leader to have an official dinner in the palace since the founding of the People's Republic in 1949.
>
> Dining in the Forbidden City will be a significant honor for Trump, in keeping with what China's Ambassador to the US Cui Tiankai promised would be a "state visit-plus."[1]

Another 2017 CNN article highlighted Trump participating in the "ceremonial sword dance in the Kingdom of Saudi Arabia...outside the Murabba Palace....The traditional men's sword dance is known as the ardah....The performance combines dance, drumming and chanting poetry, and it signifies the start of notable occasions like religious holidays or weddings."[2] Trump joined just two other world leaders to have participated in the dance before: King Charles III (the former Prince of Wales) and President George W. Bush.

Then, in 2019, Trump did what no one expected: he crossed into North Korea in front of the eyes of the world at a time when the world stood on the brink of nuclear war.

In the run-up to this historic meeting, North Korean leader Kim Jong-un had threatened America and Israel with nuclear attack, at one point saying any country that "dares hurt the dignity of its supreme leadership" will face "merciless, thousand-fold punishment."[3]

In an NBC News article about the visit, it was noted that Trump took an "unprecedented step onto North Korean soil....Side-by-side with Kim in the heavily-fortified demilitarized zone, Trump became the first sitting U.S. president to cross the 1953 armistice line separating North and South Korea, then joined Kim for a roughly 50-minute meeting."[4]

Despite Trump's meeting with the North Korean leader, which defused nuclear tensions, the United States and North Korea did not make concrete progress on denuclearization of the Korean peninsula.

Now—amid the Biden administration's disastrous foreign policies and weakness leading to the chaotic withdrawal from Afghanistan in 2021, the Russia-Ukraine war that has claimed hundreds of thousands of lives, and China's threats to attack Taiwan, bringing the world to the brink of World War III—Jong-un has resumed his nuclear threats, ordering his military to "thoroughly annihilate" the United States and South Korea if provoked.[5]

For so many, *unprecedented* seems to be the word to describe Trump and how God has used and is using him in the United States and throughout the world.

THE TRUMP PROPHECIES

While many prophecies about the 2020 president election and Trump didn't come true, the flow of prophetic words and revelations about Trump,

America, and the future of our world are pouring out at an even greater rate today.

Dr. Michael Brown, host of the nationally syndicated *Line of Fire* radio program, delved into this topic in his recent *Charisma* article, "Enough Already With the Pro-Trump Prophecies!"

> There is still egg on our faces because of the 2020 debacle. (When I say "our faces" it is because I am a leader in the Pentecostal/charismatic church. And even though I worked hard with others to call for prophetic accountability and to rebuke the false prophecies about Trump, this is my family, so there is egg on all of our faces. This is my mess too.)
>
> Tragically and inexcusably, there is still denial and deception and duplicity about the failed prophecies, all in the name of the Lord. There is still excuse making and finger pointing and blame shifting without any accountability and integrity, to the point that some of the "prophets" who blew it most egregiously—I mean prophesying specific dates and timelines that flatly did not pan out—have continued to prophesy about Trump to this day, without correction or apology....
>
> What the larger body of Christ (and certainly the secular world) may not know is that some of the most respected charismatic prophets did *not* prophesy a Trump victory. They offered no prophetic words at all about the elections, recognizing that God had not spoken to them about it....
>
> I even have colleagues who don't claim to be prophets who reached out to me some months before November 2020, saying that God showed them that Biden would be president, one reason being the degree to which many Christians had made Trump into an idol. These voices, however, were totally obscured by the landslide of pro-Trump prophecies, and in the days to come, you can expect to hear these pro-Trump "prophets" shouting from the rooftops again.[6]

A February 2021 Politico article, "The Christian Prophets Who Say Trump Is Coming Again," quoted Johnny Enlow, cofounder of the Restore7 ministry, noting more than one hundred "credible" Christian prophets had declared that Trump would soon be restored to the presidency in early 2021 following his loss to Biden.

"Indeed, Enlow was not alone out on that limb," Julia Duin wrote. "Greg Locke, a Nashville pastor with a massive social media following, said after Trump's loss that he would '100 percent remain president of the United States for another term.' Kat Kerr, a pink-haired preacher from Jacksonville, Florida, declared repeatedly last month that Trump had won the election 'by a landslide' and that God had told her he would serve for eight years. In his video, Enlow went further. 'There's not going to be just Trump coming back,' he said. 'There's going to be at least two more Trumps that will be in office in some way.'"[7]

And even though a recent Monmouth University poll found 30 percent of Americans—and 68 percent of Republicans—"believe that Joe Biden only won the presidency because of voter fraud," believers need to follow Scripture to discern between authentic prophetic words and inauthentic ones.[8]

How Can I Know If a Prophetic Word Is True?

Under the New Covenant—the promise God has made with humanity that He will forgive our sins and restore communion with those who accept Jesus Christ as their Savior—prophecies need to be tested, judged, and weighed.

In 1 Corinthians 12–14, the apostle Paul wrote about the gifts of the Holy Spirit—wisdom, knowledge, faith, healing, miracles, prophecy, discerning of spirits, speaking in tongues, and interpretation of tongues—encouraging believers to exercise these gifts in love and wisdom.

First Corinthians 14:1–3 (NKJV) says, "Pursue love, and desire spiritual gifts, but especially that you may prophesy. For he who speaks in a tongue does not speak to men but to God, for no one understands him; however, in the spirit he speaks mysteries. But he who prophesies speaks edification and exhortation and comfort to men."

The Bible lays out nine principles to determine whether a prophetic word is true. As the 2020 presidential election obviously demonstrated, not all prophecies are from God. Here are two Bible verses that set the standard for determining whether a prophetic word is true:

> Let two or three prophets speak, and let the others judge.
>
> —1 Corinthians 14:29, NKJV

Beloved, do not believe every spirit, but test the spirits, whether they are of God; because many false prophets have gone out into the world.

—1 JOHN 4:1, NKJV

The apostle Paul instructed us to "test the spirits" because every prophetic word comes from God or the flesh or a demon.

"When truth is denied, deception is released," wrote John C. Hagee in the *Prophecy Study Bible*. "False prophets and false prophecy abound in the world today. False prophecy leads to deception and makes the believer the object of manipulation or domination by false prophets who have ungodly motives and a hidden agenda."[9]

Hagee's *Prophecy Study Bible* lays out nine principles for judging prophecies:

1. "The purpose of New Testament prophecy is to edify, exhort, and comfort (1 Cor. 14:3)."

2. "Prophecy agrees with the Word of God!"

3. "Prophecy must bear fruit and agree with the Holy Spirit in conduct and character."

4. "If prophecy contains predictions that do not come true, the prophecy was false. Deuteronomy 18:22 says, 'When a prophet speaks in the name of the LORD, if the thing does not happen or come to pass, that is the thing which the LORD has not spoken; the prophet has spoken it presumptuously.'"

5. "If a prophecy comes true and promotes disobedience against God or Scripture, it is not a true prophecy."

6. "True prophecy produces liberty and not bondage."

7. "True prophecy injects fresh life into the meeting of believers."

8. "True prophecy given by the Holy Spirit will bear witness with your spirit. The Bible says, 'And it is the Spirit who bears witness, because the Spirit is truth' (1 John 5:6b)."

9. "Any prophecy that comes true but does not give glory and honor to the Lord Jesus Christ is the spirit of divination. The

fact that a prophecy comes true is not proof it came from God. (See Deuteronomy 13:1–3.)"[10]

"I would encourage every person to take prophecy before the Lord in prayer and to examine it according to the Scripture and compare the message that's being preached to what's preached in the Word of God before you run with that specific prophecy," Troy Black, a Christian author and prophetic voice, said during an interview with Charisma Media founder Stephen E. Strang.[11]

"I'M STILL USING TRUMP"

During the interview, Strang said some prophetic voices prophesied a decade ago that Trump would be president for two terms, and while he was elected in 2016, he wasn't reelected in 2020. "So what specifically are you hearing about Donald Trump?" Strang asked Black. He answered:

> I've been hearing different prophecies about Donald Trump specifi- cally and about the elections...over the last three or four years. And I've shared several words publicly. And one of the main things that I've heard about Donald Trump specifically is the Lord saying, "I'm still using him. I'm still using Trump."...There's a specific reason why God is using Donald Trump during this hour, during this time, and why He's not done with him. And I say that not out of a place of opinion, but I say that based on the words that I've been hearing from the Holy Spirit. God's still saying, "I'm not done with him, I'm not done with him."
>
> And does that mean that he's going to win this year specifi- cally? To be honest, I don't know. I'm praying that he does....As a conservative Christian, I'm praying that he gets reelected. Based on what I've heard from the Lord, I believe he's going to be, but the Lord hasn't clearly and specifically stated that he's going to be reelected....I would warn every believer this year as well: there are going to be more and more prophecies about Donald Trump coming out this year, still to come from many different voices across the spec- trum. And my warning in love would be, be careful with connecting dots that the Lord is not connecting. Make sure that it's something the Holy Spirit's actually said. And then also, if it's coming from

somebody that you don't know if you can trust or not, take it with a grain of salt and pray about it before you move forward with that.[12]

Over the last two decades we have seen many prophets arise—and many of them speak accurately about Trump and his role in the future of America. While well documented by Strang in his book *God and Donald Trump*, it's worth mentioning again Kim Clement's prophetic words in 2007, directed right at Trump; they still ring deeply true:

> "Trump shall become a trumpet," says the Lord. "No, you didn't hear Me. Trump shall become a trumpet. Are you listening to Me? I will raise up the Trump to become a trumpet."
>
> "There will be a praying president, not a religious one, for I will fool the people," says the Lord. "I will fool the people. Yes, I will." God says, "The one that is chosen shall go in, and they shall say, 'He has hot blood,' for the Spirit of God says, 'Yes, he may have hot blood, but he will bring the walls of protection on this country in a greater way, and the economy of this country shall change rapidly,'" says the Lord of hosts. Listen to the word of the Lord. God says, "I will put at your helm for two terms, a president that will pray, but he will not be a praying president when he starts. I will put him in office, and then I will baptize him with the Holy Spirit and My power," says the Lord.[13]

Take a moment to read through those words again, stated many years before Trump announced his candidacy. What didn't come to pass in his election and time in office?

Then, in the months before the 2016 presidential election, Lance Wallnau took a bold stand and pronounced that Trump would be the forty-fifth president of the United States. This was foolish in the eyes of the political world and the common man; at the time Wallnau announced it, Trump was down by over ten points in the race against Hillary Clinton.

In a CBN News interview in 2017, Wallnau said that God revealed to him that Trump is Cyrus, the Persian king who allowed the Jews living in captivity in ancient Babylon to return to Israel and rebuild the temple.

"I heard the Lord say, 'Donald Trump is a wrecking ball to the spirit of political correctness,'" Wallnau says.

"After I met him I heard the Lord say, 'Isaiah 45 will be the 45th president,'" he explains. "I go check it out; Isaiah 45 is Cyrus."[14]

Written about one hundred years before the reign of Cyrus, Isaiah 45:1–5 (NKJV) says:

> Thus says the LORD to His anointed, to Cyrus, whose right hand I have held—to subdue nations before him and loose the armor of kings, to open before him the double doors, so that the gates will not be shut: "I will go before you and make the crooked places straight; I will break in pieces the gates of bronze and cut the bars of iron. I will give you the treasures of darkness and hidden riches of secret places, that you may know that I, the LORD, who call you by your name, am the God of Israel. For Jacob My servant's sake, and Israel My elect, I have even called you by your name; I have named you, though you have not known Me. I am the LORD, and there is no other; there is no God besides Me. I will gird you, though you have not known Me."

Wallnau pointed out that just like Cyrus didn't know the Lord, Trump also didn't know God the way an evangelical would typically define it. But Wallnau also noted that he believes Trump has a "fear of God," and just like God positioned Cyrus for the sake of Israel, He also positioned Trump for the sake of His people.[15]

USA Today noted that Wallnau is one of only a few evangelical leaders to have accurately predicted Donald Trump's presidency.[16]

WILL TRUMP APPOINT FIVE SUPREME COURT JUSTICES?

One of the other leaders to be accurate regarding God's work involving Trump and America was not someone considered a "normal" prophet. A retired third-generation firefighter, Mark Taylor revealed in 2016 that God had told him Trump would be president.

Beginning in 2011, he received prophetic words that Trump would be elected and that he would appoint five Supreme Court justices.[17] He saw three new justices put into office under Trump. During Trump's first term, he appointed Amy Coney Barrett, Brett Kavanaugh, and Neil Gorsuch to the high court. Maybe it's not a coincidence that the Biden administration has only appointed one justice to the Supreme Court—Ketanji Brown Jackson, the first black woman to serve on the court, replacing Stephen Breyer—and God is saving the last two for Trump's return. Time will tell.

In fact, at a campaign fundraiser in Los Angeles that raised $28 million and was attended by George Clooney, Julia Roberts, and Barack Obama, Biden said the winner of the 2024 presidential election will likely have the chance to fill two vacancies on the Supreme Court, which he described as "one of the scariest parts" if Trump is successful in his bid for a second term.[18]

In an interview with Strang, evangelist Mario Murillo spoke about prophetic things he wrote about in *It's Our Turn Now: God's Plan to Restore America Is Within Our Reach*. The Holy Spirit had shown him sparks of revival breaking out.

> I wrote that a campus miracle would start somewhere in America, and certainly we saw [that] at the beginning of [2023] in Asbury. I also said that there would be transitions because…woke people will become so miserable that they'll reject woke. Then the Bud Light thing happened. Then *Jesus Revolution* came out. Now Hollywood is reeling under the impact of the *Sound of Freedom*, and now we're watching further changes in the culture. People are hungry.
>
> Jesus said, "You say there cannot be a harvest yet for a few months." John 4:35. "But I tell you that vast numbers of human souls are ripening all around you." I saw that; that's why in our crusades…we've had as many as 1,400 volunteers come to attend, many of them thinking they're not going to have enough to do. And the altar calls are so vast that every one of them are used up. That's how many people want to be saved right now.[19]

In *It's Our Turn Now*, Murillo wrote that a "golden opportunity is churning amid America's moral and physical disaster."

> The call from God is clear and strong: "Come and let Me make you fit to seize this golden opportunity." The Spirit of God is telling us it is our turn now.

Political, corporate, and media villains have had their day and their say. It is our turn now.

It is our turn now because the misery caused by the Left and Wokeness will ignite the largest influx of conversions to Christ we have seen in our lifetime. The billions of dollars spent to erase the Christian faith will prove to be an utter waste. We are entering a season where Christian influence in America will greatly increase.

He who holds power to reverse plots, make plans backfire, and cause the wrath of man to boomerang has been quietly working. Soon His handiwork will be revealed. It is a massive harvest of souls that are being ripened by misery, corruption, and tyranny. How do I know this is true? Because I have already seen it.

I wrote this book because something shocking and unexplainable started happening in our tent crusades. At the height of a pandemic lockdown—in California, the bluest state in America—thousands were being converted to Christ.

You can barely get Californians to a Christian meeting when it is *convenient*. But then they started coming during a lockdown. It filled me with questions: Why were they overflowing the tent now that leaving their house was almost impossible? What was happening? Why was it happening?

It's our turn now. That phrase kept repeating in my heart. It was a clue of some kind. The feeling kept growing within that I would witness some great event. Then the scales fell off my eyes.

I realized that as glorious as our tent crusades are, they are only a small part of a great and widespread phenomenon brewing nationwide. That is why I believe there is an urgent warning from the throne of God to get ready for harvest.[20]

THE LAST-DAYS MESSAGE OF BILLY GRAHAM

The world-renowned evangelist Billy Graham, the preacher who delivered the gospel message to millions of people around the world, gave sound wisdom on what was to come in the future—for the world and for America.

When people asked him if we are living in the end times the Bible describes so vividly, he pointed to the fact that the end the Bible talks about is the present world we live in, a system dominated by evil.

We have to ask ourselves: Is this the end times that the Bible describes so graphically? Is this the final storm that will sweep away everything in its path? The Scriptures definitely teach that there will be an end to human history as we know it, and most biblical scholars believe that it is coming soon. It will not be the end of the world, but it will be the end of the present world system that has been dominated by evil.

The Bible teaches that Satan is actually "the prince of this world" (John 12:31) and "the ruler of the kingdom of the air, the spirit who is now at work in those who are disobedient" (Ephesians 2:2). As long as he is still at large, in constant conflict with God and pursuing his deadly plan, be assured that wars will continue and death and disaster will multiply. Without God there will be no hope for humanity.[21]

He then pointed out easily discernable signs that will occur as we near the end of the age, drawn from Jesus' teaching in Matthew 24:

- Famines
- Pestilences
- Earthquakes
- Betrayal
- Hate
- False prophets
- Increased wickedness
- Love of man growing cold
- The gospel reaching the ends of the earth[22]

While history has been full of a lot of the signs Jesus pointed out, they all seem to be growing and compounding in our day and age—especially the rise of false prophets.

FALSE PROPHETS: THEN AND NOW

What did Jesus say about false prophets?

> Watch out for false prophets. They come to you in sheep's clothing, but inwardly they are ferocious wolves. By their fruit you will recognize them. Do people pick grapes from thornbushes, or figs from thistles? Likewise, every good tree bears good fruit, but a bad tree bears bad fruit. A good tree cannot bear bad fruit, and a bad tree cannot bear good fruit. Every tree that does not bear good fruit is cut down and thrown into the fire. Thus, by their fruit you will recognize them.
>
> —MATTHEW 7:15–20

Jesus' words are to the point. Why? Because the deception of the enemy is very subtle and deceptive, as John Bevere wrote in his book *Thus Saith the Lord*. The false prophets "come dressed as sheep, not wolves. With appearances so similar it is hard to distinguish the true from false. Jesus said there would be many, not a few (Matt. 24:11), and that, if possible, even the elect would be deceived by them because of their supernatural gifts. How do we rightly divide between the true and the false? Jesus said their fruit would tell the story."[23]

But what does that fruit look like? Is it more than accuracy of prophetic words? "The Lord explained that a prophet could speak a word, and it could come to pass, but he is to be rejected if he leads you into idolatry, covetousness, or rebellion (Deut. 13:1–5; Col. 3:5)."[24]

So what is the fruit we are to look out for? James 3:14–16 lays out two fruits we can spot easily if we look close enough: jealousy and selfish ambition. Or, as Bevere said, "Both are summed up in the term self-seeking."[25]

This typically comes to the surface when prophets are challenged on a word they have spoken. In an interview, Murillo spoke out against the rise of false prophets in the last days.

Driven to speak out against those the Holy Spirit had highlighted to him as giving inauthentic prophetic words, Murillo, in speaking with Strang, said, "I share this with a broken heart. I believe that people are being destroyed by false prophets, and I believe that the wave of this that we're seeing right now deserves our undivided attention."[26]

Murillo stated that it is the Bible judging these wolves in sheep's clothing, not him—or anyone else. "We're doing what the Bible says, what Jesus said, and what Paul said: 'Beware of false prophets.'"[27] He went on to address those who aren't comfortable confronting false prophets.

When asked by Strang how to judge false versus true prophets, Murillo stated that we:

- Use the Word of God as the basis of all "truth" being spoken. "We're in a time of biblical illiteracy," he pointed out. We can "simply read the Bible and see how off this person or that person is."

- Watch for threats against people who disagree with the "prophet."[28]

Murillo then tied the false prophets back to Trump, saying he believes that Satan is using the false declarations as weapons against the president, leading to his indictments—four major ones as of this writing, and one having declared him guilty. By declaring that "God's got it in the bank, the election is won, don't worry about it, God's got this," these prophets have sown apathy into the hearts of millions. Murillo said:

> God doesn't have this: the church has to repent. We have to get to work. We have to realize that Donald Trump needs our prayers and fasting because we are locked in a spiritual war, and we don't need these false prophets putting apathy in us. That's dangerous and ungodly.[29]

Strang added that Satan will try to persuade people to stop going to church, stop reading their Bibles, and stop being interested in the things of the Lord. "He'll get you to go off the cliff with some of these leaders with all this nonsense, and part of it is that, after a while…people do wake up, and their eyes are open, and they're disillusioned, and then they don't want anything to do with God."[30]

That is the biggest danger of false prophets: giving undue hope, creating apathy in the lives of God's people, allowing Satan to sneak in and destroy a culture, and then before people realize what has happened, they fall further away from Christ.

CREATING THE FUTURE

While there are true and false prophets, there is also a group of people that fall into neither category. They need to be addressed by the praying and fasting church as well. These are people who want to create a future of their own making. They have a theory of change that revolves around a dialectic, a "dialogue between people holding different points of view about a subject but wishing to arrive at the truth through reasoned argumentation,"[31] and alchemical methods, or changing something from one substance to another through words.[32]

According to James Lindsay, founder of New Discourses, people in great power aren't interested in prophecies about what might be happening in the near or distant future, and they don't care about deceiving people for money or profit (although they gain both), but instead they want to create the future, shaping and forming it as they see fit to do so.

The elite understand that nations like the United States will only undergo transformative change, historically, during times of chaos when people are searching for "guideposts for what the future will bring." These behind-the-scenes puppet masters use lies as seeds, sown over and over again through media, art, and other parts of culture, to create thought patterns people will agree with and follow without question.[33]

These lies, stated over and over again, force people—even though most are unaware of what's happening—to make decisions that eventually change the course of the nation and its history.

Lindsay says that changing history is simple. It only takes three steps:

> Step 1: "Plunge society into chaos (say, by funding lots of things that destabilize communities)."
>
> Step 2: "Build 'reflexive' potential so that the people driven into chaos work in ways favorable to your agendas."
>
> Step 3: "When chaos ignites, place strategic 'guideposts' that lead desperate people to make exactly the kinds of mistakes that take them where you want them to go."[34]

Examples of this practice can be seen in the communist takeover of Russia in 1917 under charismatic lawyer Vladimir Lenin, the communist takeover of China in 1949 under Mao Tse-tung, and the global financial takeover occurring today under the World Economic Forum's Great Reset plan by financial movers and shakers.[35]

People working to reshape the world in their image was predicted in the Bible. The most important and first time we see it was in the beginning, in the Garden of Eden.

Satan initiated his plan with the first step—create chaos—as he asked Eve, "Did God really say, 'You must not eat from any tree in the garden'?" (Gen. 3:1).

Immediately, he was flipping over Eve's (and Adam's) world. He wanted them to question reality—God's Word—and throw their lives into a tailspin. And it worked. Eve responded with an altered version of God's words to them:

> We may eat fruit from the trees in the garden, but God did say, "You must not eat fruit from the tree that is in the middle of the garden, and you must not touch it, or you will die."
>
> —GENESIS 3:2–3

Eve added the part about not touching it. God only said don't eat it. Chaos had arrived; truth had been altered. So Satan pushed it further:

> "You will not certainly die," the serpent said to the woman. "For God knows that when you eat from it your eyes will be opened, and you will be like God, knowing good and evil."
>
> —GENESIS 3:4–5

PART TWO

THE LAST PRESIDENT
AND AMERICA'S FUTURE

CHAPTER SEVEN

THE BIBLICAL STANDARD OF TRUTH

Preach the word; be prepared in season and out of season; correct, rebuke and encourage—with great patience and careful instruction. For the time will come when people will not put up with sound doctrine. Instead, to suit their own desires, they will gather around them a great number of teachers to say what their itching ears want to hear. They will turn their ears away from the truth and turn aside to myths.

—2 TIMOTHY 4:2–4

When we accept a lie, no matter how Satan got us to believe it, we transfer our belief from one Father (God) to believing another father (the enemy of our souls).

—CHUCK D. PIERCE AND REBECCA WAGNER SYTSEMA, *POSSESSING YOUR INHERITANCE: TAKE HOLD OF GOD'S DESTINY FOR YOUR LIFE*

CONSIDERING THE AMOUNT of deception that we see unfolding second by second in our time, we need to know how to navigate the stormy seas we find ourselves in. We need to know what the biblical standard of truth is, how we hold on to it, and how we avoid deception.

In the book *Possessing Your Inheritance: Take Hold of God's Destiny for Your Life*, Chuck D. Pierce and Rebecca Wagner Sytsema point out how we fall into deception and how we stay anchored in the truth:

The two things that will hold us in deception are ignorance and pride. First, we must realize that God does not desire that we be ignorant. Our primary source of truth is the Word of God. You may be believing something abou God, yourself or others that is contrary to the Bible. That is one reason we as Christians must know the Bible. The more we know what it really says, the less of an opening Satan has to lie to us. The belt of truth and the sword of the Spirit, which is the Word of God (see Eph. 6:14, 17) are, therefore, two very important elements of our spiritual armor as Christians.

Pride also works to hold us in deception. This happens when we refuse to acknowledge that we have been deceived because, after all, we know better. Pride is an especially vulnerable area for those who may have grown up in church or have pursued higher Christian education. Satan can be holding us in bondage to sin that we refuse to see.[1]

In Christ's Image Training (ICIT) leader Francis Frangipane wrote that God has called us to be "dedicated to the way of truth. Indeed, each of us has been conditioned by decades of unbelief, fear, and an unbridled thought life, which has reinforced deception."[2]

Too many Christians tend to think or assume that they are unable to be deceived because they have come to Christ. But this itself is a deception. Frangipane continued:

> Let us stay humble and not presume that the *calling* of God and the *choosing* of God are alike. "Many are called," Jesus taught, "but few are chosen" (Matt. 22:14). Many tests await the called before they are equipped by God and become His chosen; not the least of these tests is becoming free from deception.[3]

Because we live in a natural world where honesty and truth must be enforced by laws, where media companies continually distort the facts, advertising agencies promise the impossible, and people are wrapped up in fantasy worlds of books, video games, television shows, movies, and more, everywhere we look we face lies, deception, and distortions of the truth.

Thankfully there are ways to rise above the cascading tide of deception: a revelation to know the truth of God's Word. Frangipane wrote, "Deception and confusion so fill this world that in order for us to discern what is right, Scriptures command us to 'seek' for, 'love,' and 'buy truth' (Prov. 2:1–5; 2 Thess. 2:10; Prov. 23:23)."[4]

Frangipane gave us the remedy to deception when he wrote,

> Jesus prayed, "[Father,] sanctify them in the truth; Your word is truth" (John 17:17). He was saying, "Father, purify them of the lies and illusions of this age through Your penetrating Word." In Ephesians, Paul tells us that Christ sanctifies the church by cleansing her "by

the washing of water with the word…that she would be holy and blameless" (Eph. 5:26–27).

This then, embracing the truth and allowing the Word of Truth to do its work of sanctification, cleansing and purification in our lives is the process through which we become holy. Loving the truth is the beginning of our freedom.[5]

So what is truth?

WHAT IS THE TRUTH OF GOD'S WORD?

Truth can be defined as "that which conforms with fact or reality." Truth can also be seen as "genuineness, veracity, or actuality. In a word, truth is reality. It is how things actually are. Theologically, truth is that which is consistent with the mind, will, character, glory, and being of God. Truth is the self-disclosure of God Himself. It is what it is because God declares it so and made it so. All truth must be defined in terms of God, whose very nature is truth," wrote Dr. Steven J. Lawson, professor of preaching at the Master's Seminary.[6]

In Scripture, we see:

- God is the God of truth (Ps. 31:5; Isa. 65:16).

- Grace and truth filled Jesus (John 1:14).

- Jesus is the truth (John 14:6).

- The Spirit of truth is the Holy Spirit (John 14:17; 15:26; 16:13).[7]

A further look shows us that:

- "Truth is divine." Since God is the God of truth, Jesus is the truth, and the Holy Spirit is the Spirit of truth, truth comes from the divine source of all life: God.

- "Truth is absolute." Despite the movement of the last two hundred years to declare that truth does not exist, it will never go away. Truth is final and absolute because the Creator of all things declared it to be so.

- "Truth is singular." Jesus declared He is the truth. Therefore, anything that appears outside of Him and His known character is not the truth.

- "Truth is objective." Truth can't be found by feelings, by emotions, or in the sayings of others who are not grounded in the truth—Jesus Christ. Truth isn't malleable; it is not dependent on us. It flows from the heart of Father God and is real, tangible, and alive in the living presence of Jesus Christ.

- "Truth is immutable." Truth can't change. God doesn't lie, and He doesn't change. Since truth comes from Him and is embodied in Christ, it will never change.

- "Truth is authoritative." Jesus said that the truth will make us free as we come to know Him—the truth (John 8:32). He is the source of the authority that truth carries. And because He is the Word of God (John 1:1–2), it is His life as the Word of God that will cleanse us from deception and sin (John 17:17). Nothing can ultimately stand in the light of His truth.[8]

As we pray and ponder the prophetic words, stories, ideas, dreams, and visions being promoted in Christendom regarding the future of President Donald Trump, America, and the world, we must remember these things above. We also need to lean into the Holy Spirit, the Spirit of truth, who enters our lives and guides us into all truth. John 16:13 (NKJV) says, "However, when He, the Spirit of truth, has come, He will guide you into all truth; for He will not speak on His own authority, but whatever He hears He will speak; and He will tell you things to come."

The Holy Spirit wants to tell us what will happen, but it will always be according to the truth, for that is the only reality there is in this life. He helps us discover the truth—or reality—by leading us to Jesus (John 16:13), by initiating direct, divine encounters that alter how we see the Word and God (Acts 9), by calling us to walk with Him each day (Gal. 5), and by helping us see all the connections in Scripture, as Jesus did with the disciples on the road to Emmaus and Philip did with the eunuch (Luke 24:13–35; Acts 8:26–40).

Additionally, we can pray the apostle Paul's prayer over our lives each day, trusting the Holy Spirit will enlighten us with His knowledge:

> I keep asking that the God of our Lord Jesus Christ, the glorious Father, may give you the Spirit of wisdom and revelation, so that you may know him better. I pray that the eyes of your heart may be enlightened in order that you may know the hope to which he has called you, the riches of his glorious inheritance in his holy people.
> —Ephesians 1:17–18

What Is Deception?

Yet we can't be ignorant of the devil's schemes. He uses a multitude of things to keep us from knowing the truth. As noted by Mark Virkler, founder of Communion With God Ministries, the devil wants you to believe:

- We don't need to hear from God. The devil lies and tells us we don't need to hear God's voice; you can know things on your own, making you a god through your own efforts.

- Things in the Bible are not for today. The devil tries to convince us that much of Scripture is for another time, and "you can't apply or live it in this age" (dispensationalism).

- Events in the Bible aren't real. The devil wants us to believe that the supernatural stories in the Bible are myths created by men, and not reality.

- We will be rejected. If you embrace the truth of the Bible, the devil asserts, you will lose your job and your social position (think of Nicodemus, for example).

- We don't have a high enough intelligence level to understand the Bible.

- Or, we understand all the Bible. The devil wants us to think we know more than anyone else.

- Whatever our faith leader says, goes: "I must submit to what my leader tells me to believe."[9]

These lies work in us because from the moment we humans can speak, we can lie. Mark Twain once joked that "a man is never more truthful than when he acknowledges himself a liar."[10]

All of us have embellished stories or told white lies. In a time when up is down, left is right, good is bad, and bad is good, it can be easy to overlook lying in our lives. But we know that God hates lying (Prov. 12:22). He loves the truth, and He is so committed to overcoming the lies of the enemy that He sent His Son, truth incarnate, the Word of God in the flesh, to "destroy the devil's work" (1 John 3:8), which is predominantly done through lies (John 8:44).

But lying, the deliberate act of deceiving someone through untruths, using words, gestures, events, or even silence, is a tool of the devil in every possible manner of speaking. Yet we are too scared to call lying, lying. We say things like, "Oh, they just misrepresented the truth," "They fabricated the evidence," or, "They told a white lie."

Lying is lying. Period. And the church's inability to call it as such has led the world away from the truth and toward one of the things God hates the most and into an era of extreme deception.

"A woman came to evangelist Billy Sunday on one occasion and asked, 'Reverend Sunday, how can I stop exaggerating?' He looked at her and said, 'Call it lying.' It is the same way with the 'little white lies.' There is no such thing as 'a little white lie.' Lies are lies," Christian Broadcasting Network founder Pat Robertson wrote in *Answers to 200 of Life's Most Probing Questions*.

> Yet lying is a part of society. We train our children to lie. For example, suppose you go to someone's house for dinner, and they give you a delicious meal. If you say, "That was delicious," you have told the truth and everything is fine. But what if you go to someone's house and they serve you something that is absolutely terrible, and you say, "That was the most delicious meal I have ever had"? You are lying.

You may have done it for a good reason—a white lie—but you still lied. Honestly praise something, or be silent; but do not lie!

...We must begin to be truthful to God and to one another. There is no way that the Holy Spirit can operate in someone's life if there is a lack of truth. The Spirit of God is the spirit of truth. Jesus Christ is "the way, *the truth*, and the life" (John 14:6)....We only honor God when we exhibit truth and integrity in everything we do.[11]

God established a law that would govern lying in communities. Deuteronomy 19:16–21 (ESV) says:

If a malicious witness arises to accuse a person of wrongdoing, then both parties to the dispute shall appear before the LORD, before the priests and the judges who are in office in those days. The judges shall inquire diligently, and if the witness is a false witness and has accused his brother falsely, then you shall do to him as he had meant to do to his brother. So you shall purge the evil from your midst. And the rest shall hear and fear, and shall never again commit any such evil among you. Your eye shall not pity. It shall be life for life, eye for eye, tooth for tooth, hand for hand, foot for foot.

This would be unthinkable in today's church. The American church is very forgiving of those who have declared false things against other believers, against the government, against the culture, and so on.

NAVIGATING PROPHECY AND DECEPTION

Bringing this back to how we navigate the world of prophecies and deception, we need to turn to the Bible and the apostle Paul. In his first letter to the church in Thessalonica, Paul warned them to "not quench the Spirit. Do not treat prophecies with contempt but test them all; hold on to what is good, reject every kind of evil" (1 Thess. 5:19–22).

When Paul says to "not quench the Spirit" (v. 19), he is likely warning about disobeying the Holy Spirit by immoral behavior. We resist the Spirit's work in our sanctification when we sin. The quenching of the Spirit likely also involved the despising of prophecies (v. 20). "Paul's answer was that they should not neglect the prophets but rather test every supposed prophetic utterance to see if the one delivering it was a true prophet" (v. 21). Paul also said to reject even the appearance of evil (v. 22), "most likely a warning not to entertain those who were false prophets, though Christians have the general duty not to engage in moral evil."[12]

What are some practical ways to discern what God is saying through all the prophets out there—some proven and some not? This is especially key when their messages contradict each other. R. Loren Sandford, author, pastor, and prophetic leader, stated:

> Lately, prominent voices have prophesied words concerning national and world events that would seem to be at odds with one another. For instance, some prophesy an imminent and catastrophic economic crash, while others have prophesied a season of economic prosperity, especially for Christians.
>
> What is a believer to do when well-known prophetic people speak conflicting words? How can we sort the true word from the spirit of error?...
>
> The apostle Paul instituted a structure for testing prophetic words spoken in the public assembly. First Corinthians 14:29 says, "Let two or three prophets speak, and let the others pass judgment" (NASB).... New Testament prophetic people didn't always deliver 100 percent accurate words [so] their words therefore needed evaluation to separate the good from the bad....
>
> It follows that prophetic words, whether spoken in the public assembly, promoted through electronic media or published in print, must be tested and that we believers therefore carry a responsibility to sort out what we hear.[13]

SIX WORD TESTS TO DISCERN PROPHETIC WORDS

Sandford then presented us with six "word tests" we can use to know if the prophetic message is from God.

Test 1: Scripture

True prophetic words never contradict any portion of Scripture, meaning we need to be "biblically literate as believers lest we render ourselves vulnerable to deception packaged and presented as anointed revelation."[14]

Test 2: The Revealed Nature and Character of God

When looking at prophetic words about "God's wrathful judgment in catastrophic economic or natural disasters, we must begin with God's essential nature." Who is God as He revealed Himself in Scripture? Predominantly, He shows Himself to be "a loving Father who sends ample warnings over extended periods of time, again and again calling His children to turn from destructive ways."[15]

Test 3: Reality Check

We need to think rationally rather than be carried along with our emotions. God is all-knowing, and all intelligence comes from Him. He wants us to use our brains. As the apostle Paul wrote in Romans 12:3 (NASB):

> For through the grace given to me I say to everyone among you not to think more highly of himself than he ought to think; but to think so as to have sound judgment, as God has allotted to each a measure of faith.

Sandford said to look at prophetic words about the coming revival that will "sweep America and restore the nation to its Christian foundations."

> Forget for a moment who is prophesying such a revival and do the reality check. Where is the surrounding culture headed? What elements need to be present in the culture for there to be that kind of revival, and are those elements present? Are those conditions in place today? Would it therefore be a culture-sweeping revival or something that would manifest in certain islands of glory amid a continuing sea of darkness?
>
> At this point I'm not judging the accuracy of these prophecies of culture-changing revival. I'm saying that as we evaluate the accuracy of any prophetic word, we need to realistically assess the culture in which we live in order to wisely adjust our focus and strategy.[16]

Test 4: Concrete Realities

Flowing from test 3, there will often be tangible signs "confirming reality embedded in or accompanying the prophecy itself." Think of Moses at the burning bush accompanying God's call on his life, or Paul's blindness when Jesus redirected his life.[17]

Test 5: Filter Out Emotions

Whether a word is positive or negative, true or false, it will pass through our emotions and magnify and distort them. It is vital that we "seek and live in intimacy with the Lord, not the excitement generated by any positive or negative prophetic pronouncement."[18]

Test 6: The Speaker's Fulfillment Track Record

Before you receive any prophetic word as truth, evaluate the track record and character of the speaker.

> In Acts 11:28, Agabus accurately prophesied a famine so that the body of Christ could prepare in advance. Later, in Acts 21:11, he told Paul that the Jews would arrest him if he went to Jerusalem.
>
> One hundred percent accurate? Not quite. The Romans, not the Jews, arrested him, although they did it in response to Jewish pressure. Agabus' track record for accuracy fell just short of 100 percent, but he was certainly accurate in substance.
>
> Deuteronomy 18:21–22 addresses this kind of scenario: "You may say in your heart, 'How will we know the word which the Lord has not spoken?' When a prophet speaks in the name of the Lord, if the thing does not come about or come true, that is the thing which the Lord has not spoken. The prophet has spoken it presumptuously; you shall not be afraid of him."[19]

UPGRADING PROPHETIC WORDS

In 2011, Francis Frangipane issued a call for Christians to upgrade the prophetic in the body of Christ.

> To me there is a difference between a false prophet and a wrong prophet. Yet when will we honestly look at this issue? False alarms have repeatedly misrepresented the Lord's coming over the last 40 years.
>
> On the front end of these apocalyptic warnings, evangelists report significant benefits: increased participation in altar calls and certainly more prayer and repentance among Christians who respond. Yet when the preannounced date passes uneventfully, the effect of being wrongly warned leaves many hearts hardened.

Meanwhile, the nonbelieving world observes the self-induced anxieties spilling from the evangelical world. In response, they fortify themselves against a religion that, to them, has symptoms of mental illness.[20]

Frangipane then laid out biblical principles that need to be followed that will increase the accuracy of prophetic words and bring God the proper glory.

1. Prophecy comes from God and flows through humble people.

First, let's remember that it was God who placed prophets in the church (see 1 Cor. 14). The power released by a humble, accurate prophet can be a revelation of the Lord Himself, one that causes people to fall on their faces in worship (see v. 25).[21]

2. True prophetic words are confirmed by two or more people.

Jesus sent His disciples out in twos. He also spoke of the power that is released when two or three disciples gathered in His name. Revelation also tells us that the last great prophetic move will be heralded by two prophets (not one) speaking and ministering together (Rev. 11).

Paul again repeats the principle of two or three in his second letter to the Corinthians: "By the mouth of two or three witnesses every word [*rhema*] shall be established" (2 Cor. 13:1). It is important to note that when it comes to discerning an actual word from the Lord the best indicator a prophet has, typically, is a witness of an unseen reality; he does not have a completed "word from the Lord."...

If you are being ministered to by a prophet and have any question about what is being said, give the Holy Spirit time to confirm His word through one or two more people (unless you have an immediate confirmation in your spirit that the word is God's).[22]

3. Check with other, mature believers before issuing warnings to large groups of people.

What if you have a national ministry and believe you have a warning to issue? There may be exceptions to this, but I'd suggest you speak it first privately to your peers, as well as to the church leaders in the region where the warning applies. Let someone outside your local ministry team confirm it independently. Give God time to arrange a supernatural presentation of His will. The witness of two or three different national ministries, spoken independently yet confirmed supernaturally, is a powerful catalyst for faith.

The restraints I suggest are not to hamper the prophetic but to place prophets as background players on a stage where the Word of God is the featured star.[23]

CHAPTER EIGHT

WHAT LOCKWOOD SAW CONCERNING 2024

And yet, at this moment when the night air quivered with the mad vocifera-
tions of the "common people," that the Lord had been good to them; that the
wicked money-changers had been driven from the temple, that the stony-hearted
usurers were beaten at last, that the "People's William" was at the helm now...

—INGERSOLL LOCKWOOD, *1900: OR, THE LAST PRESIDENT*

INGERSOLL LOCKWOOD'S NOVEL *1900: or, The Last President* tells the story of a time when chaos engulfs America following the election of an outsider candidate. As the story unfolds, it becomes clear that the candidate is immensely popular with the common people.

In a Charisma News article, Jessilyn Lancaster highlighted that some internet sleuths and dedicated Trump followers believe Lockwood was forewarning of future events.[1]

Pastor Paul Begley pondered this possibility:

> Could God be saying that this will be the last duly-elected-by-the-people president of the United States, the greatest empire that's ever been on the planet because it's the only nation that founded their nation's culture on the Word of God? Israel [is] the only nation created by God. Every empire, Babylonian, the Egyptians, the Persians, the Romans, the British Empire…eventually failed because they weren't founded on the Word of God. Could this be the last president? Could God have been speaking through [Lockwood]?[2]

Begley questioned if Lockwood's novels were prophetic, suggesting that Trump's 2016 victory might represent the last legitimate election, even if he does not return to office.

I think that's very possible, and it's a sad thought, but the beast kingdom is coming, this new world order. This could be the last time, or we might have already, and...the world is racing toward a one-world government and World War III, which could create this one world government.[3]

Lockwood's novel contains hauntingly prescient passages about a tumultuous night in New York City on November 3, 1896. As the news of the president's election spreads, the city is thrown into chaos, led by anarchists and socialists. The police struggle to contain the rioters, and a sense of dread and upheaval grips the city. Lockwood describes the scene:

That was a terrible night for the great City of New York—the night of Tuesday, November 3rd, 1896. The city staggered under the blow like a huge ocean liner which plunges, full speed, with terrific crash into a mighty iceberg, and recoils shattered and trembling like an aspen.

The people were gathered, light-hearted and confident, at the evening meal, when the news burst upon them. It was like a thunder bolt out of an azure sky: "Altgeld holds Illinois hard and fast in the Democratic line. This elects Bryan President of the United States!"

Strange to say, the people in the upper portion of the city made no movement to rush out of their houses and collect in the public squares, although the night was clear and beautiful. They sat as if paralyzed with a nameless dread, and when they conversed it was with bated breath and throbbing hearts.

In less than half an hour, mounted policemen dashed through the streets calling out: "Keep within your houses; close your doors and barricade them. The entire East side is in a state of uproar. Mobs of vast size are organizing under the lead of Anarchists and Socialists, and threaten to plunder and despoil the houses of the rich who have wronged and oppressed them for so many years. Keep within doors. Extinguish all lights."

...About nine o'clock, with deafening outcries, the mob, like a four-headed monster breathing fire and flame, raced, tore, burst, raged into Union Square.

The police force was exhausted, but their front was still like a wall of stone, save that it was movable. The mob crowded it steadily to the north, while the air quivered and was rent with mad vociferations of the victors: "Bryan is elected! Bryan is elected! Our day has come at last. Down with our oppressors! Death to the rich man! Death to the gold bugs! Death to the capitalists! Give us back the money you have ground out of us. Give us back the marrow of our bones which you have used to grease the wheels of your chariots."[4]

Reflecting on Trump's initial election victory, we see that while it did not incite riots, it sparked significant protests, such as the Women's March, in major cities. Despite fierce opposition from elites, Trump's popularity among the general public soared, with his rallies drawing unprecedented crowds.

His support was even evidenced by large rallies in traditionally Democratic strongholds. In his run in 2020 for reelection, Trump was drawing crowds upwards of twenty thousand people.

His popularity has continued since then. The *Epoch Times* reported, "Despite being held in a state that has been reliably Democrat, a rally for the Republican former president set a record for New Jersey, a congressman said....Overhead photographs showed that the May 11 [2024] crowd filled much of a quarter-mile span between Mariner's Pier and the Adventure Pier; attendance estimates varied widely, from 40,000 to 100,000."[5]

In 2020, riots erupted in major cities following George Floyd's death, mirroring the chaos described in Lockwood's narrative. This raises the question: Could Lockwood's fiction also foreshadow the 2024 election?

Does God communicate through fiction? This compelling possibility urges us to consider the intersection of prophetic fiction and reality in today's world, challenging us to remain vigilant and discerning in these uncertain times.

USING FICTION AS A MESSENGER

During the last 120 years, numerous novels have eerily foreshadowed future events. Aldous Huxley's 1932 novel, *Brave New World*, is one such example, with its visions increasingly mirrored in our reality.

Huxley's work, described by the *Wall Street Journal* as "one of the most prophetic dystopian works," depicts a future society known as the World State.[6] This society is governed by science and efficiency, with emotions and individual desires bred out of children from a young age. Relationships are shallow, as "every one belongs to every one else."[7]

The novel opens at the Central London Hatchery and Conditioning

Centre, where children are created outside the human womb and cloned to expedite population growth. Huxley introduces concepts such as:

- The sorting of embryos into classes and subjecting them to specific chemicals and hormones to condition them for their designated roles

- The existence of five human classes, including Alpha (bred and conditioned to be leaders), Beta, Gamma, Delta, and Epsilon (bred and conditioned for menial jobs)[8]

Huxley's dystopian vision, devoid of hope, mirrors current advancements. We now have:

- Synthetic wombs with technology enabling the growth of embryos outside the human body

- Children conceived through in vitro fertilization

- Genetic engineering, or the manipulation of an organism's genes using biotechnology

George Orwell's famous and prophetic novel *Nineteen Eighty-Four*, published in 1949, also foreshadows our current trajectory. Set in Oceania, a totalitarian state perpetually at war with Eurasia and Eastasia, the novel introduces the concept of the Party, a tyrannical group led by Big Brother that brainwashes its population through mass media and the restrictive language of Newspeak. Orwell's concept of doublethink and slogans such as "War is peace," "Freedom is slavery," and "Ignorance is strength" resonate today.[9] The Thought Police and constant surveillance maintain the regime's control, suppressing free thought and ideas.[10] Orwell's protagonist, who rewrites history, offers a chilling glimpse into a future where AI could dictate interpretations of the Bible, history, and foundational societal pillars.

Fast-forward to the 1980s and 1990s, when Tom Clancy emerged as a prescient author with his techno-thrillers about geopolitics, espionage, and terrorism. *Foreign Policy* magazine hailed Clancy for his "incredible predictive power." Clancy's military and intelligence community connections lent his works an eerie authenticity. The article noted Clancy's "enthusiasm for the endless advance of technology in warfare" and his "outrageous plots" that often seemed to predict real-world events.[11]

Here are some prophetic events from Clancy's novels:

The 9/11 Attacks

Clancy's 1994 novel, *Debt of Honor*, eerily prefigured the 9/11 attacks. In the book, a Japan Air Lines pilot crashes a 747 into the Capitol, killing almost the entire American government. National security officials were aware of Clancy's predictions but "never took them particularly seriously."[12]

The Middle East–Latin America Connection

Iran's plot in 2011 to assassinate the Saudi ambassador to the United States using a Mexican drug cartel mirrored Clancy's 2003 novel, *The Teeth of the Tiger*. In the novel, Islamic terrorists team up with a Mexican cartel to launch attacks in the US.[13]

The Osama bin Laden Raid

Clancy's 2010 novel, *Dead or Alive*, paralleled the hunt for Osama bin Laden, depicting US forces tracking a bin Laden–like terrorist hiding in a city.[14]

THE 2024 PRESIDENTIAL ELECTION

Headlines suggest major news outlets anticipate significant chaos during the 2024 presidential election. There is heightened focus on the election certification process, with expectations of numerous issues.

In response to concerns about the 2020 presidential election, the Trump campaign and Republican National Committee (RNC) plan to deploy one hundred thousand attorneys and volunteers to "protect the vote and ensure a big win" in November. Republican poll watchers will monitor ballot casting and counting, ready to report irregularities. RNC Chief Counsel Charlie Spies stated, "The Democrat tricks from 2020 won't work this time....We will aggressively take them to court if they don't follow rules or try to change them at the last minute. President Trump has said that the Republican victory in November needs to be too big to rig. The political team will be working to ensure a huge victory for Republicans at all levels, and RNC legal is committed to making sure that victory can't be rigged."[15]

RNC Co-Chair Lara Trump added, "Every ballot. Every precinct. Every processing center. Every county. Every battleground state. We will be there.

The RNC is hiring hundreds of election integrity staff across the map...recruiting thousands of more observers to protect the vote in 2024."[16]

Jason Yates of My Faith Votes expressed confidence in the election's integrity, predicting an enormous conservative win in 2024.

"I don't think we're going to have any shenanigans," Yates said. "There may be attempts, but there's a lot of people paying attention....I really think at the end of the day, Christians will look around and say, 'There's just too much nonsense happening in this nation. There's too much at risk today. I'm going to show up regardless of whether it's Donald Trump or not. I'm going to vote for those biblical values, and I'm going to vote, even though I'm concerned about election integrity, because I know that the only thing that's really going to stop those concerns is if I show up and vote.'"[17]

The Associated Press reported on election-related lawsuits in states like Michigan and Nevada, highlighting a "shadow war for the 2024 election."[18] According to another Associated Press story, election officials foresee a wide range of threats, from cyberattacks to international interference.[19]

Outside of voter issues in the 2024 election cycle, the media have been predicting other kinds of chaos. *The Economist* magazine declared in November 2023 that "Donald Trump poses the biggest danger to the world in 2024." The world-renowned international magazine said in its thirty-eighth annual predictive guide "The World Ahead 2024":

> A shadow looms over the world....That a Trump victory next November is a coin-toss probability is beginning to sink in. Mr Trump dominates the Republican primary....In the primaries, at least, civil lawsuits and criminal prosecutions have only strengthened Mr Trump. For decades Democrats have relied on support among black and Hispanic voters, but a meaningful number are abandoning the party. In the next 12 months a stumble by either candidate could determine the race—and thus upend the world. This is a perilous moment for a man like Mr Trump to be back knocking on the door of the Oval Office.[20]

Bloomberg advised preparing for a second Trump term, stressing the importance of teaching the military to obey the Constitution rather than the president. The opinion piece declared, "Prospect of a Second Trump Term Demands Preparation, Not Panic." They went as far as saying that the key to stopping

Trump from overtaking American life is "to teach and re-teach the military at all levels that principle of civilian control is about obeying the Constitution, not the president."[21]

Given that we saw Trump—an unpopular candidate with the elites—elected, we witnessed riots during his run in 2020, and major media and news outlets are preparing for unrest in the days ahead, it doesn't appear a stretch to say that Lockwood's novels were prophetic, especially when they seem to line up with words from modern-day prophets.

TRUMPOCALYPSE AND THE ATTEMPTED ASSASSINATION OF PRESIDENT TRUMP

In my second book, *Trumpocalypse: The End-Times President, a Battle Against the Globalist Elite, and the Countdown to Armageddon*, Paul McGuire and I wrote about how a high-ranking Republican leader told Rodney Howard-Browne, pastor at The River Church in Tampa Bay, Florida, during Trump's first term in office that there was a "plot on Capitol Hill to remove Trump suddenly from office" and that this leader specifically meant via assassination.[22]

The book set out to expose "the chilling truth about the fierce opposition to the Trump presidency, and why the globalist elite and Deep State will stop at nothing—assassination, military coup, staged economic collapse, or worse—to overthrow him."[23]

While most of the news coverage and statements from federal officials seemed to suggest, as of late July 2024, that twenty-year-old Thomas Matthew Crooks acted alone in the July 13 attempted assassination of Trump, given all the deep-state attacks on Trump over the last eight years, it's logical to ask whether this assertion is true.

The news reports seemed to place the blame on security failures and the incompetence of the US Secret Service and local law enforcement officials for missing opportunities to stop Crooks before he was able to fire several rounds at Trump, grazing the former president's ear, killing volunteer firefighter Corey Comperatore, and wounding two other rallygoers.[24]

Did Crooks act alone, or was this a coordinated assassination attempt involving the deep state? In an article, "The Plot to Kill Trump Goes to the Top," Cliff Kincaid, a journalist and media critic, raised this question, noting it was the primary job of the Secret Service to prevent someone like Crooks from climbing up a ladder and getting on top of a building where he was able to shoot at the former president from only one hundred thirty yards away. The head of "the Secret Service also says they didn't have an agent on the roof of the building because the roof wasn't flat and was 'sloped.' This is absurd," Kincaid wrote. "The excuses demonstrate that something more sinister occurred here. Firing the DEI hire in charge of the Secret Service doesn't get rid of the root of the problem—a Deep State that has an enforcement arm which carries out what the Russians call 'wet work.' Let's face facts. Our federal government is a tyranny with corrupt agencies, some of them supposedly 'protecting' Trump and now investigating themselves....Trump's life is still in mortal danger. Prior to the murder attempt, we had urged the Trump campaign to hire a private security firm because we didn't trust Biden's Secret Service to protect our former president. Sadly, we were proven to be correct....The current plan is to kill Trump and plunge the U.S. into a Civil War."[25]

Only time will tell if Kincaid is correct, but let's pray this doesn't happen, asking God to confound the plans of the enemy and to protect Trump and America from this type of chaos.

During a July 17, 2024, event hosted in Milwaukee by the Heritage Foundation, conservative commentator and former Fox News talk show host Tucker Carlson captured the zeitgeist of the moment, saying the attempted assassination of Trump is proof there is a "spiritual attack underway" in the United States. "There is no logical way to understand what we're seeing now in temporal terms; you just can't," Carlson said. "These are not political divides. There are forces—and they're very obvious now, they've decided, for whatever reason, to take off the mask—whose only goal is chaos, violence, destruction.... What group do they dislike most? What group are they absolutely terrified of and hoping to eliminate? Well, it's Christians, that's who it is. It's Christians."[26]

The apostle Paul told us in Ephesians 6:10–19 how to achieve victory in this spiritual battle now underway in America and the world:

> Finally, be strong in the Lord and in his mighty power. Put on the full armor of God, so that you can take your stand against the devil's schemes. For our struggle is not against flesh and blood, but against the rulers, against the authorities, against the powers of this dark world and against the spiritual forces of evil in the heavenly realms. Therefore put on the full armor of God, so that when the day of evil

comes, you may be able to stand your ground, and after you have done everything, to stand. Stand firm then, with the belt of truth buckled around your waist, with the breastplate of righteousness in place, and with your feet fitted with the readiness that comes from the gospel of peace. In addition to all this, take up the shield of faith, with which you can extinguish all the flaming arrows of the evil one. Take the helmet of salvation and the sword of the Spirit, which is the word of God. And pray in the Spirit on all occasions with all kinds of prayers and requests. With this in mind, be alert and always keep on praying for all the Lord's people.

Preparing for the Future

In light of these concerns, it is crucial for citizens, policymakers, and institutions to remain vigilant, to be proactive, and to engage in regular prayer. Also, ensuring the integrity of the election process and safeguarding democratic principles are paramount.

The lessons from fiction, combined with real-world observations, provide valuable insights. The 2024 presidential election will not only shape the future of the United States but also influence the global landscape.

The prophetic visions of authors like Huxley, Orwell, Clancy, and Lockwood serve as powerful reminders of the potential paths our society could take. Their works encourage us to reflect on the direction we are heading and to take steps to ensure a future that upholds the values of freedom, liberty, and human dignity.

As we prepare for the 2024 presidential election, let us strive to create a world that reflects America's and Scripture's highest ideals.

A Dream of America's Future

Chris Reed, president and CEO of MorningStar Ministries, released a dream he had on March 9, 2024, in which he foresaw an assassination attempt in the coming months:

> I was moving fast in time, starting in April 2024 (with the eclipse that crossed over Texas, which people have been talking about; it seemed Texas was pulled into this). A conception happened at this

time and coincided with this eclipse, leading to something serious happening in the nation before the elections in November 2024.

This "event" caused absolute chaos and affected the elections in the U.S. in November 2024. It seemed like an epic "October surprise," and pandemonium ensued.

I knew President Biden had fizzled out, and they had tried hard to prop him up. This "event" caused a major division of America right before and during the election time. It intensified the division to a very scary and intense level.

And then the dream shifted, and it was somehow 1968, and I was given an old newspaper which said "assassination of two major leaders in the same year of the Chicago convention" (I knew that was Robert Kennedy Sr. and Martin Luther King Jr. who were both killed in 1968). (The Democratic convention is scheduled for Chicago in 2024 as well.) But through all of this painful chaos in the streets, economy and on the news, America had a huge awakening of awareness of the evil and corruption going on in America. It was like the vast majority of the nation said, "We can never let this happen again...we can't!"

The dream ended, and at the end of the dream it was July 2025 (July 11, was highlighted to me). It seemed like most of the chaos ended in the nation, and things started to heal by July 2025. It had all started in April/May 2024 (with the eclipse/conception) and was 40 weeks of pregnancy with intense birth pangs intensifying before the delivery, and then there were complications before the birth AND after the (40 weeks) birth. (The birth was in January 2025, and was placed in an incubator.) The baby lived, and it was beautiful. The baby was named "America."

We need to pray about all of this. I think this is a warning, and a call to the intercessors and to the people of God to take this serious. Because in the dream referencing the 1968 Democratic Convention in Chicago, referencing knowing Martin Luther King Jr. and of course Bobby Kennedy were both killed, I felt that the warning was there, [it] seems to be an indication of a coming assassination attempt sometime during this 16-month process from April 2024 till July 2025.[27]

Reed's prophecy—like the ones of prophet Brandon Biggs on March 14, 2024, foreseeing "an attempt on [Trump's] life that this bullet flew by his ear, and it came so close to his head that it busted his eardrum,"[28] and of Joseph Z on August 18, 2022, urging people to pray for Trump because he saw a vision about an attempt on Trump's life, along with his teaching on July 7, 2024, that the "shot heard around the world" would signal the beginning of a "great shaking"[29]—was fulfilled by the attempted assassination of Trump on July 13, 2024, when Crooks opened fire on him at a Trump rally in Butler, Pennsylvania, grazing the former president in the ear.

Calling for the church to join him in prayer for America, Reed hopes that a spirit of repentance from the people of America may divert the nation from its path of destruction, echoing what Billy Graham told me in an interview over a decade ago regarding America's Nineveh moment.

"Just as the judgment of Nineveh was averted due to their obedience, submission and repentance before the Lord, so too can the judgment of America be diverted if her people will submit once again to the ways of God and repent of our collective sin against Him," Reed said.[30]

Offering some sound wisdom regarding what might take place, Dr. Michael L. Brown, host of the nationally syndicated *Line of Fire* radio program and author of *Revival or We Die: A Great Awakening Is Our Only Hope*, wrote that "elections do matter, and political leaders, especially presidents, can do tremendous harm or good. Absolutely. But we must keep everything in context, and only the Gospel can save a lost soul or bring forgiveness to the guilty or heal a broken heart."[31]

His advice for the days ahead, leading up to the presidential election, is:

- Look to the Word of God, not people, for directions as our election guide.

- Focus on how we live today for Jesus, and don't worry about what will happen tomorrow.

- Our eyes must be on Jesus, and we must unite around Him in our witness to America and the world.

- Keep in mind that there are no political saviors, and that the gospel is the only thing that can save people.

- Avoid getting wrapped up in election fever or hype.

- Stay involved in the political process, especially if that is where God has called you to be.

- Pray for God's will to be done in your city, county, state, region, and country.

- Let God take care of the rest.[32]

These insights emphasize the importance of faith, prayer, and a focus on the gospel as America approaches a pivotal moment in its history. As Reed's dream and Dr. Brown's advice highlight, the future of the nation hinges not only on political outcomes but on the spiritual awakening and repentance of people.

CHAPTER NINE

THE GREAT NORTH AMERICAN ECLIPSE AND THE FUTURE OF AMERICA

There's a great deal to say in the Bible about the signs we're to watch for and when these signs all converge at one place we can be sure that we're close to the end of the age. And those signs, in my judgment, are converging now for the first time since Jesus made those predictions.

—BILLY GRAHAM, INTERVIEW BY THE AUTHOR

Is GOD SENDING a message to America? What does the Bible say about America's future? How does President Donald J. Trump fit into unfolding end-times prophecies?

These are pressing questions many seek to answer through prayer, prophetic gifts, and biblical research. Notably, the total solar eclipse on April 8, 2024, appeared to be a prophetic sign of what is to come for America and the 2024 presidential election.

The prophetic significance of the total solar eclipses in 2017 and 2024 is intensely debated among Christians seeking hope in chaotic times. Some see a glimmer of hope in the natural signs that God has sent to our country over the last seven years. Many believe He is speaking through the sun, moon, and stars, with the two eclipses symbolizing peace and repentance intertwined.

When Jesus' disciples asked Him two thousand years ago about signs of His return, Christ told them there would be "great earthquakes, famines and pestilences in various places, and fearful events and great signs from heaven" (Luke 21:11). He continued, saying:

> There will be signs in the sun, moon and stars. On the earth, nations will be in anguish and perplexity at the roaring and tossing of the

sea. People will faint from terror, apprehensive of what is coming on the world, for the heavenly bodies will be shaken.

—LUKE 21:25–26

A TOTAL ECLIPSE OF THE SUN: AMERICA'S NINEVEH MOMENT

Genesis 1:14 (NKJV) states that God created "lights in the firmament of the heavens" for "signs and seasons." Psalm 19:1–2 declares, "The heavens declare the glory of God; the skies proclaim the work of his hands. Day after day they pour forth speech; night after night they reveal knowledge."

The Great North American Eclipse of 2024 combined with the Great American Eclipse of 2017 formed a giant X in the middle of America, centered in Carbondale, Illinois, famously known as "Little Egypt."[1] We know from Scripture and history that Egypt was the enslaver of Israel. Throughout the Bible the country represents an enslaving power. We also know that God set Israel free from their bondage in Egypt through supernatural signs and wonders, including the ten plagues.

The total solar eclipse in 2024 traversed the United States from Texas to Maine, just days after a planetary alignment, captivating millions. Remarkably, there was a partial or total eclipse in seven towns named Nineveh (or Ninevah) in the United States and one in Nova Scotia, Canada; two of those were in the path of totality, along with Jonah, Texas.[2] Nineveh was the great city in the Bible that repented because Jonah told them they were about to be judged by God. Nineveh experienced a total solar eclipse on June 15, 763 BC, which may have been not long before Jonah arrived to pronounce judgment.[3]

During the Great American Eclipse of 2017, which crossed only the United States, five towns named Salem (meaning peace or wholeness), from the same Hebrew word as Jerusalem (meaning city of peace), were in the path of totality.[4]

"[Eclipses] are absolutely huge," said Pastor Mark Biltz, founder of El Shaddai Ministries. "You have to realize how God communicates with us. Just like with one if by land, two if by sea lantern lights…God made signs for us if we know when and where to look for them. The number one reason He says is for signs. It doesn't say light. It doesn't say heat. It says signs, and that refers completely to eclipses."[5]

Between the eclipses of 2017 and 2024, an annular eclipse occurred on

October 14, 2023, a week after the October 7, 2023, Hamas attack on Israel. An annular eclipse occurs when the moon passes directly between the earth and sun but does not completely cover the sun. The annular eclipse started in Oregon, just like the 2017 eclipse, and went down through Texas, crossing the corner of an area known as the Texas Triangle, the number one sex trafficking area in the US, said Biltz.[6]

The paths of the eclipses in 2017, 2023, and 2024 formed the letters Aleph and Tav, the first and last letters in the Hebrew alphabet—or "Alpha and the Omega, the First and the Last, the Beginning and the End," the title of Jesus Christ in Revelation 22:13.[7]

"I think God always warns before He strikes," said Biltz. "He gave us a seven-year warning...from the 2017 eclipse, and this one is His final warning. This *X* is also the font of the ancient letter Tav. Tav in Hebrew means sign. OK, so this is the *X* marks the spot that is God's signature....The scientific thing about this is so amazing....Every Hebrew letter has a numerical value like Roman numerals. The letter Tav is four hundred, and God said He uses eclipses for signs [Gen. 1:14]. Tav means sign. The only reason we can have an eclipse is because the sun is exactly four hundred times larger than the moon and four hundred times further away. So this is definitely God ordained— God's sign that judgment is coming. And I pray that the people repent, but I believe the church today is asleep."[8]

Was the April 8, 2024, eclipse the Nineveh moment Billy Graham foresaw? Is God telling our nation, shortly before the presidential election on November 5, that we're facing judgment—or revival? These signs remind us that God communicates through the heavens, urging us to repent and prepare for what is to come. The total solar eclipses serve as significant markers, inviting us to discern the times and respond to God's call.

Is War Coming to America?

In his book *America at War 2024–2026*, Biltz explored the prophetic significance of recent blood moons and eclipses. He believes that war is imminent for the United States.

According to Biltz, this won't be an ordinary war. "It will be a horrific war that is coming to the United States homeland that will be unlike any other," Biltz wrote. "This war will involve enemies' boots on the ground here, causing chaos from both within and without. I firmly believe we will see suicide bombers within our borders this next year. Imagine a suicide bomber blowing themselves up at a gas station while you're filling your car, or in the aisles of your grocery store. Picture this happening in your community! What if someone hacks into the electrical grid and takes it down or uses an EMP [electromagnetic pulse] from a foreign nation while all this chaos is unfolding simultaneously?"[9]

Biltz believes the eclipses are signs of "many flash points of judgments" that will start falling over the next few years.

> This year we have the 2024 elections. There is a huge political divide between the left and the right with a volatility that could very easily explode after the primaries....It has also been reported that the Biden Administration's "nightmare scenario" involves the possibility of an all-out war in the Middle East during the upcoming elections in the U.S. There is a volatile religious divide with the Israel/Hamas war going on and there is a very high potential for Antisemitic attacks between those who support Israel and those who want them dead.... There's also a big ethnic divide going on between Black Lives Matter and white supremacists. In the midst of a civil war coming from several directions, and society in complete chaos and while we are at our weakest point, China could attack Taiwan, Iran could attack both Israel and the United States, and North Korea attacks South Korea! On top of that, God's judgment could fall on us with earthquakes or an asteroid hit in the midst of it all!...There are so many threats right now for the U.S. internally, as well as externally, that we need to be on guard in every area. Yet our nation is totally asleep.[10]

Biltz suggested that God is using these eclipses as signs in the heavens to call us to repentance, potentially freeing us from our slavery to world systems that control our lives.

God is showing us through these heavenly signs that He is calling us to repent and turn away from our sins as a nation—sins like abortion (Prov. 6:16–19), the love of money (1 Tim. 6:10), cowardice (Rev. 21:8), sexual immorality (1 Cor. 6:18), mistreatment of the poor (Prov. 14:31), hatred (Matt. 5:22), and more. He's also inviting us to join in His movement to see America and the nations turn back to Jesus Christ.

We are living in a divine moment, one when Jesus is standing at the door to our hearts and saying, "'Here I am! I stand at the door and knock. If anyone hears my voice and opens the door, I will come in and eat with that person, and they with me'" (Rev. 3:20).

BILLY GRAHAM CALLS FOR GREAT SPIRITUAL AWAKENING

In an interview for a WND.com series, evangelist Billy Graham discussed the story of Jonah and the need for global repentance, saying the world is "coming toward the end of the age."

> The Bible indicates that as the time for Christ's return approaches, evil and social chaos may well intensify. Are we living in those days? Only God knows the future and the answer to that question; the Bible makes it clear that we aren't to predict the exact time of Christ's return or claim to know when it will happen.
>
> At the same time, many of the signs or events that Jesus said must take place before His return are certainly in place. Never before, for example, has it been possible to penetrate virtually every corner of the world with the Gospel, as Jesus predicted (see Matthew 24:14).
>
> The fourth and last watch is the coldest hour before the dawn. It's the one that most people dread because it is so cold and you're still sleepy. I think that we're in the fourth watch in our world. We're coming toward the end of the age, not the end of the world or the earth but the end of the age—the period that God has set aside for this particular time....
>
> Make it your goal to be faithful to Christ, no matter what happens in the world around you. We may be tempted to withdraw, or to react negatively to those who don't agree with us. But God loves them, and He wants to use us to share the good news of Christ's forgiveness and new life with them. Remember Jesus' words: "As long as it is day, we must do the work of him who sent me. Night is coming, when no one can work" (John 9:4).[11]

Before his passing in 2018, Graham called for an end-times "great spiritual awakening."[12]

Graham compared America to Nineveh, the lone superpower of its time. When Jonah traveled to Nineveh and proclaimed God's warning, the people repented and escaped judgment. Graham believed the same could happen today.

As I mentioned earlier, that interview inspired the call for a day of national repentance in *Trumpocalypse*, leading to The Return: National and Global Day of Prayer and Repentance on September 26, 2020. In conjunction with the event, President Donald Trump issued a proclamation for a "National Day of Prayer and Return":

> The trials and tribulations the American people have faced over the past several months have been great. Yet, as we have seen time and again, the resolve of our citizenry—fortified by our faith in God—has guided us through these hardships and helped to unite us as one Nation under God. As we continue to combat the challenges ahead of us, we must remember the sage words of President George Washington during his first Presidential Address: "propitious smiles of heaven can never be expected on a nation that disregards the eternal rules of order and right, which Heaven itself has ordained." As a country and a people, let us renew our commitment to these abiding and timeless principles. Today, I am pleased to join my voice to yours in thanking God for blessing this nation with great power and responsibility. With reverence, humility, and thanksgiving, we beg for His continued guidance and protection.[13]

Paul McGuire said he had a vision on July 4, 2012, where the Lord showed him that the great spiritual awakening Graham called for is contingent upon whether people choose to obey, repent earnestly, and "really stop playing church and cry out to Me in fervent and in intense prayer."

> We're facing the greatest spiritual battle in the history of mankind. Signs of the return of Christ are everywhere. The world is shaking on the verge of World War III, pandemics, nukes, directed energy weapons, and on and on, and the most tumultuous election or non-election we've ever had in the history of America. America is literally on the edge of a cliff and is moments from judgment, not because God wants it, but because of the hardness of the hearts of God's people....
> There are conservative secular radio talk show hosts, social media

stars...authors—a whole movement has raised up calling for a third Great Awakening as the only solution to the new world order or the Great Reset....Many of these people aren't saved....I believe it's a case of if God called His own people, His own leadership, His own pastors to carry this message, and they refuse to do it, well, God will raise up rocks to preach to America....I pray [*The Trump Code*] and our books will be like a sledgehammer that breaks that stone.[14]

Pastor Paul Begley wondered if the April 8 eclipse could be the prophesied Nineveh moment that Billy Graham foresaw, signaling either judgment or revival before the presidential election. Begley believes America has wandered from God's Word and set up laws that now protect those who don't follow His standards.[15]

Begley sees the eclipse as part of the fulfillment of Luke 21:25–28: "There will be signs in the sun, moon and stars. On the earth, nations will be in anguish and perplexity at the roaring and tossing of the sea. People will faint from terror, apprehensive of what is coming on the world, for the heavenly bodies will be shaken. At that time, they will see the Son of Man coming in a cloud with power and great glory. When these things begin to take place, stand up and lift up your heads, because your redemption is drawing near."

Begley believes God communicates through major global events and heavenly signs, sparking interest from those who don't usually follow biblical prophecy. He emphasized the need to recognize the signs and awaken spiritually.

People "are curious to know the meaning and significance of this remarkable event and whether it is an indication of something special or another sign," Begley said. "So we really need to let people know, look, we're getting closer, and closer, and closer [to the end times]. We don't know the day or the hour. It would be crazy to try to predict that. But what we can do is point out the signs. It's not really a timeline. It's a sign line."[16]

IS AMERICA IN END-TIMES PROPHECY?

As the author of seven biblical prophecy books, I'm frequently asked whether the Bible includes prophecies about the future of America. I explored this question in depth in my first book, *The Babylon Code*, an investigative book that deciphers a prophetic enigma in the Bible—"Mystery, Babylon" in Revelation 17–18—linking it to contemporary global developments.

In the book, McGuire and I delved into the idea that a code is embedded in the Bible, revealing the formation of a global government, cashless society, and universal religion in the end times. We began by questioning if current global events signify the world is moving into the last days as predicted in Scripture. This prophetic mystery starts with the Tower of Babel in Genesis and culminates with the battle of Armageddon in Revelation. We argued that an elite group of globalists is orchestrating the creation of what many world leaders have called the new world order, echoing the apostle John's "Mystery, Babylon" in Revelation. We explored whether this group, comprising powerful international entities, is working to create a unified global system or a one-world government.

The book highlighted a convergence of dozens of end-times signs, including geopolitical turmoil, economic instability, technological advances, and moral decay. We presented evidence suggesting that today's global crises—such as natural disasters, economic meltdowns, and geopolitical tensions—are harbingers of the apocalyptic events prophesied in the Bible. These signs indicate the rapid approach of the predicted seven-year tribulation period, marked by widespread chaos and the rise of a global dictator—the Antichrist.

We also examined how ancient Babylonian occult practices have influenced secret societies throughout history, contributing to the current push for global governance. Ultimately, we urged people to recognize these signs and be ready for Christ's return, when He will overthrow the false new world order and establish a new, divine order during His millennial reign on earth, followed by judgment day and the creation of a new earth, new Jerusalem, and new heaven.

While the Bible doesn't specifically mention the United States, many Bible scholars and faith leaders in recent decades have asked whether America is destroyed or seriously diminished in a nuclear attack or some other major catastrophe before the tribulation and the rise of the Antichrist.

After the September 11, 2001, terrorist attacks, the late Times Square Church Pastor David Wilkerson, author of the bestselling book *The Cross and the Switchblade*, told his congregation that he believed America was the end-times Babylon. He predicted that the church in America would see a final awakening from a major calamity, followed by one last revival. This revival would shake the world, bringing down the "Babylonian system of greed" in a short period.[17]

Though not directly referenced in the Bible, the United States could possibly be seen in the unfolding events involving "Mystery, Babylon the Great" in Revelation 17–18. In these chapters, world merchants are trading with the nation of Babylon. Then, in one hour, Babylon is judged by fire. As it burns, the merchants aboard their ships stay far away and watch, saddened that their center of trade and prosperity is gone.

Wilkerson noted that these chapters refer to the "great harlot who sits on many waters" (Rev. 17:1, NKJV) that is destroyed in one hour (Rev. 18:10)—"utterly burned with fire" (Rev. 18:8, NKJV)—while the merchants of the earth who "became rich by her" (Rev. 18:15, NKJV) "weep and mourn over her" destruction (Rev. 18:11, NKJV), staying "at a distance for fear of her torment" (Rev. 18:15, NKJV), raising the question of whether this is describing a nuclear attack on America. After all, Russia, China, and North Korea have repeatedly threatened to attack the United States with nuclear weapons in recent years.

For example, in a recent US Naval Institute article, "The Next Taiwan Crisis Will (Almost) Certainly Involve Nuclear Threats," James H. Anderson wrote that a Chinese attack on Taiwan could involve a simultaneous electromagnetic pulse (EMP) attack on Taiwan and a nuclear attack on the United States. "It is more plausible to imagine Beijing launching an electromagnetic pulse attack over Taiwan," Anderson wrote. "In theory, such a weapon could paralyze the island's communication networks. Inflicting such a sudden and massive psychological blow might, in turn, shock Taipei's political leaders into capitulation. China also could use nuclear threats to dissuade the United States from rendering military assistance to Taiwan during a crisis. Here, it is worth recalling that senior Chinese officials have already issued such threats against the United States, as happened during the Taiwan crisis in 1996 and again in 2005. What is more, Chinese military publications and journals have mentioned—on multiple occasions—the potential for nuclear first strikes against the United States as part of various Taiwan invasion scenarios."[18]

In explaining America's seeming absence from Bible prophecies, some have asked if it's possible that so many Christians disappear in the rapture—the eschatological belief that followers of Jesus will ascend into heaven at some point prior to or during the tribulation—that the United States would cease to be the global economic and military superpower, thus playing a limited role as end-times events unfold.

Others point to America's soaring levels of national debt—$34.9 trillion and rising by about $1 trillion every hundred days—as a potential cause for an economic collapse that could plunge the United States into financial and societal chaos, diminishing its role in global events.[19]

Randy DeSoto, writing in the Western Journal, noted that we live in a time of "signs in the heavens, wars and rumors of wars, [and] earthquakes" that may very well point to the soon return of Christ. If we are entering the end times, DeSoto asked, "What role might the United States play?"

> The Bible speaks of a time at the end of the present age in the books of Daniel, Revelation, and Matthew—among others—when there will be seven years of tribulation culminating in the battle of Armageddon in Israel and the return of Jesus Christ to earth. The United States, currently the most powerful nation in the world, is not clearly referenced in any of this, and there may be multiple reasons why—some bad, some good—according to Bible experts.[20]

While only God knows for certain how world events will play out in the months and years ahead, it's interesting that Ingersoll Lockwood's book is titled *The Last President*. Was it prophetic? Could Donald Trump be America's final president, or at least, the last legitimately elected president?

While many Bible scholars don't find the United States in Scripture, Paul Begley believes "a reference to eagle's wings in the book of Revelation just might have to do with the United States." Begley pointed out that the prophet Daniel wrote about four empires, including one like a lion with eagle's wings, along with a bear, a leopard, and a beast more powerful than the others with iron teeth. Begley noted that the apostle John wrote in Revelation 13 of a beast that embodies the empires Daniel mentioned, with elements of a lion, bear, and leopard but without eagle's wings. However, in Revelation 12, eagle's wings are given to a woman (who represents Israel) so she can escape the dragon, or the devil. Given that the bald eagle is symbolic of America, it's interesting that the eagle is the only beast from Daniel that isn't part of the one-world government.[21]

DeSoto noted that other scholars believe the United States can be seen in Ezekiel 38, which depicts an epic battle between Gog and Magog, in which Persia (modern-day Iran) joins forces with other nations, possibly including Russia and Turkey, to attack Israel. Ezekiel 38:13 refers to Tarshish (possibly the modern-day United Kingdom) and "all their young lions" protesting the invasion. The young lions could include the United States, as offspring of the UK, since "both Britain and the United States played a pivotal role in the birth of modern Israel after World War II."[22]

Another possible scenario for the United States is a massive nationwide revival, as has happened several times in the past. Charisma News and CBN News have chronicled the beginnings of such a revival, which could be the next great awakening America needs.

WE'VE GOT TWO YEARS

In May 2024, prophet and author Chuck Pierce issued a prophetic message during an interview with Strang on the *Strang Report*. Pierce declared, "God said, 'America, I'm going to give you two years...to make choices to realign with My covenant plan.'"[23]

Pierce emphasized that these times are escalating, with God sending signs and calling His people to rise up in unprecedented ways. He noted, "We have to understand that these times are escalating...[rather] than thinking we're just coming to the end of things and either we're going to be raptured or the world's going to come to an end." Pierce felt the April 8, 2024, eclipse was a significant sign for America:

> I just see times escalating, and God is sending signs, and sending an order for His kingdom people to rise up in ways they have never arisen, and really come forth at this time throughout the Earth, nation by nation by nation....
>
> The [2024] eclipse was assigned to America....The very place where the eclipse began in Eagle Pass Del Rio, and then that path formed all the way across America touching fifteen states, and I felt the Lord was telling me, "I am creating a path of choice for America at this time. I am giving America, starting at this time, the ability to make choices to realign fully in My purposes."[24]

Pierce explained that God is giving America two years to make clear decisions, particularly in voting according to the Word of God.

> I believe what happened...on April 8th with the eclipse was that God said, "America, I'm going to give you two years of clear decisions, and...how you vote [with the Word of God as your foundation]...is how [I will] visit [you]. And I'm going to give you two years to make choices to realign with My covenant plan."[25]

Pierce believes that God is going to visit each state individually, beginning with Passover 2024, to see how they will respond to Him. God is looking for those who will turn to Him and will be His remnant in those states in this hour.

Pierce compared America's current state to the time of the prophet Jeremiah, when people were in captivity. Today America is held captive by a failing economic system, rising debt, Big Tech control, and spiritual oppression. Yet God still has a "door of hope for America" for anyone who responds to Him in covenant.[26]

Pierce provided ways to respond to God in covenant:

- Vote according to the Word of God.

- Lift up our voices to God and ask for leaders who have His voice in their mouths. "This whole decade is about the voice [of God's people] coming forth....That's the real problem with Washington, DC: we don't have a clear voice that's coming forth, and we don't have confidence that the voice will stand in the time of trouble, or stand in the battle at the gate.... What we can do, as God's children, is say, 'Lord, bring our deliverer, bring our advocate in. Bring that one and set [them] in place that can lead us with a clear voice in the days ahead and have a clear voice toward Israel, your covenant nation, where there isn't a compromise with what we're really about.'"[27]

Reiterating the two-year timeframe, Pierce stressed the importance of recognizing God's signs indicating a righteous return to His plan for America.

The eclipse, forming a path across America, symbolizes that the Lord is giving us a new path if we choose His way.

SIGNS OF HOPE

Are there signs of hope amidst our current turmoil? Can we see change beginning now? While preachers often lead people to Christ, it's noteworthy when a converted Wiccan spearheads one of the biggest revivals in America.

At the end of May 2024, thousands of Texans reported radical life changes after participating in a major revival led by an unexpected source: Jenny Weaver, a former Wiccan turned Christian minister. Using a water fountain outside Trinity Church in Cedar Hill, Texas, Weaver baptized "hundreds and hundreds" of people. According to CBN News, Weaver is at the forefront of a significant move of God in the United States during the summer of 2024. "I heard the Lord say in March 'This will be the SUMMER OF BAPTISMS,' and this word has come to pass," she shared on social media. "2000 people and the power of God met us!" Earlier in May, thousands joined Weaver and her husband, Stephen, on Siesta Key Beach in Sarasota, Florida, for an event on Mother's Day weekend. Weaver described the event as "Absolutely a move of God!"[28]

MASSIVE CALIFORNIA BAPTISMS

In California, a statewide revival is underway, largely unreported by mainstream media. Oceans Church continues to hold massive baptism services on beaches. In 2023, the church held "Baptize SoCal," gathering over four thousand people at Pirates Cove in Newport Beach—the site where Calvary Chapel Costa Mesa Pastor Chuck Smith baptized thousands during the Jesus Movement of the 1960s and 1970s, as shown in the hit movie *Jesus Revolution*.[29]

Oceans Church, joined by three hundred congregations from across the state, aimed to "Baptize California" with a goal of thirty thousand baptisms on Pentecost Sunday. While the exact number reached isn't specified, photos show a powerful move of God, with people baptized in tubs and the ocean to accommodate the masses.

Oceans Church Pastor Mark Francey expressed the church's desire for revival to spread throughout California and the nation. "We want to see

God awakened. We're tired of the darkness in California. We believe that God wants people to know about it, and if we put our money where our frustration is, that God could do something great....What God's doing in California is not going to stop here. It's going to go to all of America."[30]

TENT REVIVALS AND MIRACLES

Thousands are coming to Christ, being healed, and experiencing freedom at Mario Murillo tent crusades nationwide. Murillo has witnessed God releasing miracles and healings in astounding ways during these events.

"The miracles that we are seeing are happening on hearts, bodies, nerves, growths, people that have been hopelessly ill that had been healed by the power of God," Murillo said. "In the tent itself, people have been healed and left, found out later that their symptoms had vanished. [They] went to their doctor, doctors found out that growths were no longer in their body."[31]

Murillo's messages boldly proclaim Christ as Savior, healer, and giver of the Holy Spirit. He urges believers to ask God for miracles so the news spreads through families, neighborhoods, cities, and states, drawing people to God.

In an article titled "Is Revival in America Now Impossible?" Murillo warned of a dangerous belief gripping American Christians: that revival is impossible. He explained that Satan has paralyzed the church with this lie, creating misunderstandings about revival, with believers "convinced that America is beyond hope."[32]

"Let me hit the biggest lie," Murillo wrote. "We do not realize that mercy causes revival. Yes, we must repent. Yes, there must be fervent prayer. But revival is—in the final definition—an act of mercy. Yes, we must do our part, but the real victory comes directly from the hand of God. And it will come yet again, in America. Why? It is what He does whenever evil is exalted. When evil is exalted, God looks for deliverers."

Murillo noted that there are over four hundred thousand ministers in the United States. Quoting Isaiah 59:14–16 (AMPC), he highlighted the impact of clergy silence:

> Justice is turned away backward, and righteousness (uprightness and right standing with God) stands far off; for truth has fallen in the street (the city's forum), and uprightness cannot enter [the courts of

justice]. Yes, truth is lacking, and he who departs from evil makes himself a prey. And the Lord saw it, and it displeased Him that there was no justice. And He saw that there was no man and wondered that there was no intercessor [no one to intervene on behalf of truth and right]; therefore, His own arm brought Him victory, and His own righteousness [having the Spirit without measure] sustained Him.

"If only once they would speak out against evil, it would turn the tide," Murillo wrote. "Many Christians believe that Isaiah 59:16 is only about prayer. But it is not. It is about speaking out against wickedness and injustice. It is about silence: 'no one to intervene on behalf of truth and right.'... Notice that in Isaiah's day God was shocked by the silence. And He is also shocked today!...But notice what God did next: '...therefore, His own arm brought Him victory.' Revival will still come because a righteous core is still praying, and God will act out of love and mercy for our nation."[33]

BORDER REVIVAL

On the United States' border in Texas, God is at work through prayer and tent meetings. Pastor Tony Suarez, creator of Revival on the Border, aimed to see five thousand people encounter God in El Paso and McAllen, Texas. God exceeded that number, with about nine thousand people having "an experience with the Lord" during the tent meetings in late March 2024. God's peace was tangible on the border, with meetings so packed they brought in two hundred extra seats just on the first night. Even border patrol agents sought prayer.[34]

CONTINUING IMPACT OF THE ASBURY REVIVAL

Fourteen months after the beginning of the Asbury Revival, it's now labeled an "outpouring." Dr. Sarah Thomas Baldwin, author of *Generation Awakened: An Eyewitness Account of the Powerful Outpouring of God at Asbury*, noted that "hardly a day has gone by" without hearing about how the revival reached people worldwide.[35]

Baldwin shared how her students still carry the "spirit of revival," with God continuing to work deeply in their lives. "Immediately after the outpouring…our campus really was exhausted," she said. "I like to say that the flood of the outpouring came up, and when the waters receded, there was some debris on the beach."[36]

However, months later, during the fall semester, students returned to Asbury "with a renewed energy and fervor." The students returned to campus with the spirit still alive in them. They stayed after chapel to worship and pray. They talked more openly and regularly about Jesus, and the sense of a deep walk with God has now become more regular in campus life.[37]

Are these moves of God just a foretaste for what is to come for our country, and is Asbury a forerunner for what God wants to do with our youth?

Let's pray that it is so.

CHAPTER TEN

PROPHETIC DESTINY— THE TRUMP LEGACY

Then Daniel praised the God of heaven and said: "Praise be to the name of God for ever and ever; wisdom and power are his. He changes times and seasons; he deposes kings and raises up others. He gives wisdom to the wise and knowledge to the discerning. He reveals deep and hidden things; he knows what lies in darkness, and light dwells with him. I thank and praise you, God of my ancestors: You have given me wisdom and power, you have made known to me what we asked of you, you have made known to us the dream of the king."

—Daniel 2:19–23

A S THE PROPHET Daniel wrote thousands of years ago, wisdom and power belong to God. He is the One who knows what will happen in the future, and He controls the presidential election in November 2024. He deposes kings and raises others. Only He can reveal what is deep and hidden.

The last eight years have been a turbulent roller coaster for our country, but when we step back and get a God's-eye view, we see His hand moving, His power and wisdom ruling in the affairs of this country.

I firmly believe that God raised Donald Trump in 2016 to be president. From the time he took office, many deep, hidden things have been brought to light: Russiagate, the COVID-19 unraveling, the 2020 riots, ongoing lawfare, the crackdown on parents who try to keep their children safe, and more.

Only God knows if Trump will win in November. The hopes and prayers of millions are for God to intervene and set our country on the right track again.

Trump seems to be the man to do that—if God wills it. And that is how we should be praying: "Your kingdom come, your will be done, on earth as it is in heaven" (Matt. 6:10).

"YOUR WILL BE DONE ON EARTH AS IT IS IN HEAVEN"

Paul McGuire says the Lord's miraculous intervention is the only answer for the quagmire the world finds itself in today.

"You see what an impossible situation we're in with the prospect of World War III, Russia, Ukraine, the prospect of the Great Reset and their digital totalitarian state and cashless society, the possibility of a major conflict between Israel and Gaza and Middle Eastern nations," McGuire said. "We are stuck in so many impossible conflicts and problems, and we're walking on very thin ice. So if we are going to look at the world purely as materialists that only believe in the physical dimension of reality, then the conclusion would be total despair and hopelessness."[1]

Consequently, McGuire said he started crying out to the Lord about a year before the COVID-19 pandemic, asking God how we can turn things around:

> I keep saying, "God, there must be something we can do. There has to be a plan because I don't believe in my heart...that God has brought us, His children, to be here for such a time as this in the last days just to allow us to be engulfed in total annihilation and destruction."[2]

As he continued to pray, slowly the Lord began to answer him.

> I sensed the Lord telling me there is a way out. "There is a way for My people to achieve victory. I didn't appoint them to be slaughtered.... Your doorway to get out of the nightmare is Me. Your answers—the downloads that you need, the favor that you need, the finances that you need, the angelic armies that you need, the power that you need to overthrow the Luciferian deep state and so on and so forth—it's all embodied in Me. And if My people will seek Me like they've never sought Me before, if My people will begin that seeking with repentance like they've never repented before, I will turn the paradigm therein violently in their favor. I will turn it around. I will make a way where there is no way. When I said...that all things are possible with God, I meant exactly what I said. All things are possible with God. There's no loophole....So when you totally give yourself over

to Me and totally open yourself up to the miraculous based on [My] Word, when you worship Me and then enter into a divine synchronization between Me and My people, I will release My power. I will release My chariots of fire. I will release the armies of God. I will release the technology of God. I will release My people."[3]

2024 PLATFORM PLEDGE TO AMERICAN CITIZENS

Trump has stated what he will do in his second term if reelected. In July 2024, Trump released his "2024 Platform Pledge to American Citizens," outlining his plan if he takes office on January 20, 2025. The platform includes twenty key promises that "will allow Americans to rise above this economic disaster that they are presently living under." These include:

1. Seal the border and end the migrant invasion

2. Carry out the largest deportation operation in the nation's history

3. End inflation and make America affordable again

4. Make America the dominant energy producer in the world, by far!

5. Stop outsourcing and turn the United States into a manufacturing superpower

6. Large tax cuts for workers, and no tax on tips!

7. Defend our Constitution, our Bill of Rights, and our fundamental freedoms, including freedom of speech, freedom of religion, and the right to keep and bear arms

8. Prevent World War Three, restore peace in Europe and in the Middle East, and build a great Iron Dome missile defense shield over our entire country—all made in America

9. End the weaponization of government against the American people

10. Stop the migrant crime epidemic, demolish the foreign drug cartels, crush gang violence, and lock up violent offenders

11. Rebuild our cities, including Washington D.C., making them safe, clean, and beautiful again

12. Strengthen and modernize our military, making it, without question, the strongest and most powerful in the world

13. Keep the U.S. dollar as the world's reserve currency

14. Fight for and protect Social Security and Medicare with no cuts, including no changes to the retirement age

15. Cancel the electric vehicle mandate and cut costly and burdensome regulations

16. Cut federal funding for any school pushing critical race theory, radical gender ideology, and other inappropriate racial, sexual, or political content on our children

17. Keep men out of women's sports

18. Deport pro-Hamas radicals and make our college campuses safe and patriotic again

19. Secure our elections, including same day voting, voter identification, paper ballots, and proof of citizenship

20. Unite our country by bringing it to new and record levels of success[4]

Trump's platform for his second term could make major inroads in turning around the nation. But what interests us here is what will follow a second Trump term.

Specifically, if Trump wins in November, could his son Barron Trump be president one day? Is that ultimately what Ingersoll Lockwood was seeing when he wrote his novels about Baron Trump?

WHO IS BARRON TRUMP?

Barron Trump is the youngest son of President Trump and his only child with Melania Trump. He turned eighteen on March 20, 2024, and graduated high school in May. As a minor, Barron was mostly kept out of the media spotlight, protected by his mother, Melania, which allowed him to live a relatively normal childhood.[5]

Recent photos show Barron towering above his father and everyone else he meets. He is six feet seven inches tall, with only his half-brother Eric and Donald Sr. coming close in height.

Barron grew up mostly in Manhattan, spending winters in Palm Beach, Florida, and periods in Bedminster, New Jersey. During his father's early presidency, Barron and his mother stayed in New York so he could finish the school year at the Columbia Grammar & Preparatory School. He later attended school near the White House and graduated from Oxbridge Academy in West Palm Beach.

When it comes to sports, it would be a natural thought that Barron would love basketball because of his height. But it seems his favorite sport is soccer. He played for the D.C. United U-12 soccer team as a midfielder. He was even able to meet Wayne Rooney, a former Manchester United soccer star.

Donald Trump has mentioned Barron's proficiency with computers, even joking that Barron hacked his "locked computer during a CPAC conference in 2022." Trump has also said Barron could have created a better website for the nation's healthcare system, which had technical glitches when it was first launched. During the 2022 Conservative Political Action Conference in Orlando, Donald Trump stated Barron "can make his computer sing."[6]

If you take all of this together, looking at it from the outside, it would seem that Donald and Melania have shepherded their child in a godly way, keeping him from the limelight and helping him pursue a "normal" life outside of the world of glamour and fame, and he has developed skills, talents, and hobbies that reflect what most of us would classify as middle-class, middle-America staples: computers and soccer. Who didn't play soccer as a kid?

Does any of this point to Barron being a natural leader, one picked by God to be a major player on the world stage as Ingersoll Lockwood's novels may suggest?

In a recent Slate article, "The Blank Slate of Barron Trump," Luke Winkie pointed out that "Barron Trump and Alexander the Great share remarkably similar jawlines." Winkie wrote that Barron, despite his remoteness, is building a nascent fandom.

The boy, who is the only child Donald Trump sired with his third wife, Melania, became a man this past March. Barron is now 18, and thus far he has maintained separation from the political project of his father's clan, especially compared to Trump's other sons—Eric and Don Jr.—who have each grifted their way toward conservative celebrity status. Barron is not on Twitter or Instagram, he has never given an interview, and he recently declined an invitation to serve as one of the delegates cementing Trump's presidential renomination. And yet, despite his remoteness, we are living in the midst of a nascent Barron fandom. The 18-year-old shall be bequeathed with the weight of the Trump legacy, whether he likes it or not.[7]

COULD BARRON TRUMP BE PRESIDENT ONE DAY?

In Lockwood's novels about Baron Trump, we find that the young man is a mover and shaker, a world-traveling, influential young man. He has great influence with world leaders and uses it to discover the truth about hidden realms. Are these prophetic signs about the real Barron Trump's future?

Daniel 2:20–22 says, "Praise be to the name of God for ever and ever; wisdom and power are his. He changes times and seasons; he deposes kings and raises up others. He gives wisdom to the wise and knowledge to the discerning. He reveals deep and hidden things; he knows what lies in darkness, and light dwells with him."

God is the one who raises up leaders and deposes them. He alone knows who the future president of America will be. Historically, God has twice placed fathers and then sons in office to guide America—John Adams and John Quincy Adams, and George H. W. Bush and George W. Bush. While this doesn't guarantee anything regarding Barron Trump's future, there is a pattern of God putting fathers and sons into office.

Major news outlets announced in May 2024 that Barron Trump would step into the political arena as a Florida delegate during the Republican National Convention. Though he withdrew from the delegation, citing "prior commitments," this initial interest could signal future political involvement. The story noted that a "campaign official told ABC News that Barron 'is very interested in our nation's political process.'"[8]

This isn't surprising given that Trump has stated that Barron likes politics and even gives him advice. "He's a smart one," Trump said. "He doesn't have to hear much, but he's a great guy. He's a little on the tall side. I will tell you, he's a tall one. But he's a good-looking guy, and he's really been a great student and he does like politics....It's sort of funny, he'll tell me sometimes, 'Dad, this is what you have to do.' So anyway, he's a good guy."[9]

While we don't know what the future holds, his initial interest and the fact he was selected by Florida Republicans could be a signal that he will one day enter the arena as his father has before him.

At a July 9, 2024, campaign rally at his golf club in Doral, Florida, Donald Trump called Barron to the stage, where he was met with cheers.

> "Welcome to the scene," Trump said. "This is the first time he's ever done it. Where is Barron? Stand up. Look at him!" Barron...then stood and proudly waved to the adoring crowd. "You're pretty popular," Trump gushed. "He may be more popular than Don and Eric. We gotta talk about this."[10]

In a story titled "Long Forgotten Novels From 19th-Century Author Ingersoll Lockwood Were Called 'The Last President' And 'The Baron Trump', How's That for Conspiracy?" Geoffrey Grider asked if Lockwood's books have anything to do with Donald and Barron Trump.

Referencing Lockwood's novels and Barron's rally debut, Grider wrote that Barron "is very tall, quite handsome and has a serious 'beyond his years' expression....From a conspiracy perspective, as the saying goes, the 'kid is a natural.' Is he about to come onto the political scene?" With the current turmoil in the country, a book called *The Last President* would be timely, the article stated.[11]

What does Barron's interest in politics show regarding the future of our country amongst the youth of America? Is God moving on the hearts of the young to get involved in the life and future of this country?

"Young people are being assaulted by the powers and principalities, the chaos, confusion, perversion, identity issues, suicide, depression, all this kind of stuff," says Sean Feucht. "But yet at the same time, we're also seeing a great harvest. And every altar call that we do, every time we go after God moving in Gen Z and Gen Alpha, their response has been phenomenal. We've seen God come and set so many people free [and] release deliverance, freedom, and hope. I have four kids that are in that group. And so to me, it's really personal. We're not going to stop until we see a Gen Z set free and on fire for Jesus."[12]

WHAT IS HAPPENING AMONG YOUTH?

Barron Trump is part of Generation Z, a generation that has grown up in an "always on" technological environment. The oldest people in Gen Z are currently in their mid to late twenties.

They have not known life without iPhones, iPads, lightning-fast internet, and instant everything. They are used to connecting with peers and others via Zoom, Instagram, and other online tools. Because of this, "research has shown that Gen Z's attitudes towards dating and sex have evolved from the generations before them; they take an especially pragmatic approach to love and sex, and subsequently aren't prioritising establishing committed romantic relationships the same way their older peers once did."[13]

In a time when dating, chatting, and relating seems to be all digital, wouldn't it be just like God to begin encountering them in personal ways in large group settings?

In recent gatherings around the country, like the revivals taking place at Asbury and Auburn, thousands of students—all in the Gen Z age range—are getting together, hearing the Word preached, and being baptized. Public universities, which many have given up on as bastions of Marxism and lost causes, are seeing evangelistic campaigns sweeping hundreds into God's family. Just in the first half of 2024:

- Florida State University had around 300 baptisms.

- The University of Alabama had around 260 baptisms.

- The University of Georgia saw 150 people baptized "in the beds of pickup trucks for want of a traditional baptismal setting."[14]

The organizer of the events taking college campuses by storm, Tonya Prewett, said that her organization, Unite US, "was birthed from a vision God gave me after mentoring college students and hearing about their pain, anxiety and depression." It began with a vision of thousands of students worshipping together in an arena. She shared the vision with local pastors and ministry leaders. "Every leader joined in the vision and in about six weeks Unite Auburn took place. Almost five thousand students showed up for the event, and around two hundred ended up getting baptized." She credits the hundreds of baptisms of students in need of truth and hope to "a move of God that can only be explained by Him."[15]

A pastor who spoke at the Georgia gathering, Jonathan Pokluda, said revival may be brewing on college campuses because young people "are tired of mundane faith sitting in the periphery of cafeteria visits and late-night benders." Pokluda said they want faith that is more than just going to church on Sunday. They want faith that is part of every day, something more than religious rituals. Because of that, "universities are pregnant with revival."[16]

It seems the flame of revival was lit at the revival that began at Asbury University in Wilmore, Kentucky, on February 8, 2023. It began during a Wednesday morning chapel service, turning into a multiweek outpouring involving Holy Spirit–led worship, prayer, and repentance. Since then, it has spread to secular campuses, churches, and youth events all over the country, and Jesus is being proclaimed, souls are being converted, and baptisms are happening. It's no coincidence that Asbury and the *Jesus Revolution* movie hit the country in the same year. It was a 1970 revival at the Asbury campus that is seen "as a significant driver behind the Jesus Movement of the '70s."[17]

Videos from places like Oahu, Hawaii, show young adults being touched by God, people coming to Christ, and the Holy Spirit moving. Nearly four thousand miles away from Hawaii, in Norman, Oklahoma, on the University of Oklahoma's campus, the eighty-six-thousand-seat football stadium was rented for the largest student-led outreach in the area, another indication God is up to something miraculous and nation-changing.

CBN News made a list of known locations where outpourings have occurred already, as of March 2023:

- Asbury University (Wilmore, Kentucky)

- Rupp Arena (Lexington, Kentucky)

- Western Kentucky University (Bowling Green, Kentucky)

- Union College (Barbourville, Kentucky)

- University of the Cumberlands (Williamsburg, Kentucky)

- Eastern Kentucky University (Richmond, Kentucky)
- Lee University (Cleveland, Tennessee)
- Grace Christian Academy (Knoxville, Tennessee)
- Samford University (Birmingham, Alabama)
- Cedarville University (Cedarville, Ohio)
- Ohio State (Columbus, Ohio)
- Indiana Wesleyan University (Marion, Indiana)
- Valley Forge College (Chester County, Pennsylvania)
- Hannibal-LaGrange University (Hannibal, Missouri)
- Texas A&M (Corpus Christi, Texas)
- Texas A&M (College Station, Texas)
- Baylor University (Waco, Texas)
- Louisiana State University (Baton Rouge, Louisiana)
- Oral Roberts University (Tulsa, Oklahoma)
- Youth event (Portland, Oregon)
- Regent University (Virginia Beach, Virginia)
- Church event (Washington, DC)[18]

Given that Donald Trump was the first president since Abraham Lincoln to declare a day of national prayer and repentance, that he announced publicly on more than one occasion that Jesus Christ is Lord of America, and that he willingly stated multiple times he is not bigger than the Man upstairs, could it be he helped provide the final push that was needed to open the gates of revival that we are now seeing fan out across America?

In a recent broadcast, Joseph Z spoke about the Lord's desire to destroy the spirit of Jezebel—a "spirit of control, domination, intimidation, and out-communicating the prophets, in a bid to shut up and intimidate the prophets"—using His anointed reformers as these pockets of revival nationwide grow.[19]

He said Christians need to stand up against this spirit because the United States is the only obstacle preventing global domination by wicked forces. He likened this conflict to the biblical confrontation between Elijah and the prophets of Baal on Mount Carmel described in 1 Kings 18:20–40. He called for Jesus' followers to take a stand against the Jezebel spirit, believing God will answer with fire, leading to a great awakening and the rise of anointed reformers:

> This is not just now in this electoral process. There's so much more to it, but you're going to begin to see this thing just begin to absolutely take off, collide....This collision is Mount Carmel. And what is Mount Carmel? Mount Carmel is the USA right now. It is America. That's where the showdown is right now. And I believe God is going to answer with fire....God is the Lion who is watching. and He is going to act during this time....
>
> All the things that people have prayed for, all the things that have come to pass and we've been waiting on, God is going to answer....I see the Spirit of the Lord bringing a great awakening through these things...and it's going to empower the spirit of Elijah....I had a vision where I saw the Lion watching the earth....He's going to begin to bring an awakening, waves of awakening and power. Hear me now. I sense it by the Spirit of the Lord that this wicked agenda will not work, and there's waves of awakening and the big word is going to be power....You're going to see...the spirit of Elijah; you're going to see it charge the prophetic....I see collision coming...so we're going into this cycle, and I see the Lord shedding His grace on the United States. I see this time of mercy....The Lord is releasing this power to charge this [spirit of Elijah], and this is where the reformers will come in and offset this hit [by the spirit of Jezebel].[20]

COULD AMERICA EXPERIENCE A LAST-DAYS REVIVAL?

Nearly all our presidents have claimed to be Christians, and many have had relationships with prominent Christian leaders like Billy Graham and others. However, there seems to be something different, prophetically, about Donald Trump and his claims that Jesus Christ is Lord and Savior not only of his life but of America.

In a Christmas service at Pastor Robert Jeffress' church, First Baptist Church in Dallas, Trump said, "Our country needs a Savior right now. And our country has a Savior. And it's not me. It's somebody much higher up than me. Much higher."[21]

He is right. We don't need a better president or better elected officials to save us—because they can't. None of them can stop sin or the rampant, devastating issues sin has unleashed on our country. Our country, for it to survive, needs one thing and one thing only: Jesus Christ.

In an interview with Tucker Carlson, pastor and author Douglas Wilson said he doesn't believe there is a political solution for America: it can only be Jesus that saves America. Wilson said many of our leaders have satanic ambitions to be like God, and some prominent evangelical Christians have become tools of the radical left because they are busy placating the cultural elite.

He said progressive secularists are threatened by people who believe their rights come from God. America's current leaders "don't believe in God, but they do believe in the devil," Wilson said. "If there is no God above the state, the state is god. The state becomes god, and it assumes the prerogatives of deity....They want to control absolutely everything, every keystroke. They want to control everything because they're aspiring to deity. The reason they're aspiring to deity is because they don't recognize any god above them."[22]

He said there is no political road to restoring a system based on Christian presuppositions in a nation that is largely no longer Christian, and that because America is suffering from a disease that is both radical and spiritual, there can only be a spiritual remedy. We need preachers to "stop being ashamed of the name of Jesus and preach the gospel...as though it's supposed to spread out into the streets after the service," he said. America needs "to repent of our sins, our arrogance, and turn back to God."[23]

What we are seeing with pastors like Wilson and students flooding football stadiums to hear about Jesus and give their lives to Him is God moving on hearts and saying America doesn't need improving—we need to be saved from our sins.

America is in a life-and-death struggle, and only Christ can save us.

In his speech at First Baptist Church, Trump acknowledged as much:

The life and death and resurrection of Jesus Christ forever changed the world. And it's impossible to think of the life of our own country without the influence of His example and of His teachings. Our miraculous founding, overcoming civil war, abolishing slavery, defeating communism and fascism, reaching boundless heights of science and discovery, so many incredible things....None of this could have ever happened without Jesus Christ and His followers and His church. None of it. And we have to remember that Jesus Christ is the ultimate source of our strength and of our hope and here and everywhere and for all time.[24]

From Abraham Lincoln to Ronald Reagan to Donald Trump

New York Times bestselling author Jonathan Cahn revealed what God had shown him about the future of America in his book *The Harbinger II*, and the Charisma Media documentary film *The Harbingers of Things to Come.* In his writing, he declared that our national judgment began on September 11, 2001, with the terrorist attacks that killed three thousand people. It gave us a window of time to repent—and if the nation didn't, greater shakings would happen.

The shakings are upon us now, but there is hope even though "America is following in the ominous footsteps of Israel. When judgment came to Israel, the first strike came in 605 BC when the armies of Babylon invaded the land."

> Yet, the greater shakings came in 586 BC as judgment ravaged the land—19 years between the two events. Following the same biblical template, America's first strike happened on September 11, 2001. Our nation's greater shaking came to America in the form of a pandemic known as COVID-19 in the year 2020—19 years after 9/11.[25]

As in every pronouncement of judgment God issued in the Bible, there is hope in Christ:

> The LORD is good, a refuge in times of trouble. He cares for those who trust in Him....This is what the LORD says: "Although they have allies and are numerous, they will be destroyed and pass away. Although I have afflicted you, Judah, I will afflict you no more.

Now I will break their yoke from your neck and tear your shackles away."

—NAHUM 1:7, 12–13

If my people, who are called by my name, will humble themselves and pray and seek my face and turn from their wicked ways, then I will hear from heaven, and I will forgive their sin and will heal their land.

—2 CHRONICLES 7:14

The key to saving America is turning back to the Lord, who is good. He is our only refuge and "he cares for those who trust in him" (Nah. 1:7). He is the only One who can set us free from the oppression we face. If we turn to Him in humble prayer, He will hear from heaven, forgive our sins, and heal our land.

We have seen Him do it before for America under President Abraham Lincoln:

> In 1863, amid the Civil War, America was almost destroyed. President Abraham Lincoln called for a national day of prayer, humility and repentance before God. Just over two months after that event, the Union experienced victory at Gettysburg on July 3, and the fall of Vicksburg under Ulysses S. Grant turned things around. That is the power of prayer![26]

In 1980 America faced another crisis, with economic troubles and the Iran hostage crisis. Jimmy Carter called for a national day of prayer.

> Two key prayers were prayed that day: first, that God would rescue our American hostages; and second, they lifted their hands to the western side of the Capitol Building and prayed that He would place in the nation's government those of His will....Two months later, there was a presidential election and a revolution in the polls. Candidates who pledged themselves to biblical values were winning across the country.
>
> The most notable was Ronald Reagan, who became the next leader of the United States of America. Reagan spoke of the need

for spiritual revival. On the same day that he took the oath of office, the hostages were released. When he was sworn in, his right hand was raised while his other hand was on the Bible on a specific verse that his mother had highlighted. It was 2 Chronicles 7:14. Shortly thereafter, the economy rebounded, the military rebounded and the Soviet Union fell.[27]

What awaits us if we humble ourselves and pray for God's intervention in the affairs of our country?

"I have no doubt that we're in [a Nineveh moment] now, [but] how long is God giving us His grace to turn back to Him as a nation?" asked Rabbi Jonathan Bernis. "I'm not a date setter. I never have been. But since COVID, there's just been a sense in my spirit that we are in a final wrap-up and God's giving us an opportunity, a final opportunity to turn around individually and corporately, as a nation and nations."[28]

If Ingersoll Lockwood was prophetic in *The Last President* and saw what was coming for America, it appears that we are about to experience another election where an unlikely candidate is picked by the people; overriding the plans of world leaders, elites, socialists, and anarchists; ushering in a president who will be a sign that:

> ...the Lord had been good to them; that the wicked money-changers had been driven from the temple, that the stony-hearted usurers were beaten at last, that the "People's William" was at the helm now, that peace and plenty would in a few moons come back to the poor man's cottage.[29]

As we look to the future, we must remember that our hope lies not in political leaders or human efforts but in the power and grace of God. Only through repentance, prayer, and a return to His ways can we see true healing and revival in our land. Let's continue to seek His guidance and trust in His promises, knowing that He is in control and has a plan for our nation.

THE LAST PRESIDENT

The unconscious democracy of America is a very fine thing. It is a true and deep and instinctive assumption of the equality of citizens, which even voting and elections have not destroyed.

—G. K. CHESTERTON, *ILLUSTRATED LONDON NEWS*, JULY 21, 1928

GIVEN THE PROPHETIC warnings from Ingersoll Lockwood, Kim Clement's prophecies, Chuck Pierce's insights, Paul McGuire's remarks, and current events, how should America and Christians respond in the upcoming election?

As many faith leaders, biblical scholars, and experts have asserted, this presidential election is crucial for the future of America, freedom, and liberty. If Vice President Kamala Harris wins, the globalist elite will likely accelerate their plans for the Great Reset and the new world order.

In addition to the Great Reset, the United Nations' Agenda 2030, which is being implemented across the US, is a major threat to liberty.[1] This plan seeks totalitarian control of the planet, including our economy, country, lives, and children.[2]

The Agenda 2030 program is based on the United Nation's Agenda 21 program, which was unveiled in 1992. The plan has 17 sustainable development goals (SDGs), along with 169 specific "targets" to be imposed on humanity. The targets include "universal health coverage," "access to...vaccines for all," and "universal access to sexual and reproductive health-care services, including for family planning [another term for abortion]."[3]

Peter Rykowski, in his article "Agenda 2030 Threatens Liberty—State Legislators Can Stop It," wrote, "It also advocates for socialist indoctrination of youth (Goal 4), global wealth redistribution (Goal 10), and radical actions to combat alleged 'climate change' (Goal 13)." He pointed out the goals are not constitutional. Although the agenda is supposedly nonbinding, it is "being implemented in communities across the United States via 'soft law,' meaning that portions of the agenda are adopted into local, state, and federal laws, thus becoming legally binding."[4]

What's the end game? An infamous World Economic Forum video, "8 Predictions for the World in 2030," features a smiling man and the caption, "You'll own nothing. And you'll be happy."[5]

As a journalist who has been investigating whether the world is moving into the end-times events predicted in Scripture since 2009, it is clear that much of what we've seen recently is preparing the world for the arrival of the Antichrist and the false prophet, who will preside over a totalitarian world government during the seven-year tribulation period.

During this unprecedented time of war, plague, famine, natural disasters, and God's escalating judgments upon the world, at least two-thirds of humanity will perish before Christ returns to defeat the armies of the Antichrist at the battle of Armageddon.

While Jesus said that only God knows the "day or hour" when these events will unfold (Matt. 24:36), He also told us to watch for the signs and be ready (Matt. 24:42–44).

Pastor Paul Begley and I detailed in our book *Revelation 911: How the Book of Revelation Intersects With Today's Headlines* that it's uncanny when you compare the fifty signs of the end times that Jesus and the prophets told us to watch for with today's headlines.[6]

Here are some of those signs:

- Increasing lawlessness and violence (Matt. 24:12)

- Increasing immorality (Matt. 24:37)

- Increasing materialism (2 Tim. 3:2)

- Calling evil good and good evil (Isa. 5:20)

- Signs in the heavens (Luke 21:11, 25)

- Weapons of mass destruction (Luke 21:26)

- Satellite technology (Rev. 11:8–9)

- Rise of Far Eastern military powers (Rev. 9:14–16; 16:12)

- Preaching of the gospel worldwide (Matt. 24:14)

- Movement toward one-world government (Dan. 7:23–26)

Begley was inspired to write *Revelation 911* following an open vision in which the Lord told him, "Revelation 9:11. It's about to happen. Warn the people....The hour is coming. It is upon mankind."[7]

"I really believe the Lord was saying that World War III is about to happen," Begley said. "I saw the letters 'Revelation 911,' just like these [on the cover of the book], bright red, suspended in the air....I went and read it in the Bible....It's about Apollyon, the destroyer, coming out of the bottomless pit, Abaddon, the place of destruction, and that he unleashed upon the earth the hordes of hell. They came as thick as locusts. They came out like smoke, darkness. He released four other fallen angels that were under the river Euphrates, and that then caused the sixth trumpet [judgment]. An angel grabbed the trumpet, sounded the sixth trumpet, which created World War III that killed a third of the world."[8]

Begley continued, "God, I believe, was telling me, 'It's about to happen.'... I feel that we're so close to this that we started writing this book. I got the vision in July of 2021; we started writing before we even [saw] Russia invade Ukraine. Israel's invaded by Hamas, which is basically Iran, China. And at the time of the taping of this interview, Putin was in North Korea...signing a pact that if anybody attacks, he'll attack them and vice versa. I mean, the axis of evil is being formed right before us."[9]

In a recent article, "Project Total Control: Everything Is a Weapon When Totalitarianism Is Normalized," John Whitehead, constitutional attorney and founder of the Rutherford Institute, and Nisha Whitehead, executive director of the Rutherford Institute, wrote that the "U.S. government is working to re-shape the country in the image of a totalitarian state."

> For years now, the government has been bombarding the citizenry with propaganda campaigns and psychological operations aimed at keeping us compliant, easily controlled and supportive of the government's various efforts abroad and domestically.
>
> The government is so confident in its Orwellian powers of manipulation that it's taken to bragging about them. For example, in 2022, the U.S. Army's 4th Psychological Operations Group, the branch of the military responsible for psychological warfare, released a recruiting video that touts its efforts to pull the strings, turn

everything they touch into a weapon, be everywhere, deceive, persuade, change, influence, and inspire.

"Have you ever wondered who's pulling the strings?" the psyops video posits. "Anything we touch is a weapon. We can deceive, persuade, change, influence, inspire. We come in many forms. We are everywhere."[10]

Given what's at stake for the future of America, the world, our children, and our grandchildren, it's vitally important that all Christians register to vote, vote, and pray for God's mercy, intervention, and His will to be done.

ENSURING A FAIR ELECTION

With the controversy around the 2020 presidential election, much effort has been put into securing the election process. Have enough measures been taken to ensure a secure election? While many report that security measures have increased, state officials are still preparing for the voting process, hoping to ensure results can be trusted. One survey found a vast majority of election officials across the nation have increased security since 2020. The Pentagon has engaged research teams from two universities to conduct a three-year risk assessment focused on the vulnerabilities of voting machines.

"We are looking at all the things that could possibly go wrong," says Dr. Natalie Scala, co-director of the Empowering Secure Elections Lab at Towson. "Those could be an actor trying to disrupt something, maybe... trying to break a machine or trying to back vote for somebody who's dead, or things like that."[11]

Despite efforts to ensure election integrity, our hope ultimately rests in Jesus Christ. Christian worship leader Sean Feucht says the "insanity that's going to ensue" during this election "is going to require the people of God to know who they are and to be unshakable. And so I'm believing for America to rise up. I'm believing for a great turnaround. I'm believing for righteousness and justice to prevail. I'm believing for the people of God to vote in America. I'm believing for the church to actually just show up and vote, which would be historic. But we also have to prepare and realize that there are a lot of things between now and then that are going to happen, surprises and twists and turns, and we've got to have our faith on a kingdom that cannot be shaken."[12]

THE IMPORTANCE OF VOTING

In the Bible, we see that we have a dual identity as Christians. We live as children and servants of God and as people under the authority of world leaders established by God.

> But you are a chosen people, a royal priesthood, a holy nation, God's special possession, that you may declare the praises of him who called you out of darkness into his wonderful light. Once you were not a people, but now you are the people of God; once you had not received mercy, but now you have received mercy....
>
> Submit yourselves for the Lord's sake to every human authority: whether to the emperor, as the supreme authority, or to governors, who are sent by him to punish those who do wrong and to commend those who do right. For it is God's will that by doing good you should silence the ignorant talk of foolish people. Live as free people, but do not use your freedom as a cover-up for evil; live as God's slaves. Show proper respect to everyone, love the family of believers, fear God, honor the emperor.
>
> —1 PETER 2:9–10, 13–17

On the show "Are Christians Obligated to Vote?" Pastor John Piper noted that the United States is a republic, a form of self-governance where citizens choose their representatives by voting for them. So the question arises: Are believers required to vote? Is voting a duty of a follower of Jesus? Would it be negligent for a Christian, as a citizen of a free society, not to vote?

Based on 1 Peter 2, Piper says Christians have a "double identity." Christians are a holy nation called the church and therefore are sojourners and exiles in every nation in the world, including the United States. The other part of that double identity involves God's call for believers to submit freely—not because earthly rulers have any final authority over us—to governors and kings, and to do good in these foreign nations where we live, like America, for the glory of God.[13]

What are the implications of this? Here are three.

1. Corporate worship is politically explosive.

"We cast a vote every week by assembling in congregational worship and singing our allegiance to Jesus as Lord over all lords, King over all kings, President over all presidents....Christ-exalting corporate worship is politically the most explosive thing we do. It is absolutely seditious in any regime that presumes to claim ultimate authority or ultimate allegiance over human beings."[14]

2. Christians want to do good works.

"There should be no question that Christians...want to do good for the people and the nation we are part of....So we bless our communities with gospel words and good deeds....Christians do not want to be part of life-ruining problems in society. We want to be a part of life-bettering solutions in society....We want to be a part of helping with the problems....This is why Peter...said that we are to be busy doing good deeds so as (1) to silence those who say Christianity is bad for the world, and (2) to make God look glorious."[15]

3. Voting is a form of good works.

"Voting is one form of doing good....We hope—by voting for worthy, competent, wise candidates—that the common good will come to more people. That's our goal."[16]

The statistics of Christians voting in the elections can improve significantly. Numbers from 2016 show about 61 percent of Christians voted.[17]

As we learned from Jason Yates of My Faith Votes, one in three evangelical Christians doesn't vote consistently. Yates encourages Christians to vote, noting there are many dangers to not voting biblical values, including national security issues.

"We all know about what's happening at the border," Yates said. "We know about potential foreign agents and foreign nations that are threats to us, and that seems to be rising....But when I think biblically, there's a number of things that if we don't get some of this right, if we don't get some of our laws, especially with an increased effort on ballot measures across the nation too that are taking place, especially with abortion, I think the moral landscape, it's sort of a permission to slip, right?

"If we don't get some of these things right, we're essentially writing a permission slip to the nation to just go further into the muck and mire of an amoral culture. And so I really do believe that who we elect to represent us [and pass] laws, and laws are based on moral codes. So if you elect people who have no standing on morals or at least have no agreement with you on morals, then you get what you deserve. Socrates said, 'Nature abhors a vacuum.' In other words, something always replaces nothing. And so, if we create a void of faith, a void of morals in the landscape of elections, then something will fill that."[18]

On top of this, Yates said many Americans have "immediate concerns and we all get it. The inflation is high, the economy, we can look at those things, and yes, those are threats and those create pain, and that is hurting families and hurting people....But I think about a verse in Psalms that says, 'When the foundations are destroyed, what will the righteous do?' And if our moral foundations are destroyed because of who's elected and the laws that they're putting in place, the amendments that they're forcing to our constitutions; if those foundations are destroyed, I'm concerned about the long-term impact of where this nation goes. It won't stand very long."[19]

Yates said they have a formula at My Faith Votes. "We say, 'Pray, think, and act.' I think it's the formula for the Christian life. We come before the Lord, we seek Him, we have a relationship with Him, we open the Word so that we think about the issues biblically, and then we put our faith into action, and we vote, and we do a lot of things, but I think that matters. And so that's my call to people, especially in 2024. Do not sit on the sidelines. Do not let your faith grow idle."[20]

Yates was reading through the Book of Proverbs recently and was struck by Proverbs 18:9.

"The New Living Translation says the lazy person is just as bad as the one who destroys things," Yates said. "And I think about that, and we can look around, we can see some of the stuff that's happening on our college campuses, we can see what happened in Israel, we can see the things where people are destroying each other, they're destroying things. But the Lord says, 'Those who sit idly by, the lazy ones who do nothing, are just as bad.' We can't sit on the sidelines in the elections. We've got to do something. We've got to vote."[21]

THE CALL TO PRAY

In his book *Christendom in Dublin*, author and apologist G. K. Chesterton wrote about attending the World Eucharistic Congress in Dublin in 1932, and then he expounded on politics, in particular democracy, which he defines as "the crowd ruling itself, like a king." He said that only people who believe in God can possibly have a democracy. He points out that self-government leads to freedom, but secular government leads to tyranny.[22]

"Lenin said that religion is the opium of the people," Chesterton wrote. "[But] it is only by believing in God that we can ever criticize the Government. Once abolish the God, and the Government becomes the God. That fact is written all across human history; but it is written most plainly across that recent history of Russia; which was created by Lenin...Lenin only fell into a slight error: he only got it the wrong way round. The truth is that irreligion is the opium of the people. Wherever the people do not believe in something beyond the world, they will worship the world."[23]

Today we have a great choice to make—freedom or tyranny. More than four centuries after the Pilgrims sailed to Plymouth, Massachusetts, aboard the *Mayflower* and dedicated America to "the glory of God, and advancement of the Christian faith," we find ourselves at a crossroads in a divided nation on the verge of judgment.[24]

As Rabbi Jonathan Cahn pointed out in his series of *New York Times* bestselling books beginning with *The Harbinger* in 2012, just as God sent prophets to ancient Israel to warn them of judgment unless they repented and turned from their sinful ways, today God has likewise sent prophets to America, warning that unless we repent and turn from our sinful ways, we will meet the same fate as ancient Israel.

Following the rule of King David in about 1000 BC, the Assyrians invaded in around 722 BC, destroying the northern kingdom of Israel. In 568 BC, the Babylonian Empire conquered Jerusalem and destroyed the temple, which was replaced by the second temple around fifty years later. In the ensuing centuries, the land of modern-day Israel was conquered and ruled by the Persians, Greeks, Romans, and others. In AD 66, the Jews led a revolt and occupied Jerusalem, initiating the first Roman-Jewish war. In AD 70, the Romans reclaimed Jerusalem and destroyed the second temple. Over the next nineteen centuries, the Jews were dispersed around the world until the rebirth of Israel in 1948.[25]

"America is replaying this ancient judgment mystery that happened in the last days of ancient Israel," Cahn said. "All the signs have appeared, and so we are now progressing in it and the template is that we've got a window of time. The Lord gives the nation a window of time to come back to Him, to either repent and go toward revival or to go away from God and head to judgment. We are now in a time where we have increasing signs that the window is coming to a close, and if we don't come back to God, we head to judgment, so this is crucial. America needs revival. It's not just a nice thing. It is the future of America. It's life and death."[26]

A RETURN TO COMMON SENSE

At this critical hour in American history—as we find ourselves deep in debt and on the precipice of economic calamity, with our enemies threatening us with nuclear war, and the wholesale rejection of the biblical values that helped America become one of the greatest experiments in freedom and liberty the world has ever known—the solution is a simple one.

We must humbly ask God to forgive us of our sins, turn back toward righteousness, and return to the Judeo-Christian roots that our ancestors fought and died for so we could enjoy the blessings of freedom and liberty.

In the preamble of "2024 GOP Platform," the authors called for a "return to common sense"—the title of the famous tract by political theorist Thomas Paine, *Common Sense: The Origin and Design of Government*, which inspired the thirteen colonies to fight for and declare independence from Great Britain in the summer of 1776.

Let's read the inspirational opening of the preamble of the Republican National Committee platform:

> Our Nation's History is filled with the stories of brave men and women who gave everything they had to build America into the Greatest Nation in the History of the World. Generations of American Patriots have summoned the American Spirit of Strength, Determination, and Love of Country to overcome seemingly insurmountable challenges. The American People have proven time and

again that we can overcome any obstacle and any force pitted against us.

In the early days of our Republic, the Founding Generation defeated what was then the most powerful Empire the World had ever seen. In the 20th Century, America vanquished Nazism and Fascism, and then triumphed over Soviet Communism after forty-four years of the Cold War.

But now we are a Nation in SERIOUS DECLINE. Our future, our identity, and our very way of life are under threat like never before. Today we must once again call upon the same American Spirit that led us to prevail through every challenge of the past if we are going to lead our Nation to a brighter future.

For decades, our politicians sold our jobs and livelihoods to the highest bidders overseas with unfair Trade Deals and a blind faith in the siren song of globalism. They insulated themselves from criticism and the consequences of their own bad actions, allowing our Borders to be overrun, our cities to be overtaken by crime, our System of Justice to be weaponized, and our young people to develop a sense of hopelessness and despair. They rejected our History and our Values. Quite simply, they did everything in their power to destroy our Country.

In 2016, President Donald J. Trump was elected as an unapologetic Champion of the American People. He reignited the American Spirit and called on us to renew our National Pride. His Policies spurred Historic Economic Growth, Job Creation, and a Resurgence of American Manufacturing. President Trump and the Republican Party led America out of the pessimism induced by decades of failed leadership, showing us that the American People want Greatness for our Country again.

Yet after nearly four years of the Biden administration, America is now rocked by Raging Inflation, Open Borders, Rampant Crime, Attacks on our Children, and Global Conflict, Chaos, and Instability.

Like the Heroes who built and defended this Nation before us, we will never give up. We will restore our Nation of, by, and for the People. We will Make America Great Again.

We will be a Nation based on Truth, Justice, and Common Sense.[27]

HOW TO PRAY FOR AMERICA

As Christians, we are first and foremost called to pray for our country. Here are eight things we can be praying for concerning the upcoming election:

1. "Thank God for our stable and lawful democracy." (See 1 Timothy 2:1–4.)

2. Repent, and "pray that God would bring about the best political outcome," that the gospel of Jesus Christ can be spread and His people won't be distracted by things beyond their control. (See 2 Peter 3:9.)

3. Pray that Christians respect and remember that "rulers are appointed by God and serve as his representatives." (See Romans 13:1, 7.)

4. Pray that government officials would act according to what God mandates. (See 1 Peter 2:13–14.)

5. Pray that Christians would fear God and trust His care of us rather than fear political happenings. (See Luke 12:4–7.)

6. Ask God for "wisdom to know when it is time to disobey or confront godless laws." (See Acts 4:18–20.)

7. Pray that Christians continue aiding and caring for vulnerable people, no matter what government is put in place. (See Galatians 6:9–10.)

8. Turn to Jesus, the real world ruler, asking Him for His purposes to prevail. (See Acts 4:24–26.)[28]

A PIVOTAL MOMENT IN HISTORY

Only God knows how this election and this country will turn out.

As of July 11, 2024, there were reports suggesting that former President Barack Obama and former US House of Representatives Speaker Nancy Pelosi were orchestrating the removal of Biden as the Democratic nominee for president.[29] A little more than a week later, Biden announced that he would not seek reelection. Anything can happen between now and Election Day.

Despite exploring biblical prophecies and the end of days in my books, I've always been an optimist. In America's darkest hours—Revolutionary War, Civil War, Great Depression, World War II, September 11—Americans have summoned an inner divine strength, pulling themselves up by their bootstraps to save the republic.

We find ourselves at a similar moment in world history, with globalism, socialism, and communism threatening to plunge the world into the nightmare described in Revelation.

Is it that time? Only God knows.

I believe He's put the ball in our court. If we pray, repent, and resist the devil's plans, we could see a turnaround in America and the world, with the fire and power of Holy Spirit–inspired revival sweeping across America and the world.

"I absolutely believe that there's going to be an outpouring…[a Joel 2] outpouring that will be transformational in this country," said Rabbi Jonathan Bernis. "And I believe throughout the Western world and beyond, it's coming. I plan to be part of it. Will it so impact the nation that there'll be a turning of policy and put us back on the right road? That I don't know. What I do know is that we're going to see a great influx of people into the kingdom of God….I believe that with all my heart. God is gracious; He's merciful. He's the Lamb of God who takes away the sins of the world. And before the Lion comes—the Lion of Judah, which is a force of destruction—you don't want to face a Lion without knowing the Lamb, right? The Lion represents vengeance and the destruction of the evil forces, the evil people that have railed against the living God.

"I want to see people embrace the Lamb before the Lion comes, and I think we're going to have that great outpouring, and very soon; I think it's already just begun, and that's what I'm living for, my friend, a final outpouring of God's Spirit that will turn many to the Lord and maybe delay God's wrath. But at some point, God's wrath is coming. So I want to just warn people again gently that the time is near, [so] don't miss the opportunity that God is providing for you to find refuge and life and eternity. There's a great way out and up; this life is just a vapor, but eternity is a glorious thing if you make the right decision now in this life, and that's where my heart is."[30]

I believe that's where God's heart is, and where all our hearts should be. He's just waiting for us to rise to the occasion to help bring in what Paul Begley calls the "great harvest revival."

If you think about it, this is one of the most exciting times in history to be a follower of Jesus. He's put all of us here at this particular moment in time when we're watching all these signs of the last days converging and accelerating at an exponential rate.

This could be our finest hour. In Matthew 9:37–38 Jesus told His disciples, "The harvest is plentiful but the workers are few. Ask the Lord of the harvest, therefore, to send out workers into his harvest field."

I'm reminded of my favorite quote from my great-grandfather-plus—poet, playwright, and philosopher Friedrich Schiller, best known for writing the poem "Ode to Joy" that Ludwig van Beethoven set to music in the final movement of Symphony No. 9.

In one of his most critically acclaimed plays, *The Death of Wallenstein*, considered Germany's version of Shakespeare's *King Lear*, Schiller wrote, "There's no such thing as chance; and what to us seems merest accident springs from the deepest source of destiny."[31]

Indeed, as we've learned in *The Trump Code*, exploring the prophetic destiny of the Trump lineage, its links to the curious works of Ingersoll Lockwood's *The Baron Trump Collection*, Donald Trump's connection to the genius of famed inventor Nikola Tesla, along with the prophecies of America's prophetic destiny, Schiller's prescient words echo those of the Master Storyteller who alone knows the destiny of Donald Trump, America, and the world:

> "For I know the plans I have for you," declares the LORD, "plans to prosper you and not to harm you, plans to give you hope and a future."
>
> —JEREMIAH 29:11

ACKNOWLEDGMENTS

I EXTEND MY HEARTFELT appreciation to Stephen and Joy Strang, founders of Charisma Media, for their insightful request to write *The Trump Code*. I am deeply thankful to Debbie Marrie, vice president of product development, and Chad Dunlap, chief operating officer at Charisma Media, for recognizing the profound connections between Ingersoll Lockwood's *The Baron Trump Collection*, Nikola Tesla, President Donald Trump and his family, and the prophetic voices of today, which served as the catalyst for this book.

I'd like to thank Adrienne Gaines, developmental editor at Charisma Media, for her excellent work in editing *The Trump Code*, as well as editor Kimberly Overcast. In addition, I'd like to thank Margarita Henry, marketing director at Charisma Media, along with publicist Jerry McGlothlin, president of Special Guests Inc., and the rest of his team. Further, I'd like to thank publicist A. J. Rice, founder of Publius PR, and his team for their enthusiasm in helping spread the word about *The Trump Code*.

Special gratitude goes to Pastor Paul Begley; his wife, Heidi; and the prayer team led by Chrystal Shields for their unwavering support and prayers throughout this journey. I am grateful to Paul McGuire for his enlightening foreword, and to McGuire, Begley, Sean Feucht, Rabbi Jonathan Bernis, Josh Peck, Marc J. Seifer, and Jason Yates for their insightful interviews and contributions featured in this book.

I'd like to thank Begley, Rabbi Bernis, Dr. Robert Jeffress, Alex Newman, and Jerry Moses for writing endorsements for *The Trump Code*.

I am also deeply grateful to God for my loving wife, Irene, whose encouragement and prayers have been a constant source of strength.

To everyone who has contributed, supported, and inspired along the way, your involvement has been deeply appreciated.

Thank you all for being a part of this journey.

NOTES

FOREWORD

1. Jonathan Cahn Official, "The Mystery Behind The Trump Assassination Attempt | Jonathan Cahn Prophetic," YouTube, July 29, 2024, https://www.youtube.com/watch?v=5vKDJ072oVs.
2. Etymology Online, s.v. "butler (n.)," accessed July 31, 2024, https://www.etymonline.com/word/butler; Anthony McConnell, "What is a Cupbearer?" Anthonymcconnell12, January 29, 2016, https://anthonymcconnell12.wordpress.com/2016/01/29/what-is-a-cupbearer/.

PREFACE

1. Joseph Z, "Prophetic Update—The Shot Heard Around the World!!" YouTube, July 14, 2024, https://www.youtube.com/watch?v=kS_BnuMJm3U.
2. "Read the Transcript of Donald J. Trump's Convention Speech," *The New York Times*, July 19, 2024, https://www.nytimes.com/2024/07/19/us/politics/trump-rnc-speech-transcript.html.
3. "Read the Transcript of Donald J. Trump's Convention Speech," *The New York Times*.
4. "Read the Transcript of Donald J. Trump's Convention Speech," *The New York Times*.
5. CBS News, "Hulk Hogan Calls Trump a 'Real American Hero,' Rips Off Shirt During RNC Speech," YouTube, July 18, 2024, https://www.youtube.com/watch?v=zg9ebwXruOY.
6. CBS News, "Hulk Hogan Calls Trump a 'Real American Hero.'"
7. Charlie McCarthy, "Trump: 'Viewpoint on Life' Changed by Shooting," Newsmax, July 18, 2024, https://www.newsmax.com/newsfront/donald-trump-viewpoint-life/2024/07/18/id/1173062/.

INTRODUCTION

1. Ingersoll Lockwood, *Baron Trump's Marvellous Underground Journey* (Boston: Lee and Shepard, 1893), 2, 22, https://archive.org/details/barontrumpsmarve00lock_0/page/2/mode/2up.
2. Mark Twain, *Following the Equator: A Journey Around the World* (Harper & Brothers, 1899), 137.
3. "The Missing Papers," PBS, accessed July 3, 2024, https://www.pbs.org/tesla/ll/ll_mispapers.html; *Encyclopaedia Britannica*, s.v. "Nikola Tesla," last updated June 16, 2024, https://www.britannica.com/biography/Nikola-Tesla.
4. Ingersoll Lockwood, *1900: or, The Last President* (American News, 1896), 12–13.
5. Emma Parry, "Back to the Future: Time Travel and Anti-Gravity Tech *Is* Possible and Could Be Used to Find Earth-Like Planets, Secret UFO Files Reveal," *The Sun*, April 11, 2022, https://www.the-sun.com/news/5097978/time-travel-anti-gravity-tech-uncovered-us-defense-studies.

CHAPTER 1

1. Lance Wallnau, *God's Chaos Candidate: Donald J. Trump and the American Unraveling* (Killer Sheep Media, 2016).
2. Michelle Fields, "Donald Trump Is the Epitome of the Washington Elite He Claims to Hate," *TIME*, June 27, 2016, https://time.com/4377225/donald-trump-washington-elite.
3. Donald Trump, "Presidential Message on the National Day of Prayer and Return, 2020," Trump White House, September 26, 2020, https://trumpwhitehouse.archives.gov/briefings-statements/presidential-message-national-day-prayer-return-2020.
4. Lawrence Hurley, "Trump's Justices Decisive in Long Campaign to Overturn Roe v. Wade," Reuters, June 24, 2022, https://www.reuters.com/legal/government/trumps-justices-decisive-long-campaign-overturn-roe-v-wade-2022-06-24.
5. Donald Trump, "Presidential Message on Easter, 2020," Trump White House, April 12, 2020, https://trumpwhitehouse.archives.gov/briefings-statements/presidential-message-easter-2020.
6. Lockwood, *Baron Trump's Marvellous Underground Journey*, 2; Ingersoll Lockwood, *Travels and Adventures of Little Baron Trump and His Wonderful Dog Bulger* (Lee and Shephard, 1890), 7.
7. Lockwood, *Baron Trump's Marvellous Underground Journey*, 22.
8. Lockwood, *Baron Trump's Marvellous Underground Journey*, 3–5.
9. Paul McGuire, interview by the author, June 24, 2024.
10. Paul Begley, interview by the author, June 19, 2024.
11. Kim Clement, "Kim Clement Trump Prophecies in 2007 | Prophetic Rewind | House Of Destiny Network," YouTube, November 13, 2022, https://www.youtube.com/watch?v=k5XEQ-RhRqY.
12. Clement, "Kim Clement Trump Prophecies in 2007."
13. Wallnau, *God's Chaos Candidate*, 7.
14. Wallnau, *God's Chaos Candidate*, 30–31.
15. Mark Taylor, "Commander in Chief," S.O.R.D., April 28, 2011, https://www.sordrescue.com/_files/ugd/c20b31_3063fc30c6e6419db41ee383ec15a7ba.pdf.
16. "Philadelphia Experiment," Naval History and Heritage Command, November 20, 2017, https://www.history.navy.mil/research/library/online-reading-room/title-list-alphabetically/p/philadelphia-experiment.html.
17. *Encyclopaedia Britannica*, s.v. "Nikola Tesla."
18. PBD Podcast, "'They'll Erase You' - Super Elites, Invention Secrecy Act, Tesla, UFOs | Dr. Steven Greer | PBD #429," YouTube, June 24, 2024, https://www.youtube.com/watch?v=wnynozKz7Aw.
19. "The Tesla Files," History, accessed July 4, 2024, https://www.history.com/shows/the-tesla-files.
20. Marc J. Seifer, interview by the author, June 21, 2024.
21. McGuire, interview by the author.
22. McGuire, interview by the author.
23. McGuire, interview by the author.
24. Sarah Scoles, "Is Time Travel Possible?," *Scientific American*, April 26, 2023, https://www.scientificamerican.com/article/is-time-travel-possible.
25. Josh Peck, "Biblical Time Travel and the Two Witnesses," *The Prophecy Watcher*, April 2024, 24–27.

26. Benjamin Lynch, "'Baron Trump' Book Theories Resurface About Donald Trump's Son," *Newsweek*, updated January 28, 2024, https://www.newsweek.com/baron-trump-book-conspiracy-theories-1863216.
27. Jonathan Bernis, interview by the author, June 26, 2024.
28. James Lindsay, "Marxism Is a Cult Religion," New Discourses, March 15, 2024, https://newdiscourses.com/2024/03/marxism-is-a-cult-religion; New Discourses, "The Reflexive Alchemy of George Soros," YouTube, April 4, 2024, https://www.youtube.com/watch?v=rI7WT4MdUz0&t=3s.
29. Troy Anderson, "Billy Graham Sounds Alarm for 2nd Coming," WND, October 20, 2013, https://www.wnd.com/2013/10/billy-graham-sounds-alarm-for-2nd-coming.
30. Aaron Blake, "Donald Trump's Strategy in Three Words: 'Americanism, Not Globalism,'" *Washington Post*, July 22, 2016, https://www.washingtonpost.com/news/the-fix/wp/2016/07/22/donald-trump-just-put-his-border-wall-around-the-entire-united-states.
31. Billy Graham, email interview by author, September 6, 2013.
32. Abraham Lincoln, "A Proclamation, For a Day of National Humiliation, Fasting and Prayer," Library of Congress, March 30, 1863, https://www.loc.gov/resource/lprbscsm.scsm0265/?st=text.
33. Paul McGuire and Troy Anderson, *Trumpocalypse: The End-Times President, a Battle Against the Globalist Elite, and the Countdown to Armageddon* (FaithWords, 2018), 271–274.
34. Trump, "Presidential Message on the National Day of Prayer and Return."
35. "National: Most Say Fundamental Rights Under Threat," Monmouth University, June 20, 2023, https://www.monmouth.edu/polling-institute/documents/monmouthpoll_us_062023.pdf.
36. Ariel Edwards-Levy and Jennifer Agiesta, "CNN Flash Poll: Majority of Debate Watchers Say Trump Outperformed Biden," CNN, June 28, 2024, https://www.cnn.com/2024/06/28/politics/debate-poll-cnn-trump-biden/index.html.
37. Stephen Collinson, "Biden's Disastrous Debate Pitches His Reelection Bid Into Crisis," CNN, updated June 28, 2024, https://www.cnn.com/2024/06/28/politics/biden-trump-presidential-debate-analysis/index.html.
38. Michael Gryboski, "Biden Announces He's Dropping Out of the Race, Endorses Kamala Harris," Christian Post, July 21, 2024, https://www.christianpost.com/news/biden-announces-hes-dropping-out-of-the-race-endorses-kamala.html.
39. Gryboski, "Biden Announces He's Dropping Out of the Race."
40. Joey Garrison et al., "Joe Biden Endorses Kamala Harris After He Drops Out of 2024 Election: Recap," *USA Today*, updated July 22, 2024, https://www.usatoday.com/story/news/politics/elections/2024/07/21/joe-biden-drops-out/74255359007.
41. Garrison et al., "Joe Biden Endorses Kamala Harris After He Drops Out of 2024 Election."
42. Bo Erickson, " Harris Holds Onto 1 Point Lead Over Trump in Latest Reuters/Ipsos Poll," Reuters, July 30, 2024, https://www.reuters.com/world/us/harris-trump-locked-tight-us-presidential-race-reutersipsos-poll-finds-2024-07-30.
43. Bill Barrow, "Barack and Michelle Obama Endorse Kamala Harris, Giving Her Expected but Crucial Support," The Associated Press, July 26, 2024, https://apnews.com/article/barack-obama-endorses-kamala-harris-joe-biden-48e38547560ae64484399d278c697a7a. .
44. Sean Feucht, interview by the author, June 26, 2024.

CHAPTER 2

1. "COVID Origins," US House of Representatives Committee on Oversight and Accountability, accessed July 23, 2024, https://oversight.house.gov/landing/covid-origins.

2. The Epoch Times, "The CIA, Biowarfare, and COVID—Dr. Robert Malone's New Book Tells the Truth | Trailer," YouTube, April 24, 2023, https://www.youtube.com/watch?v=Cr8b9DHRhY8.

3. Michael Nevradakis, "'Do Your Job. We Beg of You': FDA Officials Knew of COVID Vaccine Injuries in Early 2021 But Took No Action," Children's Health Defense, May 13, 2024, https://childrenshealthdefense.org/defender/chd-foia-fda-officials-covid-vaccine-injuries-early-2021.

4. Real Life with Jack Hibbs, "Antichrist - Coming Of The Lawless One," YouTube, June 20, 2023, https://www.youtube.com/watch?v=CRk_-DjQN2U&t=126s.

5. James Poulos, "Democracy and Despotism in a Digital Age," American Mind, October 17, 2018, https://americanmind.org/salvo/the-american-mind-online.

6. Klaus Schwab, "Now Is the Time for a 'Great Reset,'" World Economic Forum, June 3, 2020, https://www.weforum.org/agenda/2020/06/now-is-the-time-for-a-great-reset.

7. Geneva Sands, "DHS Shuts Down Disinformation Board Months After Its Efforts Were Paused," CNN, August 24, 2022, https://www.cnn.com/2022/08/24/politics/dhs-disinformation-board-shut-down/index.html.

8. Jack Kelly, "Goldman Sachs Predicts 300 Million Jobs Will Be Lost or Degraded by Artificial Intelligence," *Forbes*, March 31, 2023, https://www.forbes.com/sites/jackkelly/2023/03/31/goldman-sachs-predicts-300-million-jobs-will-be-lost-or-degraded-by-artificial-intelligence.

9. Dan Roberts et al., "Donald Trump Wins Presidential Election, Plunging US Into Uncertain Future," *The Guardian*, November 9, 2016, https://www.theguardian.com/us-news/2016/nov/09/donald-trump-wins-us-election-news.

10. Cristiano Lima, "Trump: If FBI 'Implanted' Officials in My Campaign, It Would Be 'Biggest Political Scandal' in History," Politico, May 18, 2018, https://www.politico.com/story/2018/05/18/trump-boosts-notion-fbi-implanted-official-inside-his-campaign-597529.

11. James Walsh, "'Spygate' Began on Obama's Watch," Newsmax, January 28, 2020, https://www.newsmax.com/jameswalsh/collusion-fbi-fisa-court/2020/01/28/id/951608.

12. Reuters, "Jury: Donald Trump Guilty in N.Y. Trial," Newsmax, May 30, 2024, https://www.newsmax.com/newsfront/trump-hush-money-trial-latest-05-30-2024/2024/05/30/id/1166858/#.

13. Shane Idleman, "After Guilty Verdict, Can Christians Still Support Donald Trump?" Charisma News, June 1, 2024, https://charismanews.com/culture/after-guilty-verdict-can-christians-still-support-donald-trump/.

14. Unnikrishnan Nair, "Trump Impeachment Quotes: 'They Are After You. I'm Just In The Way,'" International Business Times, December 18, 2019, https://www.ibtimes.com/trump-impeachment-quotes-they-are-after-you-im-just-way-2888493.

15. Jeremiah Poff, "FBI Opened Multiple Investigations Into Protesting Parents, GOP Lawmakers Say," Washington Examiner, May 12, 2022, https://www.washingtonexaminer.com/news/2874024/fbi-opened-multiple-investigations-into-protesting-parents-gop-lawmakers-say.

16. Andrea Hsu, "Thousands of Workers Are Opting to Get Fired, Rather Than Take the Vaccine," NPR, October 24, 2021, https://www.npr.org/2021/10/24/1047947268/covid-vaccine-workers-quitting-getting-fired-mandates.

17. Hsu, "Thousands of Workers Are Opting to Get Fired."

18. "Modest Declines in Positive Views of 'Socialism' and 'Capitalism' in U.S.," Pew Research Center, September 19, 2022, https://www.pewresearch.org/politics/2022/09/19/modest-declines-in-positive-views-of-socialism-and-capitalism-in-u-s.

19. Rikki Schlott, "Four Communist Escapees Warn: 'America Is Becoming Authoritarian Nation,'" New York Post, updated April 2, 2022, https://nypost.com/2022/04/02/america-is-becoming-authoritarian-nation-communist-escapees.

20. David Kopel, "Data on Mass Murder by Government in the 20th Century," Reason, November 9, 2022, https://reason.com/volokh/2022/11/09/data-on-mass-murder-by-government-in-the-20th-century.

21. McGuire, interview by the author.

22. Ali Vitali, "Trump Signs 'Religious Liberty' Executive Order Allowing for Broad Exemptions," NBC News, updated May 4, 2017, https://www.nbcnews.com/news/us-news/trump-signs-religious-liberty-executive-order-allowing-broad-exemptions-n754786.

23. McGuire, interview by the author.

24. "National: Public Troubled by 'Deep State,'" Monmouth University, March 19, 2018, https://www.monmouth.edu/polling-institute/documents/monmouthpoll_us_031918.pdf.

25. "National: Public Troubled by 'Deep State,'" Monmouth University.

26. "National: Public Troubled by 'Deep State,'" Monmouth University.

27. Franklin Graham, "Did God show up?," Facebook, November 10, 2016, https://www.facebook.com/permalink.php?story_fbid=pfbid02hVBjGCA7m1tExNLipziWeRR9HzrC7Q9G6jiNzs4fAPauSKtTGEciraeHEgMKVT6Tl&id=131201286936061.

28. Donald Trump, "The Inaugural Address," quoted as delivered, Trump White House, January 20, 2017, https://trumpwhitehouse.archives.gov/briefings-statements/the-inaugural-address.

29. James Poulos, "The Digital Geopolitics of Spiritual War," Succulent, October 23, 2023, https://www.succulent.vision/p/the-digital-geopolitics-of-spiritual.

30. Poulos, "The Digital Geopolitics of Spiritual War."

31. Abby Trivett, "5 Ways AI Is Summoning the Antichrist Agenda," Charisma News, March 12, 2024, https://charismanews.com/news/us/5-ways-ai-is-summoning-the-antichrist-agenda.

32. Dallas Willard, "Disappearance of Moral Knowledge—And It's Recovery by Christ Followers!" Dallas Willard Ministries, https://dwillard.org/resources/articles/disappearance-of-moral-knowledge-and-its-recovery-by-christ-followers.

33. Willard, "Disappearance of Moral Knowledge."

34. Willard, "Disappearance of Moral Knowledge."

35. New Discourses, "You Need to Love the Truth," YouTube, March 25, 2024, https://www.youtube.com/watch?v=8GXEHXM9uuc.

CHAPTER 3

1. Dan Snierson and James Mercadante, "20 Times *The Simpsons* Predicted the Future," *Entertainment Weekly*, updated July 10, 2024, https://ew.com/simpsons-predictions-that-came-true-8662708.

2. Cooper Hood, "Which Simpsons Episode Predicted President Donald Trump," Screen Rant, January 23, 2020, https://screenrant.com/simpsons-donald-trump-president-prediction-episode-bart-future.

3. Jack Hobbs, "'The Simpsons' Predicted Donald Trump's 2024 Presidential Run in 2015," *New York Post*, updated November 16, 2022, https://nypost.com/2022/11/16/the-simpsons-predicted-donald-trumps-2024-presidential-run-in-2015/.

4. Sinead Garvan, "The Simpsons: How the Show's Writers Predict the Future," BBC, July 19, 2019, https://www.bbc.com/news/newsbeat-49031845.

5. G. K. Chesterton, *The Everlasting Man* (Hodder and Stoughton, 1925), 116.

6. "10 Ways Science Fiction Predicted the Future," BBC, accessed July 11, 2024, https://www.bbc.co.uk/teach/live-lessons/articles/z6dynrd#.

7. Chris Long, "The Machine Stops: Did EM Forster Predict the Internet Age?," BBC, May 18, 2016, https://www.bbc.com/news/entertainment-arts-36289890.

8. Carl Kelsch, "Sarah Pinsker, Author of 'Song for a New Day,' on Predicting the Pandemic in Her 2019 Novel," Marie Claire, May 29, 2020, https://www.marieclaire.com/culture/a32632422/sarah-pinsker-song-for-a-new-day-book-predicted-pandemic.

9. "Mission: Impossible—Dead Reckoning Part One Plot," IMDB, accessed July 11, 2024, https://www.imdb.com/title/tt9603212/plotsummary.

10. Candice Frederick, "'Mission: Impossible—Dead Reckoning Part One' Treats AI As the Threat That It Is," HuffPost, July 12, 2023, https://www.huffpost.com/entry/mission-impossible-dead-reckoning-part-one-review-ai-threat_n_64adab24e4b07252cc1499d6.

11. Marah Eakin, "Mission: Impossible—Dead Reckoning Is the Perfect AI Panic Movie," *Wired*, July 12, 2023, https://www.wired.com/story/mission-impossible-dead-reckoning-is-the-perfect-ai-panic-movie.

12. Eakin, "Mission: Impossible."

13. Begley, interview by the author.

14. Begley, interview by the author.

15. Joanna J. Bryson, "The Future of AI's Impact on Society," *Technology Review*, December 18, 2019, https://www.technologyreview.com/2019/12/18/102365/the-future-of-ais-impact-on-society.

16. Bryson, "The Future of AI's Impact on Society."

17. Rory Cellan-Jones, "Stephen Hawking Warns Artificial Intelligence Could End Mankind," BBC, December 2, 2014, https://www.bbc.com/news/technology-30290540.

18. Eric Mack, "Elon Musk: 'We Are Summoning the Demon' With Artificial Intelligence," CNET, October 26, 2014, https://www.cnet.com/science/elon-musk-we-are-summoning-the-demon-with-artificial-intelligence.

19. Perry Stone, *Artificial Intelligence Versus God: The Final Battle for Humanity* (Voice of Evangelism Ministries, 2023), 7.

20. "Goldman Sachs: 300 Million Jobs Could Be Affected by AI," CBS News, March 30, 2023, https://www.cbsnews.com/sacramento/news/goldman-sachs-300-million-jobs-could-be-affected-by-ai.

21. Billy Hallowell, "Is Explosion of Artificial Intelligence a Threat to the Bible, Morality?," Charisma News, May 21, 2024, https://charismanews.com/is-explosion-of-artificial-intelligence-a-threat-to-the-bible-morality.

22. Billy Hallowell, "Apologist Speaks on Dangers, Uncertainties Surrounding Artificial Intelligence: 'Determining Our Future and Manipulating Us Along the Way,'" FaithWire, June 16, 2023, https://www.faithwire.com/2023/06/16/apologist-speaks-on-dangers-uncertainties-surrounding-artificial-intelligence-determining-our-future-and-manipulating-us-along-the-way.

23. Hallowell, "Apologist Speaks on Dangers."

24. Stone, *Artificial Intelligence Versus God*, 6.

25. Stone, *Artificial Intelligence Versus God*, 30–31.

26. Steve Warren, "World Economic Forum Contributor Says A.I. Could Rewrite the Bible, Create 'Correct' Religions," CBN News, June 16, 2023, https://www2.cbn.com/news/world/world-economic-forum-contributor-says-ai-could-rewrite-bible-create-correct-religions; Kirsten Grieshaber, "Can a Chatbot Preach a Good Sermon? Hundreds Attend Church Service Generated by ChatGPT to Find Out," June 10, 2023, https://apnews.com/article/germany-church-protestants-chatgpt-ai-sermon-651f21c24cfb47e3122e987a7263d348; James Lasher, "New 'AI-Generated Ouija Board' Aims to Converse With the Dead," Charisma News, May 25, 2023, https://charismanews.com/news/world/new-ai-generated-ouija-board-aims-to-converse-with-the-dead/.

27. Wikipedia, s.v. "Hugo de Garis," last edited July 1, 2024, https://en.wikipedia.org/wiki/Hugo_de_Garis.

28. Hugo de Garis, *The Artilect War: Cosmists vs. Terrans: A Bitter Controversy Concerning Whether Humanity Should Build Godlike Massively Intelligent Machines* (ETC, 2005), 1.

29. George M. Coghill, "Artificial Intelligence (and Christianity): Who? What? Where? When? Why? and How?," *Studies in Christian Ethics* 36, no. 3 (2023): 604–619, https://doi.org/10.1177/09539468231169462.

30. Thomas Horn, Joe Horn, and Allie Anderson, *Summoning the Demon: Artificial Intelligence and the Image of the Beast* (Defender Publishing, 2024), 1–2.

31. Anna Tong, "AI Threatens Humanity's Future, 61% of Americans Say: Reuters/Ipsos Poll," Reuters, May 17, 2023, https://www.reuters.com/technology/ai-threatens-humanitys-future-61-americans-say-reutersipsos-2023-05-17.

32. Horn, Horn, and Anderson, *Summoning the Demon*, 2.

33. Alex Wilkins, "AI Forecaster Can Predict the Future Better Than Humans," New Scientist, March 26, 2024, https://www.newscientist.com/article/2424121-ai-forecaster-can-predict-the-future-better-than-humans.

34. Cami Rosso, "Can AI Predict Humanity's Future Events?" *Psychology Today*, November 23, 2019, https://www.psychologytoday.com/us/blog/the-future-brain/201911/can-ai-predict-humanitys-future-events.

35. Rehan Mirza, "How AI Deepfakes Threaten the 2024 Elections," Journalist's Resource, February 16, 2024, https://journalistsresource.org/home/how-ai-deepfakes-threaten-the-2024-elections; "Science & Tech Spotlight: Deepfakes," Government Accountability Office, February 2020, https://www.gao.gov/assets/gao-20-379sp.pdf.

36. Mirza, "How AI Deepfakes Threaten the 2024 Elections."

37. Mirza, "How AI Deepfakes Threaten the 2024 Elections."

38. "How Worried Should You Be About AI Disrupting Elections?," *The Economist*, August 31, 2023, http://web.archive.org/web/20240201025836/https://www.economist.com/leaders/2023/08/31/how-artificial-intelligence-will-affect-the-elections-of-2024.

39. Jason Yates, interview by the author, May 14, 2024.

40. Yates, interview by the author.

41. "Ways You Can Act Now," My Faith Votes, accessed July 11, 2024, https://www.myfaithvotes.org/ways-to-act-now.

42. "'My Faith Votes' Launches 'Think Biblically' Video Series Designed to Bring Biblical Clarity to Christians Ahead of November Election," My Faith Votes, June 5, 2024, https://www.myfaithvotes.org/press-release/my-faith-votes-launches-think-biblically-video-series-design-to-bring-biblical-clarity-to-christians-ahead-of-november-election.

43. Yates, interview by the author.

44. Thomas Jefferson, "Jefferson's Letter to the Danbury Baptists," Library of Congress, January 1, 1802, https://www.loc.gov/loc/lcib/9806/danpre.html.

45. Mia Nelson, "Opinion: Most Americans Have a Misunderstanding of 'Separation of Church and State,'" *Liberty Champion*, March 22, 2021, https://www.liberty.edu/champion/2021/03/opinion-most-americans-have-a-misunderstanding-of-separation-of-church-and-state; Kimberly Felton, "The Truth About Separation of Church and State," *George Fox Journal*, Spring 2009, https://www.georgefox.edu/journalonline/spring09/rethinking.html.

46. Yates, interview by the author.

47. Paul Begley, "'Avi Lipkin' The Coming Apocalypse (Middle East Analysis)," YouTube, September 6, 2016, https://www.youtube.com/watch?v=6EJvjW4yRg4.

48. Begley, interview by the author.

49. Begley, interview by the author.

50. McGuire, interview by the author.

51. Oren Oppenheim, "Kamala Harris Earns Majority of Democratic Roll Call Votes, Achieving Historic Presidential Nomination," ABC News, August 6, 2024, https://abcnews.go.com/Politics/kamala-harris-nominee-DNC-majority-democratic-roll-call-votes/story?id=112580918.

52. Louis Jacobson, "Trump v. Biden 2024: Handicapping the Presidential Election," *U.S. News & World Report*, June 18, 2024, https://www.usnews.com/news/elections/articles/2024-06-18/trump-v-biden-2024-handicapping-the-presidential-election.

53. Elizabeth Beyer, "Meet Allan Lichtman, the Professor Who Predicted the President (and the Last 9)," *USA Today*, May 8, 2024, https://www.usatoday.com/story/news/politics/elections/2024/05/08/allan-lichtman-2024-election-professor-predicted-president/73613080007.

54. Jillian Smith, "Presidential Predictor Allan Lichtman Tells Democrats After Biden Drops Out: 'Get Smart and Unite,'" Fox 5, July 21, 2024, https://www.fox5dc.com/news/presidential-predictor-allan-lichtman-tells-democrats-after-biden-drops-out-get-smart-unite.

55. Tim Gombis, "Cruciformity & Christian Leadership," Faith Improvised, November 21, 2021, https://timgombis.com/2011/11/21/cruciformity-christian-leadership.

Chapter 4

1. Chris Riotta, "Did an Author From the 1800s Predict the Trumps, Russia and America's Downfall?," *Newsweek*, updated July 31, 2017, https://www.newsweek.com/donald-trump-predicted-ingersoll-lockwood-adventures-barron-melania-last-644284.

2. David Moye, "Internet Freaks Over 19th-Century Books Featuring Boy Named 'Baron Trump,'" HuffPost, August 1, 2017, https://www.huffpost.com/archive/au/entry/baron-trump-time-travel-books_au_5cd364eee4b0acea95000f4f.

3. Jessilyn Lancaster, "Did a Novelist From the 1800s Warn Us Donald Trump Would Be 'The Last President'?" Charisma News, August 7, 2017, https://www.charismanews.com/politics/opinions/did-a-novelist-from-the-1800s-warn-us-donald-trump-would-be-the-last-president.

4. Jessica Fin, "Spooky! Forgotten 19th Century Novels Feature the 'Marvellous' Adventures of a Boy Named Baron Trump Who Has a Mentor Named Don and Embarks on a Trip to Russia," *Daily Mail*, updated August 2, 2017, https://www.dailymail.co.uk/news/article-4754000/Late-1800-s-books-spooky-connections-present-day-Trumps.html.

5. Google search for "Snopes," accessed July 8, 2024, https://www.google.com/search?q=snopes.

6. Don Evon, "Is 'Baron Trump's Marvelous Underground Journey' a Real Book From the 1890s?" Snopes, August 1, 2017, https://www.snopes.com/fact-check/baron-trumps-marvelous-underground-journey.

7. Liz Martin, Brandon Vallorani, and Ingersoll Lockwood, *The 1896 Prophecies: 10 Predictions of America's Last Days* (Fidelis Books, 2023).

8. Lynch, "'Baron Trump' Book Theories Resurface About Donald Trump's Son."

9. Frederic A. Holden and E. Dunbar Lockwood, *Descendants of Robert Lockwood: Colonial and Revolutionary History of the Lockwood Family in America From A.D. 1630* (Printed privately, 1889), 552–553, 702–704; "Ingersoll Lockwood Lawyer," *The New York Times*, October 3, 1918, https://timesmachine.nytimes.com/timesmachine/1918/10/03/98271682.pdf.

10. "Ingersoll Lockwood Lawyer," *The New York Times*.

11. "Each Divorced, Both Married: Ingersoll Lockwood's Former Wife Become Mrs. Edward Johnes," *Courier-Journal*, October 25, 1892, https://www.newspapers.com/article/the-courier-journal-winifreds-divorce/3857323/.

12. Lockwood, *Baron Trump's Marvellous Underground Journey*, v–vi.

13. Lockwood, *Baron Trump's Marvellous Underground Journey*, 1–2.

14. Lockwood, *Baron Trump's Marvellous Underground Journey*, 5.

15. Lockwood, *Baron Trump's Marvellous Underground Journey*, 7–8.

16. Lockwood, *1900*, 3.

17. Lockwood, *1900*, 5, 16.

18. Lockwood, *1900*, 7–8.

19. James Griffiths, "Trump to Become First Foreign Leader to Dine in Forbidden City Since Founding of Modern China," CNN, updated November 8, 2017, https://www.cnn.com/2017/11/07/politics/trump-forbidden-city-beijing-china/index.html; Eric Levenson and Noah Gray, "Trump, White House Officials Bounce Along to Saudi Sword Dance," CNN, updated May 21, 2017, https://www.cnn.com/2017/05/20/politics/trump-saudi-arabia-dance/index.html; "Soccer Diplomacy: World Cup Host

Putin Gives Trump a Ball," Associated Press, July 16, 2018, https://www.apnews.com/article/be6ee820217b4cb6b26a4f059cf42696.

20. "Presidential Debate 2020: Why Abraham Lincoln Starred in the Final Clash," BBC, October 23, 2020, https://www.bbc.com/news/election-us-2020-54657024; Paul Bond, "Dinesh D'Souza to Compare Trump With Lincoln in Upcoming Film," Hollywood Reporter, June 11, 2018, https://www.hollywoodreporter.com/movies/movie-news/dinesh-dsouza-compare-trump-lincoln-upcoming-film-1118718.

21. Lancaster, "Did a Novelist From the 1800s Warn Us Donald Trump Would Be 'The Last President'?"

22. Bible Hub, "2332. Chavvah," accessed July 9, 2024, https://biblehub.com/hebrew/2332.htm.

23. "Meaning of the First Name Donald," Ancestry.com, https://www.ancestry.com/first-name-meaning/donald.

24. "Trump Family History," Ancestry.com, accessed July 9, 2024, https://www.ancestry.com/name-origin?surname=trump.

25. Rob Poindexter, "Kim Clement Prophesying About Donald Trump 2007," YouTube, November 24, 2016, https://www.youtube.com/watch?v=eFfFtq1fljY.

26. "Ingersoll Family History," Ancestry.com, accessed July 9, 2024, https://www.ancestry.com/name-origin?surname=ingersoll; "Lockwood Family History," Ancestry.com, accessed July 9, 2024, https://www.ancestry.com/name-origin?surname=lockwood.

27. Mordechai Rubin, "What Is Gematria?" Chabad, accessed July 9, 2024. https://www.chabad.org/library/article_cdo/aid/5541252/jewish/Everything-You-Need-to-Know-About-Gematria.htm.

28. "Donald Trump Value in Gematria Is 589," Gematrix, accessed July 9, 2024, https://www.gematrix.org/?word=Donald+Trump; "Gematria Calculator for 589," Gematrix, accessed July 9, 2024, https://www.gematrix.org/?word=589.

29. "Ingersoll Lockwood Value in Gematria Is 1408," Gematrix, accessed July 9, 2024, https://www.gematrix.org/?word=ingersoll+lockwood; "Gematria Calculator for 1408," Gematrix, accessed July 9, 2024, https://www.gematrix.org/?word=1408.

30. Bob Ortega et al., "What Trump's War on the 'Deep State' Could Mean: 'An Army of Suck-Ups,'" CNN, updated April 27, 2024, https://www.cnn.com/2024/04/27/politics/trump-federal-workers-2nd-term-invs/index.html.

31. Kevin. D. Roberts, "Taking On the New 'Big Government,'" Heritage Foundation, May 17, 2023, https://www.heritage.org/conservatism/commentary/taking-the-new-big-government.

32. Blue Letter Bible, s.v. "'aḇrām," accessed July 9, 2024, https://www.blueletterbible.org/lexicon/h87/kjv/wlc/0-1/; Blue Letter Bible, s.v. "'aḇrāhām," accessed July 9, 2024, https://www.blueletterbible.org/lexicon/h85/kjv/wlc/0-1/.

33. Ingersoll Lockwood, *Laconics of Cult* (Ingersoll Lockwood, 1910), 1.

34. Sunday Cool, "TIME LORDS? Investigating Trump & Family's Alleged Time Travel Abilities! | Ninjas Are Butterflies," YouTube, April 13, 2024, https://www.youtube.com/watch?v=D7Y32lyE5c4

35. Nicholas Goodrick-Clarke, *The Occult Roots of Nazism: Secret Aryan Cults and Their Influence on Nazi Ideology* (NYU Press, 1993), 10.

36. Karl Marx, "The Union of Believers With Christ According to John 15: 1-14, Showing Its Basis and Essence, Its Absolute Necessity, and Its Effects," Marxists Internet Archive, 1835, https://marxists.architexturez.net/archive/marx/works/1837-pre/marx/1835chris.htm.

37. Karl Marx, "Wild Songs: The Fiddler," Marxists Internet Archive, accessed July 9, 2024, https://www.marxists.org/archive/marx/works/1837-pre/verse/verse4.htm.

CHAPTER 5

1. Gary Stearman, *Time Travelers of the Bible: How Hebrew Prophets Shattered the Barries of Time-Space* (Defender, 2011), 30.
2. Ron Allen, "Does the Book of Enoch Offer Important Insight Into God's Prophetic Calendar?" Charisma News, April 3, 2019, https://www.charismanews.com/opinion/does-the-book-of-enoch-offer-important-insight-into-god-s-prophetic-calendar.
3. Joseph B. Lumpkin, *The Books of Enoch: The Angels, The Watchers, and The Nephilim* (Fifth Estate Publishers, 2011), 12.
4. Lumpkin, *The Books of Enoch*, 12.
5. Stearman, *Time Travelers of the Bible*, 33–34.
6. Phil Hornshaw, "'A Wrinkle in Time': What Is a Tesseract, and Why Does It Sound Familiar?," The Wrap, March 8, 2018, https://www.thewrap.com/wrinkle-time-tesseract-sound-familiar.
7. Hornshaw, "'A Wrinkle in Time.'"
8. Paul M. Sutter, "What Are Wormholes, and Could They Be the Answer to Time Travel?," *Discover*, July 26, 2023, https://www.discovermagazine.com/the-sciences/what-are-wormholes-and-could-they-be-the-answer-to-time-travel.
9. Sutter, "What Are Wormholes."
10. *Encyclopaedia Britannica*, s.v. "Transfiguration," accessed July 9, 2024, https://www.britannica.com/topic/Transfiguration-Christianity.
11. Herbert W. Basser, "The Jewish Roots of the Transfiguration," Biblical Archaeology Society, June 1998, https://library.biblicalarchaeology.org/article/the-jewish-roots-of-the-transfiguration.
12. Josh Peck, interview by author, June 7, 2024.
13. Michael Marshall, "Is Time Travel Really Possible? Here's What Physics Says," BBC, November 12, 2023, https://www.bbc.com/future/article/20231110-doctor-who-is-time-travel-really-possible-heres-what-physics-says.
14. Marshall, "Is Time Travel Really Possible?"
15. Marshall, "Is Time Travel Really Possible?"
16. Shannon Corbeil, "This Is the Truth Behind WWII's Creepy Philadelphia Experiment," We Are the Mighty, updated October 30, 2020, https://www.wearethemighty.com/mighty-history/philadelphia-experiment-military-conspiracy-theories/; *Encyclopaedia Britannica*, s.v. "Unified Field Theory," accessed June 15, 2024, https://www.britannica.com/science/unified-field-theory; Nick Redfern, *Cover-Ups & Secrets: The Complete Guide to Government Conspiracies, Manipulations & Deceptions* (Visible Ink Press, 2019), 393–403.
17. Corbeil, "This Is the Truth Behind WWII's Creepy Philadelphia Experiment."
18. Redfern, *Cover-Ups & Secrets*, 394.
19. Redfern, *Cover-Ups & Secrets*, 394.
20. Corbeil, "This Is the Truth Behind WWII's Creepy Philadelphia Experiment."
21. Joe Nickell, "Solving a UFOlogical 'Murder': The Case of Morris K. Jessup," Skeptical Inquirer, September/October 2021, https://skepticalinquirer.org/2021/08/solving-a-ufological-murder-the-case-of-morris-k-jessup.

22. William L. Moore and Charles Berlitz, *The Philadelphia Experiment: Project Invisibility* (Fawcett Crest, 1979), 15.
23. Nickell, "Solving a UFOlogical 'Murder.'"
24. "Philadelphia Experiment: Office of Naval Research Information Sheet," Naval History and Heritage Command, September 2, 2016, https://www.history.navy. mil/research/library/online-reading-room/title-list-alphabetically/p/philadelphia-experiment/philadelphia-experiment-onr-info-sheet.html.
25. Gideon Lewis-Kraus, "How the Pentagon Started Taking U.F.O.s Seriously," *The New Yorker*, April 20, 2021, https://www.newyorker.com/magazine/2021/05/10/how-the-pentagon-started-taking-ufos-seriously; "UFO/UAP Disclosure Press Conference," National Press Club, accessed July 10, 2024, https://www.press.org/events/ufouap-disclosure-press-conference; ABC News, "Group Calls for Disclosure of UFO Info," ABC News, May 9, 2001, https://abcnews.go.com/Technology/story?id=98572&page=1; Dr. Steven Greer, "2001 National Press Club Event (Presented by Dr. Steven Greer)," YouTube, April 24, 2017, https://www.youtube.com/watch?v=4DrcG7VGgQU&list=PLv0p0OLJ9MFykh0JpxvJR0MRV5SqglAeQ&index=.
26. Lewis-Kraus, "How the Pentagon Started Taking U.F.O.s Seriously."
27. PBD Podcast, "'They'll Erase You.'"
28. PBD Podcast, "'They'll Erase You.'"
29. PBD Podcast, "'They'll Erase You.'"
30. PBD Podcast, "'They'll Erase You.'"
31. PBD Podcast, "'They'll Erase You.'"
32. PBD Podcast, "'They'll Erase You.'"
33. PBD Podcast, "'They'll Erase You.'"
34. Hugh Ross, interview by the author, April 26, 2023.
35. Ross, interview by the author.
36. Courtney Kennedy and Arnold Lau, "Most Americans Believe in Intelligent Life Beyond Earth; Few See UFOs as a Major National Security Threat," Pew Research Center, June 30, 2021, https://www.pewresearch.org/short-reads/2021/06/30/most-americans-believe-in-intelligent-life-beyond-earth-few-see-ufos-as-a-major-national-security-threat.
37. Monroe Institute of Applied Sciences, "Gateway Intermediate Workbook," CIA, 1977, https://www.cia.gov/readingroom/docs/CIA-RDP96-00788R001700210023-7.pdf.
38. Thobey Campion, "How to Escape the Confines of Time and Space According to the CIA," Vice, February 16, 2021, https://www.vice.com/en/article/7k9qag/how-to-escape-the-confines-of-time-and-space-according-to-the-cia.
39. Campion, "How to Escape the Confines of Time and Space According to the CIA."
40. Susan Lahey, "The CIA's Secret Plan to Build a Laser Beam Powered by the Human Mind," *Popular Mechanics*, updated May 30, 2023, http://web.archive.org/web/20240229162118/https://www.popularmechanics.com/science/a43418400/cia-gateway-process-explained.
41. "Wizard: The Life and Times of Nikola Tesla," *Publishers Weekly*, accessed July 10, 2024, https://www.publishersweekly.com/9781559723299.
42. Jessica Coulon, "Did the U.S. Government Really Steal Nikola Tesla's Research Papers?," *Popular Mechanics*, June 14, 2023, https://www.popularmechanics.com/science/energy/a44197280/did-the-us-government-steal-nikola-teslas-research.

43. Matt Novak, "Nikola Tesla's Amazing Predictions for the 21st Century," *Smithsonian*, April 19, 2013, https://www.smithsonianmag.com/history/nikola-teslas-amazing-predictions-for-the-21st-century-26353702.

44. Coulon, "Did the U.S. Government Really Steal Nikola Tesla's Research Papers?"

45. Coulon, "Did the U.S. Government Really Steal Nikola Tesla's Research Papers?"

46. Marc J. Seifer, *Wizard: The Life and Times of Nikola Tesla: Biography of a Genius* (Citadel Press, 1998), 453.

47. Seifer, *Wizard*, 454–455.

48. Coulon, "Did the U.S. Government Really Steal Nikola Tesla's Research Papers?"

49. Sarah Pruitt, "The Mystery of Nikola Tesla's Missing Files," History, updated June 1, 2023, https://www.history.com/news/nikola-tesla-files-declassified-fbi.

CHAPTER 6

1. Griffiths, "Trump to Become First Foreign Leader to Dine in Forbidden City Since Founding of Modern China."

2. Levenson and Gray, "Trump, White House Officials Bounce Along to Saudi Sword Dance."

3. Laura Sigal, "North Korea Threatens Israel With 'Merciless, Thousand-Fold Punishment,'" *Jerusalem Post*, April 29, 2017, https://www.jpost.com/israel-news/north-korea-threatens-israel-with-merciless-thousand-fold-punishment-489316.

4. Josh Lederman and Hans Nichols, "Trump Meets Kim Jong Un, Becomes First Sitting U.S. President to Step Into North Korea," NBC News, updated June 30, 2019, https://www.nbcnews.com/politics/donald-trump/trump-kim-jong-un-meet-dmz-n1025041.

5. Associated Press, "North Korea's Kim Jong Un Orders Military to 'Thoroughly Annihilate' U.S. If Provoked, State Media Say," CBS News, January 1, 2024, https://www.cbsnews.com/news/north-korea-kim-jong-un-us-missile-tests-threat-nuclear-war.

6. Michael L. Brown, "Enough Already With the Pro-Trump Prophecies!," *Charisma*, January 9, 2024, https://mycharisma.com/propheticrevival/enough-already-with-the-pro-trump-prophecies.

7. Julia Duin, "The Christian Prophets Who Say Trump Is Coming Again," Politico, February 18, 2021, https://www.politico.com/news/magazine/2021/02/18/how-christian-prophets-give-credence-to-trumps-election-fantasies-469598.

8. "National: Most Say Fundamental Rights Under Threat," Monmouth University.

9. John Hagee, ed., *Prophecy Study Bible* (Thomas Nelson, 1997), 1402.

10. Hagee, *Prophecy Study Bible*, 1402–1403.

11. Strang Report, "What God Revealed About Donald Trump | Troy Black Prophecy," YouTube, June 18, 2024, https://www.youtube.com/watch?v=wwZwbPlzNQ4.

12. Strang Report, "What God Revealed About Donald Trump."

13. Clement, "Kim Clement Trump Prophecies in 2007."

14. "Lance Wallnau: Why Trump Is 'God's Chaos Candidate' and 'Wrecking Ball,'" CBN News, March 21, 2017, https://www2.cbn.com/news/us/lance-wallnau-why-trump-gods-chaos-candidate-and-wrecking-ball.

15. "Lance Wallnau," CBN News.

16. Josh Hafner, "Meet the Evangelicals Who Prophesied a Trump Win," *USA Today*, updated November 11, 2016, https://www.usatoday.com/story/news/nation-now/2016/11/10/meet-evangelicals-prophesied-trump-win/93575144/.

17. Taylor, "Commander in Chief"; Mark Taylor, "Do Not Fear America," S.O.R.D., February 24, 2016, https://www.sordrescue.com/_files/ugd/c20b31_90b7273aab984ed 1a0766063ab7203d6.pdf.

18. Deepa Shivaram, "Biden Says the Next President May Get to Name Two Supreme Court Justices," WGBH, June 17 ,2024, https://www.wgbh.org/news/ national/2024-06-17/biden-says-the-next-president-may-get-to-name-two-supreme-court-justices.

19. Strang Report, "Defending Authentic Faith: Steve Strang and Mario Murillo on Battling False Prophecy," YouTube, August 16, 2023, https://www.youtube.com/ watch?v=ZEjxeaT7hs4.

20. Mario Murillo, *It's Our Turn Now: God's Plan to Restore America Is Within Our Reach* (Charisma House, 2023), 1–2.

21. Billy Graham, "In His Own Words: Billy Graham on End Times," Billy Graham Evangelistic Association, September 8, 2017, https://billygrahamlibrary.org/in-his-own-words-billy-graham-on-end-times.

22. Graham, "In His Own Words."

23. John Bevere, *Thus Saith the Lord: How to Know When God is Speaking to You Through Another* (Charisma House, 1999), 141.

24. Bevere, *Thus Saith the Lord*, 142.

25. Bevere, *Thus Saith the Lord*, 144.

26. Strang Report, "Defending Authentic Faith."

27. Strang Report, "Defending Authentic Faith."

28. Strang Report, "Defending Authentic Faith."

29. Strang Report, "Defending Authentic Faith."

30. Strang Report, "Defending Authentic Faith."

31. Wikipedia, s.v. "dialectic," last edited April 3, 2024, https://en.wikipedia.org/wiki/ Dialectic.

32. New Discourses, "The Reflexive Alchemy of George Soros."

33. New Discourses, "The Reflexive Alchemy of George Soros."

34. New Discourses, "The Reflexive Alchemy of George Soros."

35. New Discourses, "The Reflexive Alchemy of George Soros"; Schwab, "Now Is the Time for a 'Great Reset.'"

CHAPTER 7

1. Chuck D. Pierce and Rebecca Wagner Sytsema, *Possessing Your Inheritance: Take Hold of God's Destiny for Your Life* (Chosen, 2009), 170.

2. Francis Frangipane, *Holiness, Truth, and the Presence of God* (Charisma House, 2011), 60.

3. Frangipane, *Holiness*, 60–61.

4. Frangipane, *Holiness*, 61.

5. Frangipane, *Holiness*, 61–62.

6. Steven Lawson, "What Is Truth?" Ligonier, September 1, 2010, https://www. ligonier.org/learn/articles/what-is-truth.

7. Lawson, "What Is Truth?"

8. Lawson, "What Is Truth?"

9. Mark Virkler, "How the Bible Teaches Us to Discover Truth," Charisma, June 16, 2022, https://mycharisma.com/spiritled-living/spiritual-warfare/how-the-bible-teaches-us-to-discover-truth.

10. Opie Read, *Mark Twain and I* (Folcroft Library Editions, 1973), 34.

11. Pat Robertson, *Answers to 200 of Life's Most Probing Questions* (Thomas Nelson, 1984), 207–208.

12. "Prophecies and Discernment," Ligonier, February 26, 2020, https://www.ligonier.org/learn/devotionals/prophecies-and-discernment.

13. R. Loren Sandford, "How to Discern Truth Amid a Sea of False Prophesies [sic]," *Charisma*, June 18, 2014, https://mycharisma.com/propheticrevival/propheticinsight/how-to-discern-truth-amid-a-sea-of-false-prophesies/.

14. Sandford, "How to Discern Truth Amid a Sea of False Prophesies."

15. Sandford, "How to Discern Truth Amid a Sea of False Prophesies."

16. Sandford, "How to Discern Truth Amid a Sea of False Prophesies."

17. Sandford, "How to Discern Truth Amid a Sea of False Prophesies."

18. Sandford, "How to Discern Truth Amid a Sea of False Prophesies."

19. Sandford, "How to Discern Truth Amid a Sea of False Prophesies."

20. Francis Frangipane, "It's Time to Upgrade the Prophetic," *Charisma*, July 21, 2011, https://mycharisma.com/propheticrevival/propheticinsight/its-time-to-upgrade-the-prophetic/.

21. Frangipane, "It's Time to Upgrade the Prophetic."

22. Frangipane, "It's Time to Upgrade the Prophetic."

23. Frangipane, "It's Time to Upgrade the Prophetic."

CHAPTER 8

1. Lancaster, "Did a Novelist From the 1800s Warn Us Donald Trump Would Be 'The Last President'?"

2. Begley, interview by the author.

3. Begley, interview by the author.

4. Lockwood, *1900*, 3–4, 7–8.

5. Janice Hisle, "Trump Rally Draws Tens of Thousands in Blue State New Jersey," *Epoch Times*, updated May 13, 2024, https://www.theepochtimes.com/us/trump-draws-tens-of-thousands-makes-history-in-blue-state-rally-5648508.

6. Michael Calia, "Aldous Huxley's 'Brave New World' Coming to Television," *Wall Street Journal*, August 11, 2016, https://www.wsj.com/articles/BL-SEB-96528.

7. *Encyclopaedia Britannica*, s.v. "Brave New World," accessed June 29, 2024, https://www.britannica.com/topic/Brave-New-World; Aldous Huxley, *Brave New World* (Chatto & Windus, 1932), 31.

8. *Encyclopaedia Britannica*, s.v. "Brave New World."

9. George Orwell, *Nineteen Eighty-Four* (Alfred A. Knopf, 1987), 6.

10. *Encyclopaedia Britannica*, s.v. "Nineteen Eighty-Four," accessed June 29, 2024, https://www.britannica.com/topic/Nineteen-Eighty-four.

11. Elias Groll, "The Incredible Predictive Power of Tom Clancy's Novels," *Foreign Policy*, October 2, 2013, https://foreignpolicy.com/2013/10/02/the-incredible-predictive-power-of-tom-clancys-novels.

12. Groll, "The Incredible Predictive Power of Tom Clancy's Novels."

13. Groll, "The Incredible Predictive Power of Tom Clancy's Novels."

14. Groll, "The Incredible Predictive Power of Tom Clancy's Novels."

15. Republican National Committee, "Trump Campaign and RNC Unveil Historic 100,000 Person Strong Election Integrity Program," press release, April 19, 2024, https://www.gop.com/press-release/

trump-campaign-and-rnc-unveil-historic-100000-person-strong-election-integrity-program.

16. Republican National Committee, "Trump Campaign and RNC Unveil Historic 100,000 Person Strong Election Integrity Program."

17. Yates, interview by the author.

18. Christine Fernando, "A Crush of Lawsuits Over Voting in Multiple States Is Creating a Shadow War for the 2024 Election," Associated Press, April 21, 2024, https://apnews.com/article/rnc-trump-lawsuits-2024-election-voter-rolls-c7d8943dcac776103d948532f62f2a5c.

19. Christina A. Cassidy, "Election Officials See a Range of Threats in 2024, From Hostile Countries to Conspiracy Theorists," Associated Press, December 29, 2023, https://apnews.com/article/election-security-2024-threats-cybersecurity-russia-69b130e9896a8e8a229b7a668000183f.

20. "Donald Trump Poses the Biggest Danger to the World in 2024," *The Economist*, November 16, 2023, https://www.economist.com/leaders/2023/11/16/donald-trump-poses-the-biggest-danger-to-the-world-in-2024.

21. Noah Feldman, "Prospect of a Second Trump Term Demands Preparation, Not Panic," Bloomberg, December 26, 2023, https://www.bloomberg.com/opinion/articles/2023-12-26/if-trump-wins-in-2024-we-already-know-how-to-protect-the-constitution.

22. McGuire and Anderson, *Trumpocalypse*, 154.

23. McGuire and Anderson, *Trumpocalypse*.

24. Jeanine Santucci, "1 Week After Trump Assassination Attempt: Updates on His Wound, the Shooter," *USA Today*, updated July 21, 2024, https://www.usatoday.com/story/news/nation/2024/07/20/trump-assassination-attempt-updates-shooting-investigation/74483441007.

25. Cliff Kincaid, "The Plot to Kill Trump Goes to the Top," News With Views, July 18, 2024, https://newswithviews.com/the-plot-to-kill-trump-goes-to-the-top.

26. Tré Goins-Phillips, "Tucker Carlson Says There Is 'Spiritual Battle Underway' After Trump Assassination Attempt," CBN News, July 17, 2024, https://www2.cbn.com/news/us/tucker-carlson-says-there-spiritual-battle-underway-after-trump-assassination-attempt.

27. James Lasher, "Chris Reed's Prophetic Warning: America Is Entering a Rebirth," Charisma News, March 19, 2024, https://charismanews.com/culture/prophetic-warning-america-is-entering-a-rebirth.

28. Steve Cioccolanti, "3 PROPHETS Explain 3 American SOLAR ECLIPSES | APRIL8 SIGN | Amanda Grace, Brandon Biggs Cioccolanti," YouTube, March 14, 2024, https://www.youtube.com/watch?v=Ey0qVzG8_vU.

29. Joseph Z, "PROPHETIC UPDATE—THE SHOT HEARD AROUND THE WORLD!!," YouTube, July 14, 2024, https://www.youtube.com/watch?v=kS_BnuMJm3U.

30. Lasher, "Chris Reed's Prophetic Warning."

31. Michael Brown, "A Prophetic Message Concerning the 2024 Elections," Christian Post, September 6, 2023, https://www.christianpost.com/voices/a-prophetic-message-concerning-the-2024-elections.html.

32. Brown, "A Prophetic Message Concerning the 2024 Elections."

CHAPTER 9

1. Troy Anderson, David J. Giammona, and Paul Begley, "The Great North American Eclipse," *Charisma*, March 22, 2024, https://mycharisma.com/article/the-great-north-american-eclipse.

2. "Information on the 2024 Solar Eclipse for Every Community!," Eclipse 2024, accessed July 5, 2024, https://eclipse2024.org/communities/.

3. Jessilyn Lancaster, "Solar Eclipses Omens of Significant Historic Events," Charisma News, August 17, 2017, https://charismanews.com/opinion/the-flaming-herald/solar-eclipses-omens-of-significant-historical-events.

4. "Cities That Lie in the Path of Totality," Eclipse 2024, accessed July 6, 2024, https://eclipse2024.org/2017eclipse/2017/in_the_path.htm. Note that Salem, ID, is not listed but was in the path of totality.

5. Mark Biltz, interview by the author, March 7, 2024.

6. "American Solar Eclipses," Great American Eclipse; Ashley Guio, "Human Trafficking in Eastern United States," ArcGIS StoryMaps, November 27, 2023, https://storymaps.arcgis.com/stories/b23289d0ce8e4f80a519484e8b9c5e62.

7. "American Solar Eclipses," Great American Eclipse, accessed July 6, 2024, https://www.greatamericaneclipse.com/eclipse-maps-and-globe/american-solar-eclipses-2017-to-2024.

8. Revelation Watchers, "Great American Eclipse: Pastor Mark Biltz Unveils Stunning Prophetic Significance - April 8th," YouTube, March 9, 2024, https://www.youtube.com/watch?v=gBJ_9x_VPzk&t=1336s.

9. Mark Biltz, *America at War 2024–2026: The Sons of Light vs. the Sons of Darkness* (Sumner, WA: El Shaddai Ministries, 2024), 7–9.

10. Biltz, *America at War 2024–2026*, 94–95.

11. Graham, email interview by author.

12. Anderson, "Billy Graham Sounds Alarm for 2nd Coming."

13. Donald Trump, "Presidential Message on the National Day of Prayer and Return."

14. McGuire, interview by the author.

15. "April 8th Eclipse: Is This America's 'Nineveh Moment' Billy Graham Foresaw? - Pastor Paul Begley and Troy Anderson, Authors of Revelation 911, Ready to Illuminate Its Prophetic Significance," Inspire PR Agency, March 18, 2024, https://inspirepragency.substack.com/p/april-8th-eclipse-is-this-americas.

16. Gary Lane, "'Signs in the Sun, Moon, and Stars': Does the Upcoming Solar Eclipse Point to the End Times?," CBN News, April 5, 2024, https://www2.cbn.com/news/us/signs-sun-moon-and-stars-does-upcoming-solar-eclipse-point-end-times.

17. David Wilkerson, "Quotes from David Wilkerson," *Charisma*, April 28, 2011, https://mycharisma.com/propheticrevival/evangelism2/quotes-from-david-wilkerson.

18. James H. Anderson, "The Next Taiwan Crisis Will (Almost) Certainly Involve Nuclear Threats," US Naval Institute, March 2024, https://www.usni.org/magazines/proceedings/2024/march/next-taiwan-crisis-will-almost-certainly-involve-nuclear-threats.

19. Michelle Fox, "The U.S. National Debt Is Rising by $1 Trillion About Every 100 Days," CNBC, updated March 4, 2024, https://www.cnbc.com/2024/03/01/the-us-national-debt-is-rising-by-1-trillion-about-every-100-days.html; "US National Debt," US Debt Clock, accessed July 14, 2024, https://www.usdebtclock.org/.

20. Randy DeSoto, "Is America in End Times Prophecy? Bible Experts Weigh In," *Western Journal*, April 9, 2024, https://www.westernjournal.com/america-end-times-prophecy-bible-experts-weigh.

21. DeSoto, "Is America in End Times Prophecy?"

22. DeSoto, "Is America in End Times Prophecy?"

23. Strang Report, "'America, You Have 2 YEARS!' Prophetic Warning from Chuck Pierce," YouTube, April 18, 2024, https://www.youtube.com/watch?v=mPwLAmu9qrk.

24. Strang Report, "'America.'"

25. Strang Report, "'America.'"

26. Strang Report, "'America.'"

27. Strang Report, "'America.'"

28. CBN News and Talia Wise, "Revival Is Stirring as 'Hundreds and Hundreds' Get Baptized in Texas Fountain," *Charisma News*, May 29, 2024, https://charismanews.com/news/revival-is-stirring-as-hundreds-and-hundreds-get-baptized-in-texas-fountain.

29. Abby Trivett, "California Church Experiences State-Wide Revival With 30,000 Baptisms," *Charisma News*, May 20, 2024, https://charismanews.com/culture/california-church-experiences-state-wide-revival-with-30000-baptisms.

30. Trivett, "California Church Experiences State-Wide Revival With 30,000 Baptisms."

31. Abby Trivett, "Miracle and Healing Testimonies Explode at Mario Murillo's Crusades," *Charisma News*, March 22, 2024, https://charismanews.com/news/us/miracle-and-healing-testimonies-explode-at-mario-murillo-s-crusades.

32. Mario Murillo, "Is Revival in America Now Impossible?," Mario Murillo Ministries, May 9, 2023, https://mariomurillo.org/2023/05/09/is-revival-in-america-now-impossible.

33. Murillo, "Is Revival in America Now Impossible?"

34. James Lasher, "Revival Hits US Border With 9,000 Having 'Experience With the Lord,'" *Charisma News*, April 4, 2024, https://charismanews.com/news/us/revival-hits-us-border-with-9-000-having-experience-with-the-lord.

35. Charisma Staff, "Professor Reveals Lasting Impact of Asbury Revival 14 Months Later," *Charisma News*, April 23, 2024, https://charismanews.com/news/professor-reveals-lasting-impact-of-asbury-revival-14-months-later.

36. Charisma Staff, "Professor Reveals Lasting Impact of Asbury Revival 14 Months Later."

37. Charisma Staff, "Professor Reveals Lasting Impact of Asbury Revival 14 Months Later."

CHAPTER 10

1. McGuire, interview by the author.

2. McGuire, interview by the author.

3. McGuire, interview by the author.

4. George Mentz, "Republican Party and Trump Release 2024 Platform Commitment to American Citizens," Newsmax, July 9, 2024, https://www.newsmax.com/finance/georgementz/donald-trump-platform/2024/07/09/id/1171744/?.

5. John Bisognano, "Barron Trump, Donald Trump's Youngest Son, Turns 18. Five Things to Know About Him," *Palm Beach Post*, updated April 3, 2024, https://www.palmbeachpost.com/story/news/politics/elections/2024/03/20/barron-trump-turns-18-facts-on-donalds-son-height-sports-school/72955019007.

6. Bisognano, "Barron Trump."

7. Luke Winkie, "The Blank Slate of Barron Trump," Slate, May 15, 2024, https://slate.com/life/2024/05/barron-trump-height-tall-college-donald-fans.html.

8. Michael Dorgan, "Barron Trump to Enter Politics as Florida Delegate at GOP Convention," Fox News, May 9, 2024, https://www.foxnews.com/politics/barron-trump-enter-politics-florida-delegate-gop-convention; Adriana Gomez Licon, "Barron Trump, 18, Won't Be Serving as a Florida Delegate to the Republican Convention After All," Associated Press, updated May 10, 2024, https://apnews.com/article/barron-trump-convention-delegate-president-republican-cccf0026a78e2d4485fbf6b1581bb545.

9. Brie Stimson, "Trump Says Son Barron, 18, Likes Politics and Gives Him Advice: 'He's a Smart One,'" Fox News, May 11, 2024, https://www.foxnews.com/politics/trump-says-son-barron-18-likes-politics-gives-advice-smart.

10. Kathleen Livingstone, "SOUND THE TRUMPETS Barron Trump Hypes Up Crowd in Rally Debut as Dad Donald Says 'Welcome to the Scene' and Challenges Biden to 2nd Debate," U. S. Sun, updated July 10, 2024, https://www.the-sun.com/news/11879794/trump-welcomes-barron-trump-rally-debut.

11. Geoffrey Grider, "Long Forgotten Novels From 19-Century Author Ingersoll Lockwood Were Called 'The Last President' and 'The Baron Trump', How's That For Conspiracy?," Now the End Begins, July 10, 2024, https://www.nowtheendbegins.com/long-forgotten-novels-from-19th-century-author-ingersoll-lockwood-were-called-the-last-president-and-the-baron-trump-barron-donald.

12. Feucht, interview by the author.

13. Casey Noenickx, "'Situationships': Why Gen Z Are Embracing the Grey Area," BBC, September 2, 2022, https://www.bbc.com/worklife/article/20220831-situationships-why-gen-z-are-embracing-the-grey-area.

14. Michael Gryboski, "'A Move of God': Thousands of Students Attending Revival Events, Hundreds Baptized," Christian Post, April 9, 2024, https://www.christianpost.com/news/a-move-of-god-students-attending-revival-events-100s-baptized.html.

15. Gryboski, "'A Move of God.'"

16. Gryboski, "'A Move of God.'"

17. Steve Warren, "'Revival Is in the Air': New Reports of Spiritual Awakening as Huge Event Slated for April," Faithwire, March 10, 2023, https://www.faithwire.com/2023/03/10/revival-is-in-the-air-new-reports-of-spiritual-awakening-as-huge-event-slated-for-april.

18. Warren, "'Revival Is in the Air.'"

19. Joseph Z, "JEZEBEL WILL BE DEFEATED by the REFORMERS!!," YouTube, July 8, 2024, https://www.youtube.com/watch?v=rDLt986Dhtg.

20. Joseph Z, "JEZEBEL WILL BE DEFEATED by the REFORMERS!!"

21. Shawn Akers, "What Donald Trump Said About Jesus Christ and America's Future in Robert Jeffress' Church," Charisma News, December 22, 2021, https://charismanews.com/opinion/in-the-line-of-fire/what-donald-trump-said-about-jesus-christ-and-america-s-future-in-robert-jeffress-church.

22. The_Standard, "Tucker Carlson & Pastor Doug Wilson (FULL INTERVIEW): Christian Nationalists React," YouTube, May 8, 2024, https://www.youtube.com/watch?v=0-HnY_5pkcQ.

23. The_Standard, "Tucker Carlson & Pastor Doug Wilson."

24. Akers, "What Donald Trump Said About Jesus Christ and America's Future in Robert Jeffress' Church."

25. Shawn A. Akers, "Jonathan Cahn Prophetic Documentary Reveals Mystery That Determines America's Future—And Yours," Charisma News, May 5, 2022, https://charismanews.com/culture/jonathan-cahn-prophetic-documentary-reveals-mystery-that-determines-america-s-future-and-yours.
26. Akers, "Jonathan Cahn Prophetic Documentary Reveals Mystery That Determines America's Future."
27. Akers, "Jonathan Cahn Prophetic Documentary Reveals Mystery That Determines America's Future."
28. Bernis, interview by the author.
29. Lockwood, *1900*, 7.

CONCLUSION

1. "Transforming Our World: the 2030 Agenda for Sustainable Development," United Nations, September 27, 2015, https://sdgs.un.org/2030agenda; "FACT SHEET: U.S. Action on Global Development," The White House, September 20, 2023, https://www.whitehouse.gov/briefing-room/statements-releases/2023/09/20/fact-sheet-u-s-action-on-global-development/.
2. Peter Rykowski, "Agenda 2030 Threatens Liberty—State Legislators Can Stop It," New American, November 10, 2022, https://thenewamerican.com/us/politics/agenda-2030-threatens-liberty-state-legislators-can-stop-it.
3. "Transforming Our World," United Nations.
4. Rykowski, "Agenda 2030 Threatens Liberty."
5. World Economic Forum, "8 Predictions for the World in 2030," Facebook, November 18, 2016, https://www.facebook.com/watch/?v=10153920524981479.
6. Paul Begley and Troy Anderson, *Revelation 911: How the Book of Revelation Intersects with Today's Headlines* (Salem Books, 2024), 107–109.
7. Begley and Anderson, *Revelation 911*, introduction.
8. Begley, interview by the author.
9. Begley, interview by the author.
10. John Whitehead and Nisha Whitehead, "Project Total Control: Everything Is a Weapon When Totalitarianism Is Normalized," Rutherford Institute, July 10, 2024, https://www.rutherford.org/publications_resources/john_whiteheads_commentary/project_total_control_everything_is_a_weapon_when_totalitarianism_is_normalized.
11. Caitlin Burke, "US Voting Process Under Scrutiny: 'All the Things that Could Possibly Go Wrong,'" CBN News, June 26, 2024, https://www2.cbn.com/news/politics/us-voting-process-under-scrutiny-all-things-could-possibly-go-wrong.
12. Feucht, interview by the author.
13. John Piper, "Are Christians Obligated to Vote?," Desiring God, March 3, 2023, https://www.desiringgod.org/interviews/are-christians-obligated-to-vote.
14. Piper, "Are Christians Obligated to Vote?"
15. Piper, "Are Christians Obligated to Vote?"
16. Piper, "Are Christians Obligated to Vote?"
17. John Stonestreet, "3 Reasons Why Christians Should Vote," Christian Post, September 28, 2020, https://www.christianpost.com/voices/3-reasons-why-christians-should-vote.html.
18. Yates, interview by the author.
19. Yates, interview by the author.
20. Yates, interview by the author.

21. Yates, interview by the author.
22. Dale Ahlquist, "Lecture 65: Christendom in Dublin," Society of G. K. Chesterton, https://www.chesterton.org/lecture-65.
23. Ahlquist, "Lecture 65."
24. *Encyclopaedia Britannica*, s.v. Mayflower Compact, accessed July 14, 2024, https://www.britannica.com/topic/Mayflower-Compact.
25. History.com Editors, "Israel," History, updated October 10, 2023, https://www.history.com/topics/middle-east/history-of-israel.
26. Jonathan Cahn, interview by the author, July 30, 2020.
27. "2024 GOP Platform Make America Great Again!," Republican National Committee, July 7, 2024, https://cdn.nucleusfiles.com/be/beb1a388-1d88-4389-a67d-c1e2d7f8bedf/2024-gop-platform-july-7-final.pdf.
28. Editor, "Eight Things to Pray About the Upcoming Election," Gospel Coalition, May 14, 2019, https://au.thegospelcoalition.org/article/eight-things-pray-upcoming-election.
29. R. Cort Kirkwood, "Reports: Obama, Pelosi Orchestrating Removal of Biden as Candidate," *New American*, July 11, 2024, https://thenewamerican.com/us/politics/reports-obama-pelosi-orchestrating-removal-of-biden-as-candidate/.
30. Bernis, interview by the author.
31. "Director's Words: Wallenstein," Shakespeare Theater Company, accessed July 15, 2024, https://www.shakespearetheatre.org/watch-listen/directors-words-wallenstein; Friedrich Schiller, trans. Samuel Taylor Coleridge, *The Death of Wallenstein*, 1.3, https://www.gutenberg.org/cache/epub/6787/pg6787-images.html.

ABOUT THE AUTHOR

TROY ANDERSON IS a Pulitzer Prize–nominated investigative journalist, bestselling author, founder and president of the Inspire Literary Group, vice president of Battle Ready Ministries, former executive editor of *Charisma* magazine and Charisma Media, speaker, and regular television and radio commentator. He spent two decades working as a reporter, bureau chief, and editorial writer at the *Los Angeles Daily News*, *The Press-Enterprise*, and other newspapers. He writes for *Newsmax*, Townhall, *Charisma*, Charisma News, *Human Events*, *The American Spectator*, *Outreach*, and other media outlets. He's the founder and editor-in-chief of Prophecy Investigators and cofounder of Revelation Watchers.

He appears regularly on Newsmax TV, CBN News, BlazeTV, GOD TV, Real America's Voice, Daystar Television Network's *Joni Table Talk* and *Ministry Now*, One America News Network, Salem News Channel, *Tipping Point With Jimmy Evans*, *The Jim Bakker Show*, *Jewish Voice With Jonathan Bernis*, SkyWatch TV, Cornerstone TV Network's *Real Life,* and many nationally syndicated radio programs and YouTube shows.

He's interviewed many prominent national figures, including Billy Graham, Franklin Graham, Anne Graham Lotz, Pastor Rick Warren, Dr. Tim LaHaye, Hal Lindsey, Noam Chomsky, David Horowitz, Patrick Buchanan, Dinesh D'Souza, Pastor Greg Laurie, Joel Rosenberg, Rabbi Jonathan Cahn, Sid Roth, Rabbi Jonathan Bernis, Pastor Mark Hitchcock, Nick Vujicic, Lee Strobel, Kevin Sorbo, Pat Boone, and Kirk Cameron. During his career, Anderson has received numerous journalistic accolades: more than two dozen local, state, and national writing awards; 2011 and 2012 Eddie Awards (*Folio* magazine's prestigious journalism awards); two 2015 Charlie Awards (Florida Magazine Association's top award); and a Pulitzer Prize nomination.

He's a member of the American Society of Journalists and Authors, the nation's premier association of writers of nonfiction who have met ASJA's exacting standards of professional achievement. He's also a member of the Association of Ghostwriters, Investigative Reporters & Editors, Gotham Ghostwriters, and a graduate of the Act One and Movieguide screenwriting programs. Anderson graduated from the University of Oregon in 1991 with a bachelor's degree in news-editorial journalism and a minor in political science.

He's co-author of the FaithWords/Hachette Book Group number one bestsellers *The Babylon Code* and *Trumpocalypse*, Chosen Books/Baker Publishing Group number one bestsellers *The Military Guide to Armageddon* and *The Military Guide to Disarming Deception*, and the Salem Books/Regnery Publishing number one bestseller *Revelation 911*, as well as the Chosen Books bestseller *Your Mission in God's Army*. Anderson lives with his family in Irvine, California.

Find out more at:

www.troyanderson.us

www.inspireliterary.com

www.revelationwatchers.com

www.prophecyinvestigators.com

www.battle-ready.org.